STRENGTH TRAINING
FOR
HOCKEY

NSCA®
NATIONAL STRENGTH AND
CONDITIONING ASSOCIATION

Kevin Neeld, PhD, CPSS, CSCS, RSCC*D

Brijesh Patel, MA, CSCS, RSCC*E

Editors

HUMAN KINETICS

Library of Congress Cataloging-in-Publication Data

Names: National Strength & Conditioning Association (U.S.), author. |
  Neeld, Kevin, editor. | Patel, Brijesh, editor.
Title: Strength training for hockey / NSCA National Strength and
  Conditioning Association ; Kevin Neeld, PhD, CSCS, CPSS, RSCC,*D, CMT;
  Brijesh Patel, MA, CSCS, RSCC*E, editors.
Description: Champaign, IL : Human Kinetics, [2025] | Includes
  bibliographical references and index.
Identifiers: LCCN 2024021503 (print) | LCCN 2024021504 (ebook) | ISBN
  9781718216174 (print ; alk. paper) | ISBN 9781718216181 (epub) | ISBN
  9781718216198 (pdf)
Subjects: LCSH: Hockey--Training. | Weight training. | Muscle strength. |
  BISAC: SPORTS & RECREATION / Winter Sports / Hockey | SPORTS &
  RECREATION / Training
Classification: LCC GV848.3 .S77 2025 (print) | LCC GV848.3 (ebook) | DDC
  613.7/11--dc23/eng/20240706
LC record available at https://lccn.loc.gov/2024021503
LC ebook record available at https://lccn.loc.gov/2024021504

ISBN: 978-1-7182-1617-4 (print)

Senior Acquisitions Editor: Roger W. Earle; **Managing Editor:** Kevin Matz; **Copyeditor:** Pam Eidson/E Before I Editing; **Indexer:** Ferreira Indexing, Inc.; **Permissions Manager:** Laurel Mitchell; **Graphic Designers:** Denise Lowry and Joe Buck; **Cover Designer:** Keri Evans; **Cover Design Associate:** Susan Rothermel Allen; **Photograph (cover):** Mark LoMoglio/NHLI via Getty Images; **Photographs (interior):** © Human Kinetics, unless otherwise noted; **Photographer (interior):** Alberto E. Leopizzi, unless otherwise noted; **Photo Asset Manager:** Laura Fitch; **Photo Production Coordinator:** Amy M. Rose; **Photo Production Manager:** Jason Allen; **Senior Art Manager:** Kelly Hendren; **Illustrations:** © Human Kinetics, unless otherwise noted; **Printer:** Sheridan Books

We thank Matthew Sandstead, NSCA-CPT,*D, Scott Caulfield, MA, CSCS,*D, TSAC-F,*D, RSCC*E, and the National Strength and Conditioning Association (NSCA) in Colorado Springs, Colorado, for overseeing (Matthew and Scott) and hosting (NSCA) the photo shoot for this book. We also thank and recognize Alberto Leopizzi, owner and lead photographer of A Touch of Class Images, for taking the photos for this book.

Human Kinetics books are available at special discounts for bulk purchase. Special editions or book excerpts can also be created to specification. For details, contact the Special Sales Manager at Human Kinetics.

Printed in the United States of America   10 9 8 7 6 5 4 3 2 1

The paper in this book is certified under a sustainable forestry program.

Human Kinetics
P.O. Box 5076
Champaign, IL 61825-5076
Website: www.HumanKinetics.com

United States and International
Website: **US.HumanKinetics.com**
Email: info@hkusa.com
Phone: 1-800-747-4457

Canada
Website: **Canada.HumanKinetics.com**
Email: info@hkcanada.com

E8819

STRENGTH TRAINING
FOR
HOCKEY

CONTENTS

PART III: PROGRAM DESIGN GUIDELINES AND SAMPLE PROGRAMS

FOREWORD

MEGHAN DUGGAN

I can distinctly remember a moment in late November 2014 when I was finishing a training session, by myself, late at night, in a small, dark, and dingy gym in upstate New York (just your normal Tuesday night as a women's professional hockey player at the time; far from glamorous). I was nine months removed from one of the most heartbreaking losses in my athletic career: We lost the gold medal at the 2014 Sochi Winter Olympics, after blowing a 2-0 lead late in the game and falling to Canada in overtime.

I was three years and three months away from the 2018 Olympic Games.

On this dark November night, I was recovering from wrist surgery—having had my triangular fibrocartilage complex repaired in August after years of issues with it—and finally starting to get back to training without limitations. The infamous Mike Boyle was my beloved head strength coach at the time, and I was in the middle of a set of his single-leg skater squats paired with incline dumbbell bench presses. I had done each of those exercises probably a million times before, in different gyms, countries, and cities all over the world. But that night, during that set, something changed in my mind. My approach to resistance training changed.

For my entire tenure on the national team up to this point, I had always considered myself someone who had a strong work ethic and prioritized off-ice training as an important part of my preparation with the U.S. women's national team. I was often toward the top of the group when it came to fitness testing results, I was never told I was out of shape, and I was rarely told I was weak in certain areas. But after coming up short two Olympics in a row in my lifelong dream of winning a gold medal, I knew what I had been doing was not good enough. I realized that night during the set of skater squats and incline dumbbell bench presses that how I chose to commit more wholeheartedly to resistance training for the following 3.5 years would help define my career. It would influence not only my performance but also my mentality, leadership, and accountability within our team.

I was thankful at the time I had incredible resources in the form of coaches who all played a role in my mental shift that year: Mike Boyle, Sarah Cahill, Kevin Neeld, and Mike Vaughn. I wanted to know everything—all of the *whys*. The discussion and answers following my questions led to adjusted techniques, extra reps, deeper respect for the exercises, detailed focus points on a day-to-day basis, and a more mature and professional approach to resistance training and, in turn, my hockey career.

Hockey is an incredibly dynamic and demanding sport—from a physical perspective—it combines speed, strength, acceleration, deceleration, agility, endurance (both aerobic and anaerobic), and intense physical contact. To be able to maintain performance at a high level for an extended period of time within a game, game after game during a season, and year after year over a career, a commitment to a proper strength and conditioning program is imperative. Your equipment or training space does not have to be glamorous, but with the right mindset, commitment to the details, and respect for resistance training, you can turn losses into wins. In my case, these things played a role in turning silver medals into a gold one.

I know that this book will educate all readers on the importance of resistance training for hockey and provide exercises, ideas, principles, guidelines, and programs to help hockey athletes get from one phase of their career to the next. Whatever your goal is in hockey, I am confident you can get closer to achieving it by using this book as a resource.

INTRODUCTION

BRIJESH PATEL AND KEVIN NEELD

Ice hockey may be the most physically demanding team sport in the world. The sport is highly dependent upon physical qualities such as speed, power, agility, aerobic capacity, muscular endurance, and mobility. All of these qualities require the ability to produce force at varying amounts, velocities, and ranges of motion for success. Strength is simply the expression of force and is a necessary quality for all ice hockey athletes because it plays a massive role in an athlete's performance.

Ice hockey is said to be the fastest sport played on the feet. High speeds are a by-product of high forces produced at high velocities. The repetitive nature of these forces, in combination with relatively extreme ranges of motion of the hip joint, can lead to noncontact injuries, while collisions with the opposition, the ice surface, and the surrounding boards can also result in injury. The primary goals of a well-designed resistance training program should be to improve sport performance and durability. Availability (i.e., not being injured) is essential for the individual athlete's development and for team success. As a result, hockey-specific resistance training programs should guard against common injuries within the sport by including specific work to help minimize an athlete's risk.

Ice hockey places a premium on elite skill and speed. Consequently, athletes are faster and stronger than ever before. At each ascending level, there are significant differences in the athletes' physical makeup. While developmental windows influence which qualities change more at specific ages, athletes are generally bigger, faster, stronger, and better conditioned at each successive level. Collectively, the contributors have seen these differences across youth and high school hockey, between Division I and III NCAA athletes, between women's U-18, U-22, and national team athletes, and through the varying levels of professional hockey (i.e., development camp invitees versus AHL versus NHL). In other words, athletes must not only improve their skill but must also make significant physical changes to compete at the next level.

Training can also influence an athlete's skill development and skill expression. Improving mobility and end-range strength, for example, gives athletes the opportunity to develop skill using a wider spectrum of positions and movement patterns. Having a solid foundation of resistance training and conditioning further allows athletes to avoid the technical breakdown associated with fatigue, thereby improving their ability to consistently execute their skill. By training year-round, athletes maintain a higher level of performance and accelerate their development over time.

Resistance training for ice hockey has evolved over the years. As academic and applied research have continued to shed light on the unique demands of the sport, training programs have progressed to prioritize the exercises and strategies that transfer best to on-ice performance. This book is a collaboration among some of the brightest and most experienced strength and conditioning professionals in the sport of ice hockey. In the coming pages, readers will discover

- a thorough analysis of the demands of the sport and a detailed explanation of the principles of resistance training programs for ice hockey;
- useful tests to help identify potential areas of improvement and track an athlete's progress over time;
- the most effective total body, lower body, upper body, and anatomical core resistance training exercises for hockey athletes; and
- year-round programming considerations and examples for high school, college, and professional- and national-level hockey athletes.

Whether the reader is a hockey athlete, sport coach, strength and conditioning professional, or a rehabilitation professional, this book serves as a comprehensive guide to resistance training for hockey.

PART I

PRINCIPLES OF SPORT-SPECIFIC RESISTANCE TRAINING

1

IMPORTANCE OF RESISTANCE TRAINING

ADAM DOUGLAS

Ice hockey is a sport characterized by athletes performing repeated bouts of high-intensity efforts of maximal power interspersed with periods of low-intensity movements. High-performing ice hockey athletes must have well-balanced physical and physiological systems, including robust anaerobic fitness (31), high aerobic fitness (7), and a blend of muscular strength, power, and endurance (25). These physical characteristics need to complement sport-specific skills such as skating, shooting, and passing the puck (28).

Muscular strength, power, and endurance translate directly to performance on-ice. Stronger athletes can skate faster and apply more force with each stride into the ice (20). Among high-level male skaters, high levels of horizontal leg power predict speed and agility during on-ice skating tests (11). Likewise, standing long jump power has been shown to explain approximately 8.5% of the variance in draft position among elite male skating (i.e., nongoalie) hockey athletes (8). Jumping, like skating, requires coordination of the upper and lower body to propel the athlete forward at high speeds. One hypothesis holds that the standing long jump best simulates these total body coordinated movements (8). Upper body strength is vital, because it allows athletes to shoot harder and use their bodies for positioning and body contact with another person or the boards surrounding the ice surface (28). Power metrics aside, upper and lower body strength have been shown to be positively associated with in-game statistical measures. In collegiate male ice hockey athletes, higher levels of strength measured in the preseason were associated with more favorable outcomes at the end of the season (22).

In addition to the positive relationship between resistance training and performance, the fast-paced nature of ice hockey can put athletes in precarious situations that can bring about injuries. Resistance training has been outlined as an effective method to reduce the risk of muscular injuries, with well-developed lower body strength, repeated sprint ability, and speed increasing an athlete's tolerance for practice and game demands (19).

The primary focus of this chapter is to provide the reader with a fundamental overview of how resistance training can have a positive impact on a hockey athlete's ability to be strong and powerful, move dynamically on ice, and reduce the risk of injury. The reader can then explore each training outcome in detail in the subsequent sections of the book.

Maddie Meyer/Getty Images

Muscular strength has a strong impact on skating performance. Athletes who are stronger are able to skate faster and apply more force with each stride into the ice.

INCREASE STRENGTH

On ice, the expression of strength can take many different forms, owing to the physical demands of the sport. The ability to skate faster, shoot harder, and play a physical game style is underpinned by having a requisite level of upper and lower body strength. The association between skating performance and muscular strength has been well-studied (12). Athletes who are stronger are able to skate faster and apply more force with each stride into the ice (16). Upper body strength allows athletes to shoot the puck harder and use their bodies for positioning and body contact (28).

There may be some differences in the effects of unilateral (training one limb at a time) versus bilateral (training both limbs simultaneously) resistance training for ice hockey athletes. Research indicates that greater force can be produced with unilateral exercises than with bilateral exercises (5, 17). The mechanisms behind this difference are not fully understood, but the most consistent explanation is that during bilateral exercises, there is a neural limitation that reduces maximum force production (21, 30). This phenomenon is known as the bilateral deficit and has been well documented across different muscle groups (27), populations (18), and test conditions (5).

Unilateral training can be useful for improving muscular imbalances between limbs, which can occur due to natural asymmetries or previous injuries. By training each limb independently, athletes can identify and address any imbalances and develop better overall symmetry and stability. This can be especially important for ice hockey athletes, who require strong and stable lower body muscles to perform quick turns, stops, and changes in direction on the ice.

Unilateral training, as mentioned, can also subvert the bilateral deficit, thus allowing athletes to lift more weight during a resistance training session. Greater force can be produced within a single limb when performing unilateral exercise than during bilateral training.

On the other hand, **bilateral training** can be useful for developing overall strength and power. When training both limbs together, athletes can typically lift heavier weights, which promotes improvements in overall strength and power. This can be important for ice hockey athletes who need explosive power in their skating stride and upper body strength for shooting and checking. Bilateral training provides greater stability to the body, thus leading to a greater expression of force. Training with both legs naturally provides a broader mechanical base for enhancing an athlete's strength and power compared to single-leg exercises (26). This does not mean we should disregard unilateral training when building strength. Instead, strategic unilateral programming, especially during preparation phases, complements bilateral training.

In general, both unilateral and bilateral resistance training can be effective for ice hockey athletes. The best approach may depend on the individual athlete's goals, physical characteristics, and imbalances or weaknesses. A well-designed training program that includes a combination of both types of training can help hockey athletes improve their overall strength, power, and on-ice performance.

INCREASE POWER

One of the important outcome goals of resistance training is to increase athletes' ability to produce and transmit force. Strength underpins an athlete's ability to generate force, and the expression of power can translate into improved performance on ice. **Power** is defined as the rate at which work is done. **Work**, in turn, is the outcome of applying force to an object over distance. Thus, power can be calculated by dividing work by time (9). Alternatively, power can also be expressed as the product of force and velocity, which is more commonly considered in resistance training programs and more clearly reflects the importance of strength for maximizing an athlete's power potential. Consequently, when discussing the enhancement of athletes' power, factors such as force, direction, time, and velocity should all be taken into account.

The ability to produce power allows ice hockey athletes to generate greater speed, maneuverability, and agility on ice. Power improves an athlete's ability to shoot the puck harder and change direction faster. Given that most athletic power generation involves high levels of neuromuscular activation in rotational patterns, it is important to consider the proper training that is required to prepare for the rotational nature of on-ice movements. Effective execution of movement also requires strength and power of trunk muscles. These muscles (erector spinae, abdominal obliques, and rectus abdominis) are particularly active during the acceleration phase of trunk rotations when initiating power-based movements (3). Athletes who exhibit an ability to produce large amounts of horizontal leg power have been shown in research to skate and turn at higher velocities on the ice (11). Horizontal power, evidenced through sprinting and horizontal hopping tests, is highly correlated with skating performance (14). The Wingate bike test, which is a 30-second maximum effort bout on a cycle ergometer, also has a strong correlation between skating speed and peak power (11, 23). **Peak power** is determined by the highest mechanical power generated during any 5-second interval of the test. **Mean power** is the total amount of work performed over the 30-second trial without normalizing for a full minute (4).

Power improves an athlete's ability to shoot the puck harder.

Jason Mowry/Getty Images

IMPROVE SPEED AND AGILITY

Speed and agility are two important components of athletic performance that are necessary for success on-ice. **Speed** refers to the athlete's ability to move quickly from one point to another. It can be measured in terms of straight-line speed or the time it takes to cover a set distance, such as blue line to blue line or one end of the rink to the other. **Agility** refers to an athlete's ability to change directions quickly and efficiently. It involves the ability to accelerate, decelerate, and change direction while maintaining balance and control.

Both speed and agility require a combination of physical and mental abilities including strength, power, coordination, balance, and reaction time. Training programs designed to improve speed and agility typically include exercises that focus on proving both physical and cognitive attributes through a combination of resistance training, plyometrics, change of direction drills, and sport-specific drills. By improving speed and agility, hockey athletes can gain a competitive edge on ice, allowing them to make quicker plays, evade opponents, and outmaneuver their competition.

IMPROVE BODY COMPOSITION

Body composition refers to the proportion of lean mass to fat mass within an athlete's body. Lean mass includes muscles, bones, water, tendons, ligaments, and organs, whereas fat mass includes subcutaneous fat and visceral fat surrounding the internal organs. Testing the body composition of ice hockey athletes is crucial for evaluating their physiological health and well-being. When combined with speed and power testing, body composition data can help determine the optimal weight and body composition for maximizing speed and power output. Position-specific data can help strength and conditioning professionals design individualized programs that increase lean mass or decrease fat mass. The physical and physiological characteristics of forwards, defense athletes, and goalies differ among male and female ice hockey teams. In male hockey, when comparing forwards to defense athletes, forwards tend to be smaller in stature (2, 14) and have less body mass (6). When compared to forwards and defense athletes, goalies tend to be shorter and have an increased body fat percentage (24). Geithner, Lee, and Bracko found that forwards tended to have the lowest body fat percentage among the three positions, and goalies had the highest (13).

To improve body composition, ice hockey athletes generally need to increase their lean mass, decrease their fat mass, or both. Registered dietitians should first examine and improve athletes' nutritional habits. The relation of lean tissue mass to muscle strength has been investigated (10), and a positive relationship exists between increasing lean tissue mass and increased muscle strength and power in response to a resistance training program (15). From the perspective of strength and conditioning, anaerobic exercises, such as resistance training and repeated sprint work, have proven effective in increasing lean mass while decreasing fat mass. Aerobic exercise, such as steady-state cardiovascular exercise, can also benefit ice hockey athletes by oxidizing fat for energy, contributing to an energy deficit, and reducing body fat.

PREVENT INJURIES

Ice hockey is a sport that occurs at high speed with frequent collisions. Thus, injury is a common occurrence. Injuries occur eight times as often in games as in practice (1). The most common injuries associated with this population are knee sprains and strains, concussions, shoulder ligament trauma, and groin strain injuries (1). One of the main causes of groin strains is a muscular imbalance between the adductor muscle group and the abductor muscle group, groups that are highly stressed during the unique frontal plane movement of the skating stride (29). Resistance training can work to improve the balance between these muscle groups, thus reducing the possible risk of injury. Likewise, resistance training increases lean body mass, thus providing muscle tissue that can withstand the rigors of physical play.

Anatomical core training can help reduce injury risk in ice hockey athletes by improving stability, balance, and control of the body. A strong anatomical core can help athletes maintain proper body position and posture, reducing the risk of overuse injuries such as muscle strains or low back pain (another common ailment of the population). A strong core's ability to absorb and transmit force through the body can also work to prevent acute injuries such as falls and collisions. Furthermore, anatomical core training can improve overall body mechanics and efficiency of movements that could lead to injury. For example, weak or underdeveloped core muscles can cause compensations in athletes' ability to extend their hips by creating excessive movement in their lumbar spine and can cause unnecessary weight shift in an effort to create more stability while skating or shooting, which can lead to injury. A strong and stable core can help maintain proper alignment and prevent compensatory movements, thus reducing the risk of injury.

Overall, training the anatomical core is a vital component of injury prevention in ice hockey. By strengthening the core muscles, improving balance and stability, and promoting proper body posture, athletes can reduce their risk of injury and stay healthy and competitive on the ice.

CONCLUSION

Ice hockey athletes require a well-balanced physical and physiological system that includes robust anaerobic and aerobic fitness as well as muscular strength, power, and endurance to complement their sport-specific skills. Having adequate levels of strength in the upper and lower body can positively affect an athlete's skating, shooting, and physicality. Resistance training has proven to be an effective method for reducing the risk of muscular injuries, as well as increasing an athlete's tolerance to the demands of practices and games.

Resistance training can have a positive impact on an athlete's ability to be strong, to be powerful, and to move dynamically on ice while also reducing the risk of injury. Power allows athletes to generate more speed, maneuverability, and agility on ice. Progressive overload, which involves increasing weight or resistance, sets and repetitions, and intensity of training over time, is an effective way to achieve these goals. Each subsequent section of this book provides a deeper overview of the outcome benefits of resistance training for the hockey athlete.

2

ANALYSIS OF THE SPORT AND SPORT POSITIONS

ANTHONY DONSKOV

Strength and conditioning has made important advancements throughout the years. A solid understanding of first principles such as biomechanics and physiology has fostered this growth. Gone are the yesteryears of hockey athletes using training camp to get in shape. Today's athletes are immersed in resources such as resistance, speed, and power training, which are critical components for off-season gains.

Coaches are also immersed with an abundance of information to help them in designing appropriate strength and conditioning programs. The goal of this chapter is to provide strength and conditioning professionals with the necessary information to underpin their programs with a solid foundation of scientific acumen. This chapter focuses on a biomechanical analysis of the hockey stride, as well as a physiological and position-specific analysis that may guide the practitioner in appropriate program considerations for the sport of ice hockey.

GENERAL BIOMECHANICAL ANALYSIS

Biomechanics is the study of mechanical laws relating to movement. Subareas of biomechanics include **kinetics** and **kinematics**. The former is the study of the explanation of motion, such as ground reaction forces, rate of force development, and horizontal power, while the latter is the study of the description of motion, such as orientation of body segments and joint angles. Competencies in biomechanics and exercise physiology are considered first principles for the strength and conditioning professional.

Hockey is a rare team sport played on the ice in a near frictionless environment. **Friction** is the resistance that one surface or object encounters while moving over another. Friction is antagonistic in nature and resists movement, acts parallel to the plane of contact, may be both static and dynamic, and is dependent on pressure. The properties of acting parallel to the plane of contact and depending on pressure are relevant to the environment. If a force is applied parallel to the ice surface, unlike on turf, grass, court, or cement, locomotion becomes inefficient and compromised due to the lack of friction on the ice. To make forward progress on the ice, the hockey athlete must produce a force by angling the skate blade almost perpendicular into the ice surface. The pressure between the applied force of the skate blade and the reactive force of the ice creates propulsion by producing friction. Lack of friction is why hockey is the fastest team sport on earth, why open ice hits are like small car crashes (large amounts of kinetic energy are dissipated quickly), why large amounts of protective equipment are worn by players (to redistribute forces to larger surface areas), and why the unique muscle recruitment patterns of hockey are different from any other field-based sport (8).

Hockey Stride

The hockey stride can be described as a biphasic activity involving a **support phase** and a **swing phase** (figure 2.1) (31, 40). The support phase can be subdivided into single-leg support, corresponding to glide, and double-leg support, corresponding to push-off. Propulsion occurs during the first half of single-leg support and continues during double-leg support as the hip is abducted and externally rotated and the knee is extended (26, 31).

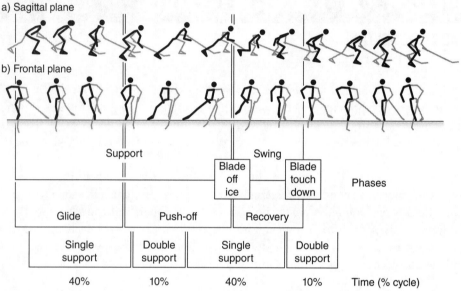

Figure 2.1 The hockey stride.

Reprinted by permission from D.J. Pearsall, R.A.Turcotte, R.A., and S.D. Murphy, "Biomechanics of Ice Hockey," in *Exercise and Sport Science*, edited by W.E. Garrett and D.T. Kirkendall (Philadelphia, PA: Lippincott, Williams & Wilkins, 2000), 675-694, permission conveyed through Copyright Clearance Center, Inc.

Support Phase (Single-Leg and Double-Leg)

- During double-leg support, the legs are in a quasi-isometric state with facilitation of the quadriceps and hamstrings in preparation for propulsion. The ankles are dorsiflexed in preparation for toe-off.
- During single-leg support the ankle is pronated and dorsiflexed with the weight shift on the inside edge of the skate boot.
- The adductors are engaged, and the glutes are preloaded and ready for propulsion in the frontal and transverse planes.

Propulsion Phase

- The glutes contract to extend, abduct, and externally rotate the femur at the hip in the frontal and transverse planes.
- During extension, the adductor complex, in particular the adductor magnus and adductor longus, work to eccentrically decelerate the powerful hip extensors in the frontal and transverse planes.

- During propulsion, the glutes and quads work as the accelerators, and the adductors work as the braking system.
- Perpendicular forces relative to the skate blade are produced in conjunction with the hip abductors and external rotators, creating stride width, which may increase forward speed by enabling a more oblique skate orientation relative to the skating surface in the frontal and transverse planes.

Run-to-Glide Action

Skating can be described as a **run-to-glide action**. The run portion consists of athletes starting from a standstill while overcoming inertia. This occurs by stopping and starting abruptly using a crossover step, pivoting and reaccelerating out of a turn, or by using a V-start, which typically occurs in on-ice testing. During the run portion, the goal is to create friction needed to overcome inertia and create propulsion. The run-to-glide transition can be identified at approximately the third stride (fifth step) (3). During glide, the goal is to take advantage of the near frictionless environment that the ice surface provides. See table 2.1 and figure 2.2 (27) for the biomechanical contrasts in run-to-glide. Energy spent during skating serves to overcome air resistance and ice friction while increasing kinetic energy (6, 7).

Table 2.1 Run-to-Glide Biomechanical Glossary

Term	Description
Propulsive angle	Angle of the skate blade relative to the ice; this angle increases during the run to create friction and decreases during glide to maximize speed
Unimodal force production	Force at touch down; occurs during the run portion of skating
Bimodal	Force at touch down and force at toe-off; occurs during the glide portion of the hockey stride
Impulse	The integral of force relative to the interval of time; think of impulse as total force
COM	Center of mass
Step width	The oblique distance between ipsilateral and contralateral foot during the hockey stride
Trunk segmental angle	Angle of the trunk relative to the horizon line

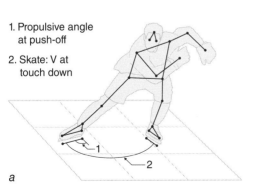

1. Propulsive angle at push-off
2. Skate: V at touch down

1. Shoulder abduction/ adduction at push-off
2. Hip abduction at push-off
3. Take off angle at push-off
4. Shoulder abduction/ adduction at touch down

a   b

Figure 2.2 Run to Glide: *(a)* run, and *(b)* glide.

Reprinted by permission from M.N. McPherson, A. Wrigley, W.J. Montelpare, D. Pearsall, and A. Ashare, "The Biomechanical Characteristics of Development-Age Hockey Players: Determining the Effects of Body Size on the Assessment of Skating Technique," ASTM Special Technical Publication (2004), 272-287.

Run

- Large propulsive angle (27, 31)
- Unimodal force production (34)
- Shallow knee angle (20)
- Large step width (3)
- Large lateral impulses create large vertical **center of mass** (COM; the average position of all parts of the system) movement (31)
- Hips abducted between 5 degrees during swing and 25 degrees at push-off (33)

Glide

- As number of strides increases, angle of the propulsion decreases to minimize friction (20)
- Body position important
- During glide, knees and hips deeper joint amplitudes to minimize air friction
- Propulsive angle decreases to maximize glide
- Bimodal force production (initial blade contact and push-off)
- Increase knee range of motion with successive push-offs of approximately 10 degrees between push-off 1 and push-off 3 (20)
- Decreased step width, which takes advantage of minimal ice friction (3)
- Low trunk segmental angle needed to reduce air friction

Skating Efficiency

What makes a great skater? This is a complex question to answer. While there is variability in skating, fundamental patterns emerge. Patterns falling outside of an acceptable range may be targeted as areas for improvement by skill coaches. Skating, like playing the guitar, is a skill. There are plenty of athletes playing at high levels that have unorthodox stride signatures. Better skating ability enables athletes to get into the right spots faster, create time and space, or decrease time and space on the defensive side of the puck. However, the game of hockey is complex, and although skating is a premium skill, one must also consider hockey sense and technical and tactical tendencies, because all contribute to success on the ice.

Skating Funnel

The **skating funnel** is composed of three qualities: genetic, physical (or trainable), and biomechanical (figure 2.3). The funnel moves from foundational to specific. All components play a part in an athlete's stride signature.

Genetics

Although certain characteristics of muscle architecture can be trained, it is highly genetically dependent. In other words, everyone has a unique ceiling. In terms of muscles and human movement, two of the most important architectural parameters are physiological cross-sectional area (PCSA) and fiber length. Muscle force is proportional to PCSA, and muscle velocity is proportional to fiber length (21). Longer muscles generate higher velocity movement, which may be critical for speed on the ice.

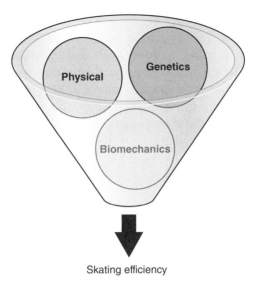

Figure 2.3   The skating funnel.

Lever length also plays an important role. Work is equal to force applied over a distance. If the length of a lever can be increased, the force needed to get work done can be reduced. Think of using a wrench to loosen a bolt. It is much easier to loosen a bolt with a longer handle than a shorter handle. Longer handles (i.e., longer levers) lead to economized efforts by working more efficiently at the job. Efficiency is maximized with longer levers. These qualities are genetically determined.

Physical or Trainable Qualities

Physical qualities in the skating funnel are trainable variables that are critical to be a fast, efficient skater. They include mobility, strength, step width, and turnover:

- **Mobility** is the efficiency of a movement or the ability to effectively reach a desired posture or position with minimal energetic cost. Aging plus the mileage accumulated during game schedule demands can cause a loss in the requisite mobility needed to attain efficiency on the ice (31a). Impulse is a product of net force and the amount of time the force is applied. An athlete who can produce force for longer periods of time can create larger impulse. A young skater who can gain a few extra inches of knee flexion can effectively increase stride length and, in turn, the amount of time that force is applied, leading to a much more efficient stride.

- To overcome inertia and accelerate, **strength** is needed to create pressure between the skate blade and the ice. Researchers have observed significant relationships between off-ice lower body strength tests and acceleration ability. For example, elite athletes jump significantly further in the single-leg broad jump than lower caliber athletes (3, 27, 33). It appears that higher levels of strength may partially differentiate elite from non-elite skaters.

- **Step width** is the oblique measurement from the ipsilateral foot relative to the contralateral foot during propulsion. Large amounts of hip abduction are needed in conjunction with large step widths to improve acceleration ability on the ice (3, 25). In order to produce large step widths, requisite strength is needed to achieve a deep knee flexion and stiffness through the lower leg to create friction during the run-to-glide phase.

- **Turnover**, or **stride rate**, is defined as how quickly the hockey athlete can recover from swing phase to stance and prepare for the next push-off. How fast can an athlete apply force? Stride rate has been found to further separate acceleration ability between elite and non-elite skaters (26). Researchers have found a correlation between stride rate and both single- and double-leg support times while skating at easy, moderate, and high velocities (26). In other words, as speed increases, support time decreases, and athletes with a superior ability to apply high force in short periods of time achieve greater velocities (26). This reinforces the concept that at higher speeds the rate of force development is critical (26, 43). Stride rates are typically much greater for higher caliber athletes (27, 34, 40, 43).

Biomechanics

As Arnold Palmer famously said, "Swing your swing. Not some idea of a swing. Not a swing you saw on TV. Not that swing you wish you had. No, swing your swing. Capable of greatness. Prized only by you. Perfect in its imperfection. Swing your swing. I know I did." Although no two skating strides, like golf swings, are the same, it is important to note if a stride pattern falls outside an acceptable range. Slight adjustments may lead to large improvements. This is much easier when working with a novice hockey athlete versus an elite athlete. Motor pattern changes are much more difficult to develop when patterns have been established for longer periods of time.

When it comes to biomechanics, there are four **heuristics**, or rules of thumb, to consider when viewing skating efficiency. As speed increases from run to glide, the following happens:

- Stride frequency increases with each step.
- Glide time increases with each step (this does not happen in land-based team sport).
- Trunk segmental angle remains low to decrease air resistance.
- The placement of the recovery leg below the hip enables effective stride length in the next push-off.

Biomechanical Considerations Related to Equipment

In the world of ice hockey, perhaps no other tool is as important as an athlete's choice in skates. The hockey skate consists of a hard outer shell, a rigid toe box to withstand the velocity of flying pucks, a padded tongue that might be manipulable for increased range of motion, an Achilles guard, a heel counter, and a skate blade. Athletes traditionally choose a skate that provides the most comfort while ensuring performance needs. The balance of this so-called performance teeter-totter typically resides in a personal choice between rigidity and range of motion. For example, defense athletes may choose a stiffer boot because backward skating (C-cut) does not have a swing phase; it only has a stance (foot is on the ice the whole time). A stiffer boot provides additional frontal plane support while also enabling rigidity during change of direction on the ice. In addition, the trunk segmental angle in forward skating is significantly less than in backward skating, which means that athletes lean their bodies forward more during forward skating than backward skating (43). This choice has a direct impact on biomechanics and foot contact within the skate because forward skating exerts more pressure on the anterior footbed of the skate (30).

The radius of contour (ROC) is more commonly referred to as the **rocker**. The ROC is the longitudinal profile of the blade and defines how much of the blade is in contact with the ice. In theory, a shorter rocker (less blade on the ice) allows for greater agility while a longer ROC is more favorable for speed (speed skates versus hockey skates).

Create a Theoretical Framework Using a Conceptual Model

Figure 2.4 shows an example of a conceptual model that targets stride efficiency. The relevant constructs are the support and swing phases, and the causal indicators of the construct are the glide, push-off, knee extension, and turnover. Fill in the indicator variables of the causal variables for on-ice skating mechanics. What is an acceptable biomechanical range for each phase, based on the four heuristics? Next, fill in the error filters of causal variables to indicate how to fix issues experienced on the ice. In other words, what baseline physical competencies and exercises serve to complement these phases within the stride? Can they be trained? See figure 2.5 for examples of the indicator variables and error filters.

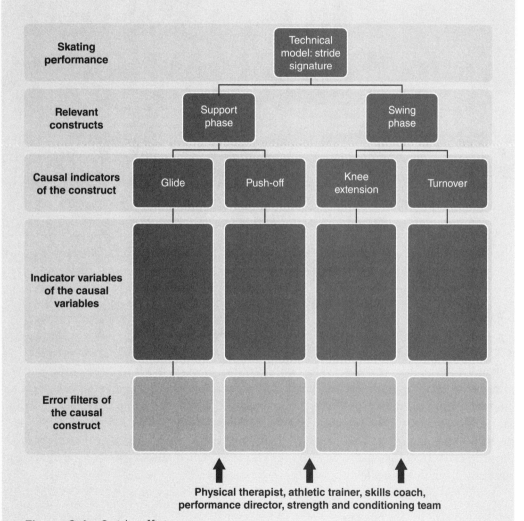

Figure 2.4   Stride efficiency.

(continued)

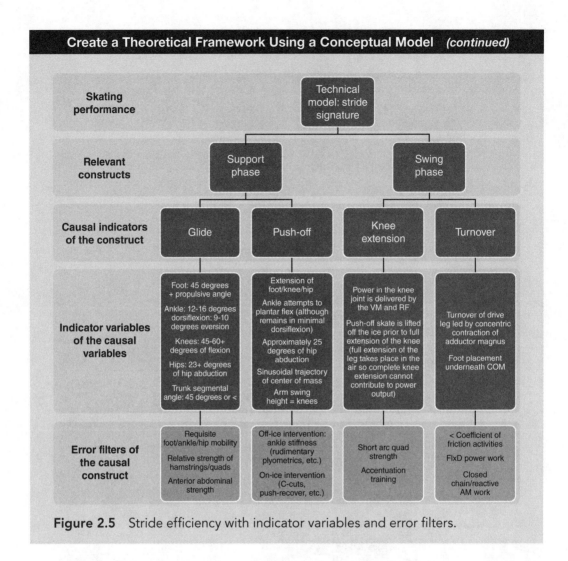

Figure 2.5 Stride efficiency with indicator variables and error filters.

Finally, the pitch of the skate is defined by the height of the blade and the position of the pivot point, or apex, of the blade. The pitch can change the lie of the skate, which can alter position. A forward pitch would place more body weight on the balls of the feet, increasing shin angles and possibly improving acceleration. Different pitches may produce different skating techniques. Using pressure sensors in the foot, researchers observed that the anterior foot showed greater peak forces at higher speeds (37). Perhaps manipulating the pitch may serve to augment these findings, allowing athletes to increase speeds on the ice.

Additional equipment-related considerations include the following:

- Ice temperature may dictate the type of **hollow** (the concave groove of the bottom surface of the skate blade; also called the **radius of hollow** [**ROH**]) to use in certain situations. Cold ice is firmer and may require a deeper hollow, whereas warm conditions may benefit from a shallower hollow.

- The ROH, ROC, and pitch allow athletes to individualize their skates based on their unique environments. It is important to educate athletes on these biomechanical underpinnings; however, the final choice in both skate boot and blade profile should be at the athletes' discretion.

- In return-to-play situations, using a shallower hollow can reduce strain on healing tissues.

- Skates are to hockey athletes as running shoes are to elite sprinters. Coaches should strive to understand the tools of the trade while educating athletes on the pros and cons of equipment setup.

- The **lie** of the hockey stick (the angle of the shaft relative to the ice surface; see figure 2.6) has biomechanical impact on the skating stride. Smaller athletes who have deeper postures on the ice may choose a lower lie to account for their crouched positions. Taller athletes with longer limb segments may choose larger lies to account for their individual anthropometrics. The most common lie is 45 degrees. Lie number typically can be found on the shaft of the hockey stick. When choosing an appropriate lie, hockey athletes should wear their skates, assume their hockey positions, and make sure the entire blade is flush to the floor. An inappropriate lie may cause kinematic issues at the ankle, knees, hips, and trunk while simultaneously compromising puck-handling skills on the ice.

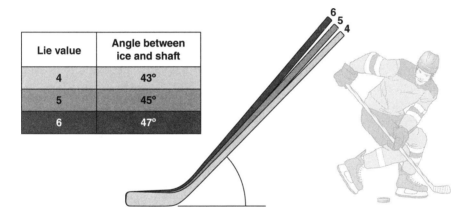

Lie value	Angle between ice and shaft
4	43°
5	45°
6	47°

Figure 2.6 Lie chart.

Understanding biomechanics enables the strength and conditioning professional to comprehend the subtle nuances that make training hockey athletes different from other field-based populations. Key takeaways include the following:

- Strive to understand biomechanics. What does a good stride look like?

- Create a simple biomechanical conceptual model. Update this model over time. Use this model as a proxy, not a mandate. Create bumper lanes and ranges around this conceptual model. Use targeted interventions, both on- and off-ice, to correct biomechanical inefficiencies that fall outside this range.

- Coach to the athletes' solution.

- Skating, like playing the guitar, is a skill. Repetition breeds success. Start at a young age, refining the skill of skating. Refining skill at a young age is easier than trying to correct skill at a later age. Stride signature is difficult to change in high training age hockey athletes in comparison to beginner and intermediate hockey athletes.

GENERAL PHYSIOLOGICAL ANALYSIS

Hockey is a game of intermittent acceleration, change of direction, strength, power, and work capacity. The hockey athlete can reach speeds of nearly 30 mph (48 km/h) with an excess of 20 pounds (9.1 kg) of additional weight in the form of protective gear. In addition to skating at very high velocities, athletes can cover distances between 2.3 and 6.8 kilometers (1.4 to 4.2 miles) per game, depending on the position (22). Defense athletes are on the ice for approximately 50% of the game, compared to an average of 35% for forwards (39). The surge in wearables, such as local positioning systems (LPS) and inertial movement analysis (IMA) devices, has also allowed for the quantification of position-specific workload (summation of all forces across all movements divided by 100) during games. Forwards had higher volumes and intensities of load during games in elite female ice hockey (10) and in men's NCAA Division I (29). To meet these demands, the hockey athlete must harness multiple biomotor abilities that can tangibly be used on the ice.

Hockey has changed over years. Athletes are bigger, faster, and stronger than ever before. Compared with athletes in the 1920s and 1930s, athletes of the early next century were an average of 17 kg (37 lb) heavier and 10 cm (3.9 in.) taller, with BMI increased by 2.3 kg/m² (28). Training camp is no longer the time to attain peak playing condition. Failure to show up in shape may result in preventable injury and loss of playing time and ultimately may cost athletes their jobs. Off-season performance training is a necessity (9).

The building blocks of successful hockey performance are mobility, speed, power, strength, and conditioning. Hockey requires a combination of these attributes unique to each athlete based on position, playing style, injury history, and role within the team. The following sections examine the physical and physiological demands of the hockey athlete and provide an overview of the requirements for successful performance on the ice.

Strength

Strength is the ability to exert force against an object. Strength and conditioning professionals focus on several different forms of strength needed to be successful on the ice. Maximal strength, relative strength, strength–speed and speed–strength can all be trained within the weight room. Strength and conditioning professionals may use various technologies, such as linear position transducers, to measure bar speed, enabling specific velocity windows to target specific adaptations (19). Pertaining to programming for the hockey athlete, simple, progressive overload programs may work wonders for young, aspiring athletes who lack requisite levels of baseline strength. Simple programs for advanced hockey athletes may also work wonders, but for different reasons. Advanced hockey athletes need to spend more time refining their craft on the ice. This comes at a physiological cost. Simple programs can also be used with great success in complementing (not competing with) on-ice workload (8). On the ice, applied force is displayed by driving down into the ice while the ice creates a reactive force (figure 2.7) (31).

Hockey requires a large amount of relative strength, which is needed to overcome inertia to create friction (3); combat centrifugal forces needed to change direction in tight, confined areas; and maintain balance on thin skate blades, all while withstanding the demands of physical contact (15). Figure 2.8 details the physics of hockey and the corresponding need for strength.

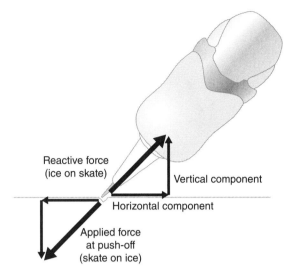

Figure 2.7 On-ice applied and reactive force.

Reprinted by permission from D.J. Pearsall, R.A.Turcotte, and S.D. Murphy, "Biomechanics of Ice Hockey," in *Exercise and Sport Science*, edited by W.E. Garrett and D.T. Kirkendall (Philadelphia, PA: Lippincott, Williams & Wilkins, 2000), 675-694, permission conveyed through Copyright Clearance Center, Inc.

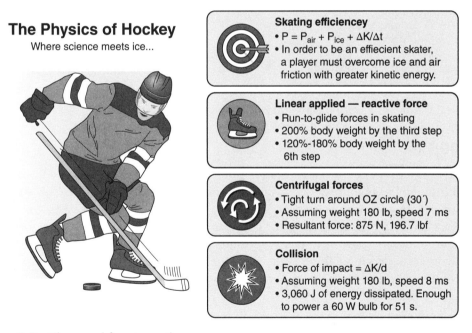

The Physics of Hockey
Where science meets ice...

Skating efficiencey
- $P = P_{air} + P_{ice} + \Delta K / \Delta t$
- In order to be an effiecient skater, a player must overcome ice and air friction with greater kinetic energy.

Linear applied — reactive force
- Run-to-glide forces in skating
- 200% body weight by the third step
- 120%-180% body weight by the 6th step

Centrifugal forces
- Tight turn around OZ circle (30′)
- Assuming weight 180 lb, speed 7 ms
- Resultant force: 875 N, 196.7 lbf

Collision
- Force of impact = $\Delta K / d$
- Assuming weight 180 lb, speed 8 ms
- 3,060 J of energy dissipated. Enough to power a 60 W bulb for 51 s.

Figure 2.8 The need for strength.

Power

Power is the ability to perform work as quickly as possible. It is a product of both force and velocity. Power is a rate-dependent motor ability (how quickly the light switch turns on), as opposed to force, which is more dependent on magnitude (how strong the light can shine). Another variable that needs to be considered in displaying power is impulse. Impulse is the integral, or portion of force, relative to the interval of time. It can be measured using a standard force plate. Think of impulse as total force. There are three ways to maximize impulse for the hockey athlete: increase peak force, increase the rate of force development, and increase the duration of force application. Skating has different ground contact profiles, or different impulse profiles, compared to field-based sports. Ground contact times in sprinting are approximately 80 to 100 milliseconds during maximum speed. Foot contact time decreases as speed increases. In contrast, contact times on the ice range from 380 to 420 milliseconds, a range roughly four to five times longer than land-based foot contact profiles (34). As speed increases on the ice, so too does ground contact time. Hockey athletes rely on longer strides to maximize the force into the ice and therefore the propulsive impulse. Separating training means into high force/high time and high force/low time is an excellent method to build an extensive library of power-based development exercises for the hockey athlete; see figure 2.9 (8). Similarly, jump progressions with higher ground contact times, such as box jumps and bounds, may be more relevant than short ground contact time jumps, such as pogo jumps, in ice hockey (1).

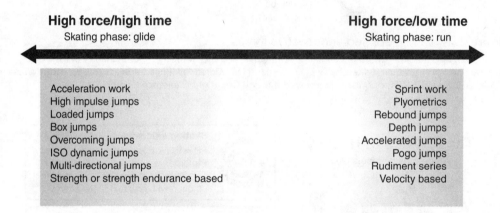

Figure 2.9   Power library for the hockey athlete.

Speed

The game has changed over time from a game of size and strength to a game of skill and speed. **Speed** is the ability to move as fast as possible from point A to point B. Speed in team sport is contingent on several variables: capacity, ability, and skill. **Capacity** describes the biomotor abilities, such as strength and power, that underpin speed. **Ability** is the linking of these capacities in a sport-specific manner, such as proper biomechanics, while passing, puck-handling, and shooting on the ice. **Skill** is the ability to use this speed during game play, which includes speed of hands, speed of feet, and speed in decision-making ability. Game speed is dependent on all three elements. A simple way to remember this is the autosport analogy. Both capacity and ability may be viewed as the car, with the goal being to build bigger, stronger, and more robust engines during key stages of athletic development. Skill may be viewed as the driver behind the wheel. How does one use this speed during the organized chaos of a hockey game?

Off-ice speed tests such as the 40-yard (37 m) dash, 30-meter (32 yd) sprint, and resisted sprinting have all been shown to have moderate to strong correlation to on-ice skating speed (12, 18, 36). Sprinting and jumping are two of the strongest predictors of on-ice speed (8). Off-ice speed may create a favorable transfer in the form of stride rate on the ice. The ability to quickly recover the stride leg prior to the opposite leg push-off is termed **stride rate**. Stride rate has been found to further separate acceleration ability between elite and non-elite skaters.

Low trajectory angle, short single-support time, and the foot placed below the hip prior to propulsion are aspects that separate average from elite athletes (26). As referenced earlier, as speed increases, support times decrease and stride rate increases. This reinforces the concept that at higher speeds the number of times the force of propulsion is applied may be more important than the force at each propulsion (26, 34, 43). Speed and power training are two important considerations for the strength and conditioning professional when constructing off-season training.

Mobility and Flexibility

Mobility, the ability to reach a desired posture or position, is context dependent, meaning that there are different demands placed on the system for different sports and activities, thereby requiring different levels of mobility. **Flexibility** is the range of motion around a joint, often limited to one or two joints and not heavily reliant on the nervous system for support. Many factors can affect mobility within the system, such as previous injury, osseous adaptation, inefficient posture, facilitated muscle groups, and poor overall movement quality or control. These can all affect the system and compromise efficiency on the ice. A dynamic movement assessment can reveal these inadequacies and prompt the strength and conditioning professional to program specific mobility exercises that enhance motor skill.

Increased mobility, enabling the hockey athlete to express efficient movement within a greater total range, is one of the quickest ways to build more efficient skaters. Elements of relative strength, mobility, and technique are important for economizing stride mechanics and building more efficient athletes.

$$\text{Hockey stride} = \text{stride length} \times \text{stride frequency}$$

During an athlete's formative years, stride length and stride frequency may be improved due to neurological development and the acquisition of improved motor skill. Gaining a useful movement database by playing multiple sports and being exposed to free play during the early years advances the physical literacy learning curve for young athletes. As the hockey athlete matures in age, the biggest improvement in stride efficiency may be a shift in focus to improving stride length. Stride length is contingent upon several factors, including mobility. Mobility during this time plays a crucial role in realizing these performance gains.

Adequate mobility of the ankles and hips can directly enhance stride length by allowing the athlete to adopt a lower skating position, which increases efficiency (output relative to the cost of input), and the ability to express force for longer periods of time. This improvement in kinematics may improve force production on the ice. Increasing range of motion allows the hockey athlete to express force into the ice for longer periods of time, which increases the propulsive impulse. Mobility has tangible effects on an athlete's ability to enhance acceleration and speed.

Energy System Use

Examining the energy system demands in ice hockey can lead to debate. **Intragame** (athlete-based decisions) and **intergame** (position, game situations, technical packages) differences all come into context when assessing which energy system dominates during competitive play. Context matters. In science, data is removed from context to study and observe, but it is the context that brings the data to life. Without context, it is possible to justify beliefs and behaviors, when, in fact, most of the debate simply depends on circumstance. For the team sport athlete, it is important to develop and maintain energy production (9).

The average hockey athlete plays between 12 and 20 shifts per game and has an average rest period of 225 seconds between shifts (9). A typical shift consists of 30- to 80-second bouts of intermittent explosive efforts (28). The rest interval between periods is 15 minutes. An estimated 70% to 80% of the energy for a hockey athlete is derived from the phosphocreatine system and glycolysis (2), but the amount varies based on the specific type of activity (table 2.2) (4). This does not take away the importance of developing a sound foundation of aerobic fitness, which can enhance processing of exercise-induced metabolic waste and enhance recovery. "All three energy systems are used during an ice hockey game, but one system will predominate depending on: individual intensity level at that moment; game situation; and the motivation of the athlete" (39, p. 44).

Table 2.2   Approximate Contribution of the Systems During the Game of Hockey

Type of activity	Phosphocreatine system (anaerobic)	Glycolytic system (anaerobic)	Oxidative system (aerobic)
5-second burst	85%	10%	5%
10 seconds of hard skating	60%	30%	10%
30 seconds of continuous activity	15%	70%	15%
1-minute shift of intermittent sprints, coasting, and stops	10%	60%	30%
Recovery between shifts and periods	5%	5%	90%

Reprinted by permission from Canadian Hockey Association, *Intermediate Level Manual,* (Ottawa, ON: Canadian Hockey Association, 1989).

Energy Production

Adenosine triphosphate (ATP) is the energy currency of the human body. It is derived from the conversion of food macronutrients (carbohydrates, protein, and fat) at the muscle cell level and allows the body to convert chemical energy into mechanical work. The breakdown of ATP into ADP + P (adenosine diphosphate + phosphate) provides the energy required for muscle contraction and performance on the ice. The intramuscular storage of ATP is limited, so to maintain work output, resynthesis is required. If ATP were not efficiently replenished it would quickly be consumed because only very small amounts are stored within the muscle. The intramuscular supply of ATP is sufficient to last for 2 seconds of maximal effort work, after which resynthesis is necessary. ATP can increase more than 100-fold in the transition from rest to maximal exercise (16). The major variable that determines this synthesis of ATP is exercise intensity. Hockey is a metabolically demanding sport, challenging the system to provide appropriate energy during intermittent play, acceleration, deceleration, change of direction, stopping, starting, gliding, and recovery between shifts and periods. It is the ability of the body to regenerate ATP that determines the hockey athlete's performance of these tasks while maintaining a high-level power output.

Aerobic System

The aerobic system is responsible for sustaining and providing submaximal levels of power output for prolonged periods of time. It is a supply and recovery system that uses oxygen, carbohydrates, and fats to resynthesize ATP. Having a strong aerobic foundation can delay fatigue caused by high-intensity anaerobic work and enable the hockey athlete to recover more efficiently in between shifts and intermissions, maintaining higher levels of performance in later stages of game play (24). Researchers assessed the relationship between the aerobic system and on-ice performance measures relative to scoring chances (14). Only $\dot{V}O_2max$ (a measure of aerobic fitness) significantly predicted scoring chances in a group of 29 Division I college hockey athletes, accounting for 17% of the variance. $\dot{V}O_2max$ has also been explored via longitudinal data collected in the National Hockey League. Fourteen years of data were collected on Montreal Canadiens athletes, revealing annual mean values ranging between 54.6 and 59.2 mL/kg/min (28). Compared to research in the 1980s (5), $\dot{V}O_2max$ has remained relatively constant, independent of body mass. Research using retrospective cross-sectional data from the 2001 and 2003 NHL drafts suggest that mean values ranged from 55.6 to 57.8 mL/kg/min (41), based on position. These numbers are relatively consistent with NCAA Division I hockey athletes, with mean values 59 ± 4 mL/kg/min (14).

Repeated sprint ability (RSA) highlights the ability of the hockey athlete to maintain maximal effort outputs with incomplete recovery (38). RSA is often trained and measured using maximal intermittent sprints, followed by short rest periods (<30 seconds). It appears that aerobic contribution increases as the number of sprints increase within the context of RSA. Gaitanos and colleagues (13) examined energy system contributions during 10 sets of maximal 6-second sprints on a cycle ergometer with 30 seconds of rest between bouts. The fall in muscle glycogen was not linear in fashion, and during the 10th sprint it was less than half that observed during the first sprint. It may be concluded that as the number of sprints increases so does the contribution of aerobic metabolism and its ability to regenerate phosphocreatine, coupled with a negligible contribution from anaerobic glycolysis. Accordingly, during the demands of a 60-minute hockey game, contribution of the aerobic system increases with time. Position-specific demands on the ice use the aerobic system at varying capacities during play. The upkeep of the aerobic system for success in ice hockey is an important performance factor for the hockey athlete.

Increased aerobic fitness is a by-product of central and peripheral adaptations that occur during training. A central adaptation occurs at the heart and lungs and is referred to as a **general adaption**. These adaptations include increased stroke volume and eccentric cardiac hypertrophy. In contrast, a peripheral adaptation occurs at the site of the musculature and is referred to as a **specific adaptation**. The central and peripheral adaptations of aerobic training are listed in table 2.3.

Table 2.3 Central Versus Peripheral Adaptations of Aerobic Training

Central	Peripheral
Eccentric cardiac hypertrophy (left chamber can fill with more blood)	Increase in oxygen kinetics
Increased stroke volume	Increased myoglobin affinity
Decreased resting heart rate	Increased mitochondria
Increased heart rate recovery	Increased capillary density
Increased hemoglobin affinity	Increase in type I slow-twitch oxidative efficiency
Increased pulmonary diffusion	Increase in type IIa oxidative efficiency
Parasympathetic drive	

Note: Central adaptation is a general adaptation and occurs at the heart and lungs.
Peripheral adaptation is a specific adaptation and occurs at the periphery musculature.

Anaerobic Systems

The phosphocreatine (PCr) system is responsible for immediate, explosive bursts of energy lasting approximately 6 to 15 seconds. This intense work is not sustainable for prolonged periods of time because the use of ATP outpaces the rate of ATP resynthesis. PCr stores in muscle can provide up to three times the amount of the stored ATP and can do so in roughly 10 seconds. PCr stores are returned to near resting levels in about 60 to 90 seconds, making PCr a reusable fuel (16). The central and peripheral adaptations of anaerobic training are listed in table 2.4.

The lactate system supports maximum power output for approximately 15 to 120 seconds. This system is of extreme importance in ice hockey. The lactate system is anaerobic in nature (does not require oxygen) and breaks down carbohydrates to resynthesize ATP at a much faster rate than by aerobic energy production. It does so by the dissimilation of glycogen to glucose, glucose to pyruvate, and finally, pyruvate to lactate.

Table 2.4   Central Versus Peripheral Adaptations of Anaerobic Training

Central	Peripheral
Left ventricle concentric hypertrophy	Increased glycolytic enzyme kinetics (glycogen phosphorylase, hexokinase, glycogen phosphofructokinase)
Rate coding	Decreased capillary density
Motor unit recruitment	Increase in type IIa oxidative efficiency
Intermuscular coordination	
Intramuscular coordination	
Sympathetic drive	

Note: Central adaptation is a general adaptation and occurs at the heart and lungs.

Peripheral adaptation is a specific adaptation and occurs at the periphery musculature.

Target Context Versus Target Environment

Many hockey athletes remember their first few days of training camp, or their first few ice touches after a long off-season. Getting "hockey legs" back is a feeling that many athletes encounter during this time period. This may be due to the peripheral demands of skating, which are different than field-based conditioning. Context refers to the parts of something; in the case of ice hockey, the skills needed to be successful. The environment encompasses the playing surface. Both context and environment must be considered in the preparation process. Lance Armstrong won the Tour de France seven consecutive times from 1999 to 2005, but finished 488th in the Boston Marathon despite being genetically gifted and training hard. This is due to training specificity and the **SAID principle** (specific adaptations to imposed demands) (35). Applying this concept to hockey means that to get skating legs back, an athlete needs to get on the ice and skate! Skating, like riding a bike, is a skill. To get more efficient at it, then do it, and do it often. Nothing is more specific than the target environment.

Intramuscular Adaptations

Central adaptations are requisite for obtaining suitable maximal aerobic function that is required as a foundation for performance. Once the foundation has been established, adaptation inside the muscle (peripheral) may be more important for metabolic clearance and respiratory capacity than the central adaptations of increasing oxygen delivery from the heart. Oxygen still needs to get there (central), but oxygen uptake allows the hockey athlete to use this oxygen for physical output from the muscular system.

When discussing intramuscular adaptations, mitochondrial density is worth more attention. Mitochondria are the powerhouse of the cell, responsible for producing ATP though respiration while regulating cellular metabolism. In response to aerobic training, human skeletal muscle undergoes an adaptive increase in both the size and number of mitochondria. The volume of mitochondria relative to the volume of myofibrils is considered a possible index of muscle respiratory capacity (23). Mitochondrial volume density (percentage of muscle fiber volume occupied by mitochondria) has been shown to correlate with increased oxidative enzyme activity (with some enzymes increasing two- to threefold, such as citrate synthase, cytochrome c, and CoA transferase), the ability to oxidize pyruvate, a decrease in lactate dehydrogenase, a slower use of carbohydrate as an energy source, and an increased maximal oxygen uptake (17).

To maximize the specificity of local mitochondrial adaptations to hockey, athletes need to integrate skating into their off-season program. This is the essence of the SAID principle: Practice in the target environment, because there is no substitution for the ice.

POSITION-SPECIFIC ANALYSIS

Hockey athletes are divided into three general positional groups: forwards, defense athletes, and goaltenders. Forwards can be further sorted into centers and wingers. Wingers are categorized as either left wing or right wing. This decision is typically made according to the hand with which the athlete shoots. For example, right-handed shooters typically play right wing, although this is not always the case. Defense athletes may also play on the left or right side of the ice. Similar to wingers, this decision is typically made by the hand with which the athlete shoots. Each position has unique physical requirements, such as anthropometrics (size), aerobic function, and physical abilities such as speed, power, and strength that should be considered in the athlete's training program.

Athlete Profiling

A profile is a short index of the physical attributes needed to play sport. Other variables can also be assessed in a profile, such as the technical and tactical elements. Profiling may also be broken down within position groups to compare team members. Studies have been performed to profile ice hockey athletes. For example, using a retrospective, cross-sectional study design with data from the 2001-2003 National Hockey League Combine, researchers were able to distinguish physical performance differences between positions; see table 2.5 (41). Newer technologies such as LPS and IMA devices have enabled practitioners to differentiate on-ice external load measures based on position (11, 22).

Forwards

In terms of off-ice physical capacities, it appears that both forwards and defense athletes have similar power and strength profiles. Among athletes in the 2001-2003 National Hockey League Combine, there were no differences between forwards or defense athletes in long jump, vertical jump, bench press, push-up, medicine ball toss, curl-up, or sit and reach performance (41). Off-ice aerobic and anaerobic measures were also similar (41).

On-ice research has also been conducted using portable multiple-camera computerized tracking. Thirty-six NHL athletes were tracked during a game, and external workloads were measured. The principal findings were that athletes were on the ice for 10 to 25 minutes and skated an average distance of 4,606 meters (5,037 yd) during a game. Forwards performed

Table 2.5   Physical Performance Differences Between Hockey Positions

Performance parameter	Forwards	Defense athletes	Goaltender
Long jump	258.8 cm ± 19.7 cm (101.9 in. ± 7.8 in.)	255.1 cm ± 14.8 cm (100.4 in. ± 5.8 in.)	245.4 cm ± 20.6 cm (96.6 in. ± 8.1 in.)
Vertical jump	62.7 cm ± 8.8 cm (24.7 in. ± 3.5 in.)	63.0 cm ± 7.2 cm (24.8 in. ± 2.8 in.)	61.0 cm ± 6.8 cm (24.0 in. ± 2.7 in.)
Bench press (reps)	7.7 ± 4.2	9.2 ± 4.3	3.3 ± 3.9[*+]
Push-up (reps)	26.5 ± 5.2	26.6 ± 5.6	22.7 ± 5.6[*+]
Push strength	119.8 kg ± 31.2 kg (264.1 lb ± 68.8 lb)	122.5 kg ± 22.2 kg (270.1 lb ± 48.9 lb)	105.0 kg ± 28.5 kg[*+] (231.5 lb ± 62.8 lb)
Pull strength	118.8 kg ± 15.3 kg (261.9 lb ± 33.7 lb)	123.1 kg ± 12.7 kg (271.4 lb ± 28.0 lb)	107.8 kg ± 15.4 kg[*+] (237.7 lb ± 34.0 lb)
Medicine ball toss	506.1 cm ± 47.8 cm (199.3 in. ± 18.8 in.)	522.2 cm ± 53.4 cm (205.6 in. ± 21.0 in.)	506.1 cm ± 47.10 cm[*+] (199.3 in. ± 18.5 in.)
Curl-up (reps)	23.8.8 ± 15.3	27.6 ± 18.1	27.0 ± 9.5
Sit and reach	38.0 cm ± 7.9 cm (15 in. ± 3.1 in.)	39.3 cm ± 8.1 cm (15.5 in. ± 3.2 in.)	44.5 cm ± 7.7 cm[#] (17.5 in. ± 3.0 in.)
Absolute peak power (W)	1,008.4 ± 128.6	1,028.6 ± 140.9	929.2 ± 99.9[*+]
Relative peak power (W/kg)	11.6 ± 1.3	11.3 ± 1.3	10.9 ± 1.2[*]
Fatigue index (%)	39.1 ± 6.2	37.6 ± 6.5	38.0 ± 7.2
$\dot{V}O_2$max (mL/kg/min)	57.8 ± 5.3	56.1 ± 5.7	55.6 ± 4.3

[*] Significantly less than forwards.
[+] Significantly less than defense athletes.
[#] Significantly greater than forwards and defense athletes.
Data from 41.

much more high-intensity skating than defense athletes. Forwards covered 54% more distance by high-intensity skating per time unit. Forwards covered 55% and 33% more distance in sprint and very fast skating compared to defense athletes (22). Based on this study, it appears that forwards are required to perform larger amounts of work at higher intensities. Research in elite women's ice hockey has also explored differences in external workload between positions (10). Forwards had higher volumes and intensities of load measures in both training and game play when compared to defense athletes. These objective measures may aid the strength and conditioning professional in developing targeted intervention strategies during off-season training and injury rehabilitation.

Forwards require large amounts of speed, power, relative strength, and muscular endurance. In addition, forwards must be able to quickly recover from the intermittent demands of high-intensity efforts by relying on a well-trained aerobic system. Training plans must be adjusted based on time of year. During an NHL hockey season, athletes may play upwards of an 82-game schedule. In contrast, Division I college hockey teams play a 34-game schedule. Programs should be structured to complement, not compete with, on-ice work during the season.

Defense Athletes

Defense athletes are heavier and taller than both forwards and goalies (41). These anthropometric features may aid in net-front battles, wall play, shot blocking, physical contact, and tactical efficiency on the ice. The defensive position relies on skating efficiency in both forward and backward directions, requiring speed, agility, strength, and aerobic fitness. Backward skating requires slight biomechanical adjustments in comparison to forward skating. In skating backward, trunk lean in the direction of movement is not possible the way it is in forward skating. The athlete must adopt a deeper hip and knee flexed posture and lead with the hips (31).

On-ice workload research suggests that defense athletes can cover as much as 29% more skating distance than forwards, while spending 47% greater time on the ice (22). However, defense athletes spend larger amounts of time skating at slower skating speeds (very slow, slow, moderate) than forwards. Defense athletes must be able to play a larger quantity of game minutes compared to forwards, therefore relying more on aerobic function. Defensive athletes have lower volumes and intensities of load measures than forwards in both training and competition (10). The larger load and athlete load per minute scores in forwards as compared to defense athletes may be the result of defense athletes spending larger portions of the game skating at submaximal speeds.

Goaltenders

One way that the goaltending position is unique is that goalies play the full 60 minutes. Goaltenders typically have higher body fat levels, lower levels of upper body strength, and lower aerobic fitness levels than both forwards and defense athletes (41). However, goaltenders have greater flexibility (41). Goaltenders require a completely different movement profile than any other position on the ice, due in large part to the butterfly technique and the reverse vertical horizontal (see later in this paragraph). The **butterfly technique** has now become a staple in goaltending. Butterfly goalies stand with their feet hip-width apart and knees flexed in the ready position. When a low shot approaches the net, a butterfly-style goaltender quickly drops to the knees while internally rotating the hips and splaying out the lower-leg pads to cover the goal net. The combined motion of hip flexion, end-range internal rotation, and tibial external rotation transfers large amounts of stress across the hip joint and knees (32). Research has suggested that this position elicits maximal hip flexion, adduction, and internal rotation angles while sustaining knee ground reaction forces greater than 1.45 times body weight (42). Landing in position of maximal flexion, adduction, and internal rotation while supporting 1.45 times their body weight places goaltenders in a more vulnerable position relative to forwards and defense athletes. Goaltenders have been reported to execute this position approximately 34 times per game and repeat this maneuver many more times in warm-ups and practice, thus consistently encountering hip angles near the range of motion limits (42).

A relatively new technique has emerged called the **reverse vertical horizontal** (RVH). This position occurs when the leg against the goalpost is horizontal relative to the ice, while the opposite leg is vertical, in order to cover more net preventing scoring opportunities in tight, confined areas. These positions come at the expense of hip health and have been associated with the onset of overuse injuries such as femoroacetabular impingement (FAI). There are two general presentations of FAI: A **cam impingement** is characterized by a decrease in the head and neck offset at the femur and may result from the neck of the femur rubbing against the acetabulum of the pelvis, and a **pincer impingement** involves an overgrowth of the acetabular hood, which increases the relative depth of the socket. Both presentations limit the amount of hip flexion that can be achieved before the femoral neck abuts the acetabular socket.

When designing a resistance training program for goalies, strength and conditioning professionals must consider the repetitive stress placed on the hips during competition and practice. Butterfly counts in both practice and games are now being monitored through various technologies, enabling improved practice planning on the ice. Off the ice, strength and conditioning professionals with a solid understanding of functional anatomy can strategically

Ethan Miller/Getty Images

Strength training for goaltenders is unique due to the combined motion of hip flexion, end-range internal rotation, and tibial external rotation that produces stress across the hip joint and knees.

program exercises that counteract the often overfacilitated patterns of the position. The tug of war between the rectus abdominis and the adductor groups may provide a starting point. The best solution for "putting down the rope," or balancing length–tension, can be accomplished through simple but effective pelvis and rib cage repositioning activities. The goal is to facilitate targeted muscle groups while inhibiting others. For goaltenders, facilitating the ribs through breathing techniques such as breath work with strong exhalations may serve to internally rotate the ribs. Internal rotation of the ribs may help increase the dome height and power potential of the diaphragm and may be accompanied by a reorientation of the pelvis from anterior to posterior, creating a better "stacked" position between the diaphragm and the pelvic floor. Focusing on the sagittal plane fibers of the gluteus maximus and hamstrings can serve the same purpose: Reorient the pelvis to a more neutral position while restoring length–tension relationships within the system. Finally, deep bilateral exercises such as heavy squatting may need to be reconsidered or used with caution when designing programs for goalies. During deep hip flexion, the femur orients inward toward internal rotation. During extension from deep squatting, the femur may again shift internally, this time due to the strong and powerful extension fibers of the adductor magnus. This places tissue stress on a pattern that is already overworked. The solution may be to program a greater number of single-leg exercises while dedicating a larger proportion of time to posterior chain work.

CONCLUSION

Hockey is an athletic sport that requires mobility, speed, power, strength, and relevant energy system efficiency. The contribution of each of these physical qualities varies depending on the playing position. Both wingers and centers require a well-developed ATP-PCr system and strong aerobic capacity because they skate at higher intensities throughout the game compared to defense athletes. On the other hand, defense athletes are often on the ice for almost half of the game. Defense athletes are typically taller and heavier and tend to engage in net-front battles, shot blocking, and wall scrums. Goaltenders place large amounts of stress on their hips due to the repetitive patterns of their position. Both the butterfly technique and RVH place the hips and knees in vulnerable positions during game play. Understanding the unique physiological requirements for each position is important to accurately prescribe exercise on a position-specific basis. The end goal is to keep athletes healthy and safe on the ice while achieving optimal performance. The best ability is availability.

TESTING PROTOCOLS AND ATHLETE ASSESSMENT

DEVAN MCCONNELL

Hockey is one of the fastest team sports in the world. Athletes routinely skate at speeds over 20 mph (32.2 km/h) at the elite level (9). Hockey has a significant physical component associated, and most leagues and levels allow for high-intensity contact and collisions. As such, the physical makeup of athletes is a crucial component of individual and team performance, along with the technical and tactical abilities inherent in the game. Physical testing and athlete assessment protocols for ice hockey should cover a large spectrum of athletic qualities, including speed, power, strength, anaerobic power, and aerobic endurance.

This chapter outlines several tests designed to provide a well-rounded picture of physiological characteristics associated with ice hockey performance. Assessments in these qualities should be carried out for the following reasons:

- Creating baseline profiles for use in return-to-play scenarios as well as individualized training programs
- Comparing elite and sub-elite physical characteristics to aid in the targeted training plans of developmental athletes
- Establishing checks and balances on the efficacy of training programs
- Assessing readiness to train and compete
- Providing physical ability and development reference points for talent identification or recruitment purposes

Testing should reflect the physiological qualities and types of exercises the strength and conditioning professional wants the athletes to focus on. Athletes often "train for the test" so to get athletes to work on sprinting speed, include tests designed to measure sprinting speed. If unilateral lower body strength is an important feature, test unilateral lower body strength. Testing for physiological components useful to the sport is a subtle way to encourage behavior.

GENERAL TESTING GUIDELINES

The order for conducting tests, how data is recorded and collected, the setup of equipment necessary for the tests, and how to spot exercises to be tested should all be considered ahead of time. Nothing is worse than getting set up on testing day only to realize the batteries for a certain

Bruce Bennett/Getty Images

Agility, speed, power, and strength are essential for top-level hockey performance.

piece of equipment have died, or not enough testing sheets have been printed out to be able to record scores or times. Though seemingly mundane, these types of details can make or break testing sessions. Having enough hands on deck to help with athlete flow, recordkeeping, setup and breakdown, and the like is a crucial, albeit often overlooked, component of a well-run testing session. Conduct a dry run of the testing day ahead of time to help ensure things go as smoothly as possible. Making sure everyone is on the same page ahead of time minimizes unforced errors.

Safety should be of paramount importance during testing sessions. A proper dynamic warm-up should be performed prior to the session, and if there are any long waits between exercises or tests, adequate time should be given to warm back up. During maximal effort tests such as sprints or weightlifting movements, a specific warm-up procedure should take place immediately prior to the exercise. For example, when testing 40-meter (44 yd) on-ice sprints, several repetitions of submaximal sprints should be performed, building up to near-maximal effort, followed by the actual testing sprints.

The remainder of this chapter outlines specific tests that provide valuable information on the physical profile and development of aspiring hockey athletes. There is a dearth of published data on hockey athletes, so normative value tables were constructed by using data acquired in applied settings by the contributors of this book. Importantly, at each level, this data comes from elite-caliber athletes (i.e., Tier I youth, NCAA Division I college, professional, and national team athletes). These values are presented with the intention of providing a reference; however, testing data becomes increasingly more useful when it is tracked over time. Organizations are encouraged to create their own testing batteries, ideally pulling from the tests in this chapter, and develop their own normative values. Similarly, while having a frame of reference for how elite athletes perform on tests is helpful, individuals should prioritize consistent incremental improvements in their personal scores over comparisons to other athletes.

Test Finder

COUNTERMOVEMENT JUMP

The countermovement jump, also commonly referred to as the *vertical jump*, is a simple assessment that can provide a large amount of useful information about an athlete's explosive abilities. Speed and power are key components of elite hockey athletes, and lower body explosiveness is a key performance indicator for hockey performance.

Purpose

By routinely measuring and monitoring the explosive abilities of athletes, the strength and conditioning professional is provided with important feedback on the adaptations achieved by the prescribed training program. The countermovement jump is often used by NHL scouts to serve as a proxy for lower body explosiveness and skating speed potential (5). Put simply, the higher an athlete can jump, the more power the athlete is able to produce. Since explosive hip, knee, and (to some degree) ankle extension are biomechanical features of the skating stride, especially for the first few pushes during acceleration, the countermovement jump provides a biomechanically similar pattern to evaluate explosive power.

Depending on the testing apparatus, jump height may be the only available metric. While yielding beneficial information, the height an athlete jumps may be achieved via different strategies. More complex tools such as force plates can provide insight into these strategies and showcase some of the underlying mechanisms that result in jump height, such as average relative force output, peak power, braking force, reactive strength, left-right asymmetry scores, and many other data points. With these more advanced metrics, the strength and conditioning professional may be able to dig deeper into how the athlete produces force and power, allowing a more nuanced and individualized training program to be developed. In addition, some of the underlying metrics associated with the countermovement jump, such as braking phase duration, countermovement depth, and time to takeoff, may provide valuable insight into the balance between fatigue and neuromuscular readiness.

Equipment

For assessing the countermovement jump, a range of options is available. The most basic version is simply using chalk and having the athlete jump and mark the wall at the highest point. However, more advanced options are arguably more accurate and becoming increasingly accessible to strength and conditioning professionals. For example, the Vertec system is commonplace. This apparatus consists of a tall pole with multiple "vanes"; the athlete jumps and attempts to "knock" a vane to display jump height. A second tool that is relatively affordable and found in many strength and conditioning settings is a contact mat. These pieces of equipment work by measuring the time the athlete is in the air during the jump, and converting this time to a jump height by considering Newton's law of universal gravitation, which states that time to rise and fall under the influence of gravity is equal. The most advanced tool commonly available to the strength and conditioning professional is a force plate. The force plate measures jump height by calculating mass times takeoff velocity. It should be noted that force plates and contact mats allow the countermovement jump to be performed with or without arm swing, while the other options require arm swing and thus are not able to differentiate between the two variations. Jumping without contribution from an arm swing reduces the height of the jump but provides better information about the power of the lower body. Also, keep in mind that all of these options technically calculate jump height differently, so comparison between the scores from different types of equipment is not advised. Pick one tool and stick to it, if possible. Again, here are the common equipment options:

- Force plate
- Alternatively, contact mat or Vertec
- If using contact mat or Vertec, testing sheets to record data

Setup

Setup for the countermovement jump is similar regardless of testing apparatus. The only difference is the arm position. This depends on whether an arm swing is part of the protocol. If not using an arm swing, then the hands should be placed on and remain on the hips for the duration of the movement. If using an arm swing, then arms should be extended overhead at the initiation of the test. As the countermovement jump is initiated, the athlete descends rapidly into the bottom portion of the loading phase (the "countermovement") and, at the same time, quickly and in sync with the rest of the body, snaps the arms down toward the floor. Upon reaching the bottom of the movement, the athlete explosively reverses the motion, driving hard off the floor and extending the arms back up overhead. If using a touch-based method such as the Vertec, the athlete reaches as high as possible to mark or brush aside the vane. If using a contact mat or force plates, the start and finish position should be as close as possible to the same spot, and hip, knee, and ankle flexion should be avoided prior to the landing. However, it is important to absorb the landing forces upon contact with the floor, so the athlete should be instructed to land on the heels with the legs straight and knees unlocked but to immediately cushion the landing by flexing the hips, knees, and ankles.

Testing Protocol

In this example, a sequential testing protocol performed on a contact mat or force plates is described.

1. The starting position is on the center of the mat, with the weight evenly distributed on both feet.
2. At a verbal cue, the athlete rapidly descends toward the floor by flexing at the ankles, knees, and hips into the countermovement portion of the jump.

3. Upon self-selected bottom depth, the athlete rapidly reverses motion and initiates the propulsive portion of the jump by extending the ankles, knees, and hips.

4. The athlete leaves the floor during the flight portion of the jump.

5. Upon landing, the athlete absorbs contact with the mat or force plates, allowing for an eccentric braking movement while slowing the downward trajectory and completing the landing portion of the jump.

Coaching Tips

- Fully explain the testing procedure, as well as the intent behind the test.
- Cue the athlete to push explosively and forcefully as hard as possible off of the floor.
- Emphasize an evenly distributed landing.
- Discard any jump with excessive flexion of the lower body prior to landing.

Descriptive Data

See table 3.1 for normative values for a vertical jump using a contact mat and table 3.2 using force plates.

Table 3.1 Normative Values for the Vertical Jump (Contact Mat)

Level	Sex*	Height (mean ± SD)
High school[a]	F	16.6 in. ± 2.9 in. (42.2 cm ± 7.4 cm)
High school[a]	M	21.8 in. ± 2.0 in. (55.4 cm ± 5.1 cm)
University[a]	F	17.3 in. ± 0.5 in. (43.9 cm ± 1.3 cm)
University[b]	M	31.4 in. ± 2.4 in. (79.8 cm ± 6.1 cm)
National level[c]	F	22.3 in. ± 2.4 in. (56.6 cm ± 6.1 cm)
Professional[d]	M	27.4 in. ± 2.6 in. (69.6 cm ± 6.6 cm)

*F = female. M = male. [a] Bendus (2023). [b] McConnell (2018). [c] Neeld (2016a). [d] Potenza (2017).

Table 3.2 Normative Values for the Vertical Jump (Force Plates)

Level	Sex*	Height (mean ± SD)
High school[a]	F	10.4 in. ± 1.9 in. (26.3 cm ± 4.8 cm)
High school[a]	M	15.0 in. ± 2.2 in. (38.1 cm ± 5.6 cm)
University[a]	F	11.7 in. ± 1.6 in. (29.7 cm ± 4.1 cm)
University[a]	M	15.7 in. ± 2.5 in. (39.8 cm ± 6.3 cm)
National level[a]	F	13.7 in. ± 1.6 in. (34.9 cm ± 4.1 cm)
Professional[b]	M	17.5 in. ± 1.8 in. (44.4 cm ± 4.6 cm)

*F = female. M = male. [a] Bendus (2023). [b] McConnell (2022).

10-METER OFF-ICE SPRINT

Rapid acceleration is a hallmark of many elite hockey athletes. Being able to accelerate explosively over short distances is an important athletic ability that can help athletes win races to loose pucks, create separation between themselves and other skaters, and gain tactical advantage in positioning.

Purpose

The 10-meter (11 yd) off-ice sprint test is an effective way to measure an athlete's ability to move rapidly over short distances.

Off-ice sprinting speed is highly correlated with on-ice skating speed (7). Assessing short sprint ability off the ice serves as a useful measurement for a hockey athlete's ability to skate fast. One of the best ways to influence on-ice speed and acceleration is to train off-ice speed and acceleration. As in many of the other tests and assessments discussed in this chapter, athletes often train for the test. By including off-ice sprinting as part of a testing battery, hockey athletes typically prioritize this type of training to perform well on testing day. As simple and redundant as it sounds, to get faster, an athlete must sprint fast. Typically, this means hitting speeds of at least 90% of their maximal velocity. While 10-meter (11 yd) sprints may not be long enough for most athletes to reach 90% of their maximal velocity, they do allow for training and assessing acceleration abilities and are typically considered short enough to minimize the chance of injury, which is higher with longer sprints if the athlete is unaccustomed to those distances. Too often, well-meaning coaches attempt to perform speed work at the end of practice, with minimal rest periods. While this may be an appropriate strategy for training anaerobic capacity, it is not appropriate for true speed development. Sprinting at or very near maximal speed is highly neurologically taxing, meaning the speeds and forces that the body is put under require near full rest and recovery between repetitions to truly bring about the desired adaptation. Sprinting while tired or fatigued is not really sprinting, it is running. To be able to get faster, the athlete must be fresh, and fatigue must be minimized.

Equipment

The equipment available for assessing 10-meter (11 yd) sprinting speed varies in complexity and technological sophistication. At the most basic, traditional, and (arguably) least reliable end of the spectrum, a simple stopwatch may be used to time athletes. At the other end of the spectrum, motorized mechanical timing systems may be used. Somewhere in the middle are timing gates, which as a product category can also be separated by technological differences. However, the basic photocell or laser timing gates are typical, relatively cost-effective, and commonplace in many strength and conditioning facilities, schools, and professional teams, so they are included here for the purposes of describing this test. Needed equipment includes:

- Timing gates—two pairs of photocell or laser gates are necessary
- Cones to mark the edges of the sprinting lane
- Recording spreadsheets

Setup

Timing gate setup for the 10-meter (11 yd) off-ice sprint test is relatively straightforward. There are a few nuances that may be debated, but the typical setup consists of two sets of gates positioned 10 meters (11 yd) apart, denoting the starting line and the finish line. The gates should be set up with approximately 4 feet (1.2 m) between each pair, to create a lane for the athlete to sprint through. Often, the laser or photocell and its accompanying receiver are attached at the top of an extendable tripod. The tripods need to be set to the same height, approximately 3 feet (0.9 m) high, to ensure the system is measuring athletes near their center of mass when they cross through the beam.

One area of contention is where exactly the first set of timing gates should be positioned relative to the starting line—and where, precisely, the athlete should start. Because most timing gates work by starting or stopping the timing mechanism when the laser beam between a transmitter and receiver is broken by the athlete crossing through, the initial gates that serve as the start do not begin timing until the athlete passes through them. The further behind the start line athletes begin, the faster they travel when crossing the beam, and therefore they can record a 10-meter (11 yd) time significantly quicker than if they had begun directly behind the line with little to no run-up. To standardize the test, the starting position for the athlete should not be more than 1 meter (about 1 yd) behind the line and the first set of timing gates. This position ensures athletes do not have enough room to ramp up significantly and are not so close to the starting gates that they unintentionally trigger the timing mechanism before starting the sprint.

Testing Protocol
The athlete sets up within 1 meter (about 1 yd) behind the start line. The athlete should begin in a slightly staggered foot position, with the opposite arm in front (i.e., if the left foot is forward, the right arm should be in front of the body). Upon a signal, the athlete explosively initiates movement and sprints as fast as possible from the starting line through the finish line. The timing mechanism is triggered as the athlete crosses between the initial pair of timing gates and notes the finish when the athlete cross through the second pair, 10 meters (11 yd) away. For testing purposes, 3 trials should be performed, with the fastest time recorded as the official score. A minimum of 2 minutes of rest should be allowed between repetitions to ensure there is no significant fatigue limiting sprint ability.

1. Perform a standardized dynamic warm-up prior to testing
2. Three build-up sprints should be performed prior to the actual test, each increasing incrementally after the first, to approximately 70%, 80%, and 90% of maximal speed.
3. Set the first pair of gates up on the starting line, approximately 4 feet (1.2 m) in width between them. Set the second pair of gates on the finish line with approximately 4 feet (1.2 m) in width between them, creating a lane to sprint down.
4. Set a pair of cones 1 meter (about 1 yd) before the starting line, where the athlete places the feet for beginning the test.
5. Gate height should be approximately 3 feet (0.9 m).
6. Have the athlete begin in a staggered start position, with the opposite arm forward.

Coaching Tips
- Emphasize the importance of accelerating rapidly and sprinting through the finish line.
- Cue the athlete to begin in a staggered foot position, with a positive shin angle for the front leg, so that the initial movement is horizontal in nature.
- Allow for adequate braking space after the finish line, so that the athlete can gradually slow down. At least 10 meters (11 yd) should be available.
- Use cones to create a visual barrier outlining the running lane, to avoid the potential for someone to walk through the testing area.

Descriptive Data
See table 3.3 for normative values for the 10-meter (11 yd) off-ice sprint.

Table 3.3   Normative Values for the 10-Meter Off-Ice Sprint

Level	Sex*	Time (s) (mean ± SD)
High school[a]	F	2.15 ± 0.16
High school[a]	M	1.97 ± 0.14
University[a]	F	2.06 ± 0.11
University[a]	M	1.82 ± 0.08
National level[a]	F	1.81 ± 0.06
Professional[b]	M	1.66 ± 0.07

*F = female. M = male. [a] Bendus (2023). [b] Potenza (2017).

30-METER ON-ICE SPRINT

Sprinting speed on the ice is one of the characteristics with the highest impact that the strength and conditioning professional can influence among hockey athletes (3).

Purpose

Testing and assessing speed in the competition modality itself (i.e., skating) is of utmost importance within a testing battery. In addition to the 30-meter (33 yd) time, which provides information on maximal velocity abilities, a 10-meter (11 yd) split time can and should be assessed to provide crucial information on acceleration abilities. Acceleration is arguably more important to a hockey athlete than maximum speed, since many plays are won or lost over just a few explosive strides. Because of this, collecting split times can be beneficial to understanding an athlete's abilities.

By assessing 30-meter sprints as well as looking at 5- and 10-meter split times, the strength and conditioning professional can glean profile information that helps when constructing speed development training plans and programs. The 5-meter (5.5 yd) split provides information on the efficiency and explosiveness over the first two or three strides. Ten-meter split times show the athlete's acceleration ability over a distance that is common in ice hockey, from about the goal line to the top of the circle on the ice. Finally, a 30-meter split is long enough for most athletes to reach maximum velocity. By gathering and assessing data from these three splits, the strength and conditioning professional can make a more informed decision on whether an athlete needs to focus on the qualities most associated with short acceleration, such as maximal force development, or more of a high-speed stimulus, like assisted sprinting.

Different budget points may allow for different levels of technology with which to measure and analyze linear speed. While the most low-tech version of timing sprints with a stopwatch certainly provides a basic level of information, more advanced tools such as timing gates or mechanical resistance machines provide a deeper level of data that can elucidate the underlying mechanisms, strengths, and weaknesses of an athlete that influence the sprint time. Being able to describe and analyze sprinting performances on a deeper level by building a force–velocity profile can provide another layer of information to the sport scientist or strength and conditioning professional.

Equipment

Testing equipment for the 30-meter on-ice sprint is the same as for the 10-meter sprint on land.

Setup

Setup for the 30-meter on-ice sprint is similar to the 10-meter sprint on land, with a couple of notable differences. First, additional timing gates may be used to capture split time data if the equipment is available. Gates set at 5 meters (5.5 yd) and 10 meters (11 yd) can provide valuable information on acceleration ability, in addition to maximal velocity data gathered from the 30-meter (33 yd) time. Second, the beginning position on the ice should be from a crossover setup. This helps to ensure that there is no rolling start from the athlete leaning into a linear start. Because of the need to create friction between the skate blade and the ice, a staggered start similar to the land-based sprint is not possible. The crossover start allows the athlete to rapidly accelerate on the ice.

Testing Protocol

The protocol for this test is similar to the 10-meter off ice sprint.

1. Perform a standardized dynamic warm-up off-ice prior to testing.
2. Perform an on-ice skating warm-up once athletes are dressed and on the ice.
3. Several build-up repetitions should be performed prior to the testing repetitions.
4. Set the first pair of gates up on the starting line, approximately 4 feet (1.2 m) in width between them. Set the second pair of gates on the finish line, approximately 4 feet (1.2 m) in width between them, creating a lane to sprint down.
5. Gate height should be approximately 3 feet (0.9 m).
6. Have the athlete begin in a crossover start position. They may self-select which side to cross over toward, but the coach should record and keep track of this for standardization in the future.
7. Allow for adequate braking space after the finish line, so that the athlete can gradually slow down. At least 10 meters (11 yd) should be available.

Coaching Tips

- Emphasize the importance of accelerating rapidly and skating through the finish line.
- Use cones to create a visual barrier outlining the running lane, to avoid the potential for someone to skate through the testing area.

Descriptive Data

See table 3.4 for normative values for the 30-meter (33 yd) on-ice sprint.

Table 3.4 Normative Values for the 30-Meter On-Ice Sprint

Level	Sex[*]	Time (s) (mean ± SD)
High school[a]	F	4.98 ± 0.22
High school[a]	M	4.43 ± 0.17
University[a]	F	4.87 ± 0.14
University[a]	M	4.32 ± 0.14
National level[a]	F	4.56 ± 0.13
Professional prospects[b]	M	4.12 ± 0.13

[*]F = female. M = male. [a]Bendus (2023). [b]Potenza (2018).

CHIN-UP

The chin-up exercise is used as a measure of upper body pulling strength.

Purpose

Aside from a general measure of upper body strength, relative balance between upper body pulling and pushing strength has been theorized to be an important factor in reducing the incidence of upper body injury (1). Chin-ups are often performed and assessed at body weight for maximum repetitions as a muscle endurance exercise. However, it is also appropriate to load the movement and evaluate the chin-up as a strength assessment for hockey athletes. Performing higher load and lower repetitions, just like any other key exercise used to develop strength, is crucial for upper body strength development. By testing and assessing the chin-up as a strength movement, as opposed to a muscular endurance movement, the strength and conditioning professional is emphasizing to the athletes that training this important movement at higher intensities is possible and important. However, because it is common practice to assess the chin-up exercise at body weight, the normative data included in table 3.5 includes only maximum repetitions at body weight. In practice, these values can still be used to estimate a 1RM for the purposes of comparing upper body pushing and pulling strength.

Having a bench press 1RM to chin-up 1RM ratio of 1:1 should be a primary goal of upper body strength development programs (1). Far too often, athletes overdevelop their anterior musculature while ignoring their posterior strength development. This can result in less than favorable length–tension relationships around joints such as the shoulder. By having large asymmetries in pushing versus pulling strength in the upper body, the athlete may unknowingly be increasing risk of musculoskeletal injury due to postural repercussions and altered kinetics. For example, an athlete with a much higher pushing versus pulling strength ratio is likely to have more anteriorly positioned shoulders, and as a repercussion, limited shoulder range of motion. This can increase the risk of injury during collisions because the shoulder joint may not be able to move into a favorable position during contact. By striving to have a 1:1 ratio of horizonal pushing to vertical pulling strength, the strength and conditioning professional is emphasizing a balanced approach to upper body strength. To achieve this ratio, consider the following example:

A hypothetical athlete can bench press 300 pounds for 1 repetition. This same athlete would be able to perform one chin-up (estimated or actual) at a total system weight of 300 pounds. **Total system weight** refers to the sum of the athlete's body weight (BW) and the external load used in the exercise. This means that if the hypothetical athlete weighed 200 pounds, the athlete would need an additional 100 pounds of external load to equal the same load achieved in the bench press 1RM calculation (200 pounds BW + 100 pounds external load = 300 pounds total system weight). This would result in a 1RM total system load for the chin-up of 300 pounds, equaling a 1:1 ratio with the 1RM bench press of 300 pounds.

Equipment

- Chin-up bar
- Chin-up or dip belt to attach weight plates
- Weight plates

Setup

The setup for the chin-up test involves having the athlete begin in a dead hang from the bar. Knees should be flexed to 90 degrees, and feet should be crossed.

Testing Protocol

1. Have the athlete begin in a dead hang from the bar, with knees flexed to 90 degrees, and feet crossed.
2. Initiation of the test may begin when the strength and conditioning professional determines the athlete is still and then gives a cue to begin.
3. Each repetition must include the chin crossing above the bar at the top, with the arms fully extended at the bottom.
4. Swinging, jerking, or kicking is not allowed, and any repetition that includes one or all of these should not be counted.

Coaching Tips

- There are typically three hand positions that can be used for a chin-up: a supinated (underhand) grip, a pronated (overhand) grip, and a neutral (palms facing each other) grip. The neutral grip version requires a chin-up bar with specialty handle positions.
- While any of these variations is useful, with hockey athletes, it is common for the neutral grip version to be best-suited to the typical mobility or injury history demands.
- Whichever version is used, stick to that one in subsequent tests to ensure valid and reliable data.
- Be strict with the protocol; chin-ups are notoriously difficult to assess because of the additional body movement many athletes are accustomed to during training.

Descriptive Data

See table 3.5 for normative values for the chin-up exercise.

Table 3.5 Normative Values for the Chin-Up

Level	Sex*	Repetitions (mean ± SD)
High school[a]	F	2.2 ± 3.0
High school[a]	M	9.1 ± 4.1
University[a]	F	2.7 ± 2.6
University[a]	M	9.6 ± 4.3
National level[a]	F	9.7 ± 4.2
Professional[b]	M	15.4 ± 4.9

*F = female. M = male. [a] Bendus (2023). [b] Potenza (2017).

BENCH PRESS

Upper body pushing strength is important for ice hockey athletes for both performance and injury mitigation.

Purpose

Structural integrity of the upper thorax and extremities is crucial at high levels due to the collision forces associated with bodychecking. At the NHL level, athletes average 6 foot, 1 inch (185 cm) and over 200 pounds (91 kg). As discussed earlier in this chapter, they often skate at over 20 mph (32.2 km/h), and the forces associated with athlete-to-athlete contact as well as athlete-to-board contact can be extremely high, reaching impact forces of over 1,500 N (20). Therefore, upper body muscular strength and hypertrophy are important for being able to withstand the impact forces and minimize the incidence of injury. From a performance perspective, a strong upper body is associated with being able to overpower opponents, maintain control of the puck while being checked, and produce high-velocity shots. The bench press is a common exercise to be included in strength and conditioning routines for ice hockey athletes, which makes it an appropriate choice for assessing upper body pressing strength.

Equipment

- Bench press bench
- Barbell
- Weight plates
- Locking collars

Setup

The athlete should lie on the bench, positioning the eyes directly under the bar. The bar should be set at a height that is approximately 2 to 3 inches (5-7 cm) below the athlete's full extension lockout height. Instruct the athlete to grip the bar just wider than shoulder-width, with thumbs wrapped around the bar. Position the spotter behind the head of the athlete with both hands gripping the bar with an over-under hand position. The spotter counts down with "3, 2, 1, lift" as the athlete and spotter unrack the bar together. The spotter remains in contact with the bar until the athlete is comfortable and the bar is directly over the chest. Only then does the spotter remove the hands from the bar, and the athlete may then initiate movement. For the repetition to count, the bar must touch the chest at the bottom of the repetition and the elbows must be fully extended at the top. The spotter should not touch the bar unless physically reracking the bar at the cessation of the exercise. If at any time the spotter or anyone else touches the bar, the test is over.

Testing Protocol

1. Perform a standardized dynamic warm-up prior to the test.
2. The athlete sets up properly on the bench. Scapulae and glutes should be in contact with the bench. The eyes should be directly under the bar while it is racked. Feet should be in contact with the floor, directly under the knees.
3. The spotter places hands on the bar and counts down with "3, 2, 1, lift," then the athlete and spotter mutually unrack the bar.
4. The spotter removes hands from the bar, at which point the athlete may begin the exercise.
5. The athlete lowers the bar, touching the chest just below the nipple line, and presses it back up vertically until the arms are fully extended and elbows are locked out.
6. Begin with a weight that the athlete expects to be able to complete for 10 repetitions. Perform 5 repetitions on the first set.
7. Progress the load in each set by no more than 10%. For each subsequent set, perform only 3 repetitions.

8. Continue performing sets of 3 repetitions, increasing load by 5% to 10%, until either no more than 3 repetitions can be performed with proper technique or (if using a velocity measuring tool) concentric speed falls below 0.3 meters per second on any repetition.

9. Use the final load completed for all 3 repetitions to establish the 3-repetition maximum score. This may be converted to an estimated 1RM score by dividing the load by 0.90. Normative values can then be converted to a relative score by dividing the estimated 1RM by the athlete's body weight so that comparisons between athletes of different sizes can be made. *Note:* Use the same unit of measurement (lb or kg) for the estimated 1RM and the athlete's body weight when calculating the relative score.

Coaching Tips

- Fully explain the intent and purpose behind the test prior to administering.
- Use the standard of **technical failure** when performing the exercise. The test ends when the technique is not ideal, not when the athlete cannot complete a repetition.
- Emphasize a controlled descent of the bar to the chest and explosive concentric action on each repetition. Bouncing the bar off the chest negates the repetition.
- Aim for the entire protocol to consist of no more than 5 sets, including the warm-up. If 5 sets have been reached and the athlete is not near the limit, the starting weight was too low. End the test and adjust the load in a subsequent session.

Descriptive Data

See table 3.6 for normative values for the bench press relative to body weight.

Table 3.6 Normative Values for the Bench Press Relative to Body Weight

Level	Sex*	1RM/BW* (mean ± SD)
High school[a]	F	0.8 ± 0.2
High school[a]	M	1.1 ± 0.2
University[a]	F	0.8 ± 0.1
University[a]	M	1.2 ± 0.2
National level[a]	F	1.0 ± 0.1
Professional[b]	M	1.2 ± 0.1

*BW = body weight. F = female. M = male. [a] Bendus (2023). [b] Potenza (2016).

ISOMETRIC BELT SQUAT

The isometric belt squat test is similar to the isometric mid-thigh pull, which may be familiar to strength and conditioning professionals.

Purpose

This test's purpose is to assess the lower body concentric peak force output. The test provides similar or greater external loading of the lower body compared to back squatting (9). The belt squat version of this isometric test removes a few extraneous variables from the assessment, allowing for a simplified assessment of maximal lower body force. For example, with the mid-thigh pull, grip can be a limiting factor in the athlete's ability to express force. Likewise, if the athlete is not familiar with the "second pull" position from resistance training, the bar placement may be unfamiliar and therefore a limiting factor in the test. The belt squat position is almost identical to the body position from the mid-thigh pull and is commonly known as the "athletic position," so most hockey athletes should know it. Furthermore, because the athlete pushes against a belt around the hips instead of pulling against a bar in the hands during the test, concerns of grip or upper body limitations are taken out of the equation. However, for the isometric belt squat, force plates are necessary, as well as a lifting belt with a chain attachment and an anchor point on the floor or on a platform designed for anchoring.

At the time of this writing, this assessment is relatively new, and as such, there is insufficient normative data. It is included in the testing battery because the future potential for this data and its relationship to ice hockey skating performance is high.

Equipment

- Force plates
- Lifting belt with chain
- Floor anchor
- Carabiner
- Goniometer

Setup

The athlete stands on the force plates with the floor anchor between the plates, in line with the midfoot. The weight belt should rest comfortably on the back of the hips, with the chain hanging in front of the athlete. The athlete squats down so that the chain can be attached via carabiner to the floor anchor. The length of the belt or chain should then be adjusted so that the athlete's hip angle is approximately 145 degrees, while the knee angle is around 135 degrees (4).

Testing Protocol

1. Perform a standardized warm-up prior to the test.
2. Once the athlete is set up on the force plates with the belt attached, the athlete should stand up gently, so that any slack is taken out of the chain. Do not yet push forcefully.
3. After instruction, and after the force plate software is running appropriately, the athlete rapidly and forcefully pushes against the force plates as if trying to stand up.
4. The athlete remains in an isometric squat, producing as much force as possible, for 3 to 5 seconds before relaxing.
5. Three repetitions should be performed, with 2 to 4 minutes of rest between them.

Coaching Tips

- Marking the chain length for athletes of different heights can speed up the setup process.
- The primary variable of interest is peak force of the best repetition.
- It may be beneficial to have hand support for balance purposes. A high hurdle placed in front of the force plates works well.

Descriptive Data

Limited descriptive data is available, but researchers have reported absolute peak force (N) values of 3,522 ± 635 in NCAA Division I male athletes (14).

TRAP BAR DEADLIFT

Lower body strength development is a key component for improving power output, which is correlated with acceleration and speed abilities in ice hockey athletes (19).

Purpose

This test is used to assess lower body concentric strength. The trap bar deadlift is a commonly used lower body strength exercise in ice hockey strength and conditioning programs. Because of the limited contribution of the stretch shortening cycle in skating compared to land-based running, concentric force output is very important in skating locomotion. Put simply, the greater the amount of concentric force a hockey athlete can apply to the ice during the skating stride, the greater displacement the athlete is able to achieve. As such, establishing strength standards with this exercise allows the strength and conditioning professional to compare relative levels of strength between athletes, as well as monitor lower body strength development over time.

Equipment

- Trap bar
- Weight plates
- Locking collars

Setup

The athlete should set up inside the trap bar, with the hands gripping the bar just below knee height when in the bottom position. This may require using either the high or low handles, depending on the height and arm length of the athlete. In the bottom portion of the exercise, while the plates are still in contact with the floor, the athlete should distribute weight evenly through the midfoot, with a rigid torso, and with no slack in the upper extremities. The athlete lifts the bar off the floor and comes to a fully extended "tall" position with the scapulae retracted and glutes fully engaged. Then, the athlete reverses the motion, under control, back to the floor. The coach must not allow the athlete to bounce the trap bar and plates off the floor but instead must ensure there is a controlled touch-and-go at the bottom portion of the exercise. The set is terminated if technical failure is reached.

Testing Protocol

1. Perform a standardized dynamic warm-up prior to the test.
2. Set up properly inside the trap bar.
3. Begin with a weight that the athlete expects to be able to complete for 10 repetitions. Perform 5 repetitions on the first set.
4. Progress in load each set by no more than 10%. For each subsequent set, perform only 3 repetitions.

5. Continue performing sets of 3 repetitions, increasing load by 5% to 10% until either no more than 3 repetitions can be performed with proper technique or, if using a velocity measuring tool, concentric speed falls below 0.3 meters per second on any repetition.

6. Use the final load completed for all 3 repetitions to establish the 3-repetition maximum score. This may be converted to an estimated 1RM score by dividing the load by 0.90. Normative values can then be converted to a relative score by dividing the estimated 1RM by the athlete's body weight so that comparisons between athletes of different sizes can be made. *Note:* Use the same unit of measurement (lb or kg) for the estimated 1RM and the athlete's body weight when calculating the relative score.

Coaching Tips

- Fully explain the intent and purpose behind the test prior to administering.
- Use the standard of technical failure when performing the exercise. The test ends when the technique is not ideal.
- Emphasize a controlled descent of the bar to the floor and explosive concentric action on each repetition. Bouncing the bar off the floor negates the repetition.
- Shoot for the entire protocol to consist of no more than 5 sets, including the warm-up. If 5 sets have been reached and the athlete is not near the limit, the starting weight was too low. End the test and adjust the load in a subsequent session.

Descriptive Data

See table 3.7 for normative values for the trap bar deadlift.

Table 3.7 Normative Values for the Trap Bar Deadlift

Level	Sex[*]	Estimated 1RM
University[a]	F	236 lb ± 39 lb (107.0 kg ± 17.7 kg)
University[a]	M	414 lb ± 46 lb (187.8 kg ± 20.9 kg)

[*]F = female. M = male. [a] Patel (2022).

BODY COMPOSITION

Body composition is an important factor for any speed or power athlete, and hockey athletes are no exception (6).

Purpose

The purpose of this test is to measure body fat as expressed by a percent of the athlete's body mass or weight. In one of the fastest collision-based team sports, the ratio of body fat to muscle mass is a crucial consideration and assessment point. Carrying excess body fat is akin to trying to compete while wearing a weight vest. Excess weight slows an athlete down. In contrast, too little body fat is associated with decreased energy levels. Because of this, assessing an athlete's body composition allows the strength and conditioning professional to monitor changes in functional mass, keep tabs on beneficial changes in body weight, and provide important information for the purpose of modifying lifestyle habits that may lead to unnecessary fat-mass gain.

Equipment

- Skinfold calipers
- Nomogram (as applicable, based on the protocol selected)
- Flexible tape measure
- Marking pen

Setup

Setup for taking body composition assessments simply requires a skinfold caliper tool and a semiprivate area to mark the skinfold sites and administer the pinches. Before doing so, a specific protocol (e.g., the 3, 4, or 7 site Jackson-Pollock method, or another similar protocol) needs to be selected so that the associated measurement sites can be identified.

Testing

1. The athlete should wear minimal loose-fitting clothes.
2. Based on the selected protocol, mark the sites where the skinfolds are to be measured.
3. Use the thumb and forefinger to pinch and pull away the skin and subcutaneous fat.
4. Use the calipers to measure the pinch, approximately one inch (2.5 cm) away from the fingers.
5. Repeat the process based on the protocol.
6. Record the caliper measurements as they are taken.

Coaching Tips

- Perform the body composition assessment first if it is a part of a testing battery.
- The athlete should have dry skin and should not have performed any intense physical activity immediately beforehand.
- Only test on the right side of the body while standing with muscles relaxed.
- Have the same individual perform all tests, as well as subsequent tests, to eliminate inter-rater error.

Descriptive Data

See table 3.8 for normative values for body composition.

Table 3.8   Normative Values for Body Composition

Level	Sex[*]	% body fat (mean ± SD)
High school[a]	F	20.5 ± 4.0
High school[b]	M	10.4 ± 2.6
University[a]	F	19.1 ± 4.1
University[c]	M	8.4 ± 2.8
National level[a]	F	18.7 ± 3.8
Professional[d]	M	10.0 ± 1.3

[*]F = female. M = male. [a]Neeld (2016a). [b]Neeld (2016b). [c]Patel (2022). [d]Potenza (2017).

CONCLUSION

Ice hockey is a fast-paced, dynamic, physical team sport. The physiological demands are broad, ranging from explosive speed and power for rapid acceleration, maximal skating speeds over 20 mph (32.2 km/h), high levels of muscular strength needed for battling opponents at net front and in the corners, anaerobic power necessary to perform repeated bouts of high-intensity skating, and aerobic capacity crucial to recover quickly from those intense efforts. Because of the wide array of physical characteristics demonstrated by high-level hockey athletes, a comprehensive testing and assessment protocol should be put in place to determine baseline abilities in these key areas, inform training programs designed to improve capacities and reduce the incidence of injury, and monitor fatigue and readiness levels throughout the in-season and off-season periods.

This chapter has outlined the key tests associated with the physical key performance indicators for ice hockey. Whether you use these tests as written or modify them slightly based on your population, training age, equipment availability, or facility logistics, this outline should serve as a template with which to consistently and reliably test, assess, and monitor your athletes as they train and develop for ice hockey.

4

SPORT-SPECIFIC PROGRAM DESIGN GUIDELINES

VICKI BENDUS

Strength and conditioning professionals who work in the sport of hockey dedicate significant portions of time to designing resistance training programs for their athletes. A first-principles approach to program design requires competency in several natural and physical sciences, including physiology, biomechanics, motor skill acquisition, and applied anatomy. Effective program design implements a systematic process of asking simple questions and using the answers to guide decision making. What does the sport demand? What does this individual athlete need? What is the best method to address those needs? Is the athlete responding to training in the expected way? These questions frame the major aspects of building a program. Specifically, the steps include creating a needs analysis for the sport, identifying key performance indicators (KPIs), profiling an athlete, setting short- and long-term training objectives, designing a periodized training plan, monitoring responses to training, and critically reflecting on the outcomes. By engaging in this process, strength and conditioning professionals can be technicians in their application of targeted resistance training to aid in the longitudinal physical performance of an athlete.

The first three chapters provided readers with the knowledge and tools to conduct the initial steps of the process. The first section of this chapter outlines the principles of training that can be globally applied to the preparation of any athlete. The second section describes the acute training variables that can be manipulated to elicit the desired physiological responses and performance outcomes following resistance training. The final section delivers sport-specific considerations for designing resistance training programs for hockey athletes.

SPECIFICITY, OVERLOAD, AND ADAPTATION

General training principles are founded on the innate ability of the human system to respond to stress. After a training stress is applied, an athlete may enter a fatigued state, resulting in decreased performance outputs. As fatigue dissipates, a higher level of performance can be realized. The changes in performance that emerge imply that the targeted physiological adaptations have occurred. The underlying neural and structural adaptations are specific to the imposed stimulus and are accounted for in program design by the **SAID principle** (specific adaptations to imposed demands). For resistance training, the muscular strength and power adaptations elicited are specific to the muscle groups, connective tissue, joints, joint angles, contraction types, forces, and velocities of contraction (43, 52, 57).

During the training process, athletes are exposed to stressors that challenge their current levels of performance. If the athlete is exposed to the same stressor in future sessions, the body's systems start to accommodate and are no longer significantly challenged. Withdrawal of the training stimulus results in **detraining**, which returns performance levels to baseline. Training dose–response curves and adaptive potential depend heavily on an athlete's training age. **Training age** refers to the number of years an athlete has participated in formal general physical training guided by a strength and conditioning professional. Low training age athletes (less than two years of training) tend to be younger and have lower levels of general strength, fitness, and movement competency when compared to moderate (two to four years of training) and high training age athletes (greater than four years). Less physically developed athletes often adapt to a training stimulus that is more general in nature and may fatigue more quickly than athletes with higher baseline levels of physical performance. Alternatively, a more intensive training stimulus is often needed to facilitate adaptation in individuals with moderate to high training ages.

The principle of **progressive overload** dictates that training load must be increased over time in order to elicit continual improvements in performance. Overload in resistance training primarily occurs via increases in volume, intensity, density, or exercise difficulty. Overloading volume may result from increasing repetitions per set, sets per training session, or training frequency per week. Overloading intensity can occur by increasing the load or movement velocity of an exercise. Overloading via density comes from increasing work completed per unit of time, which may entail doing more work within the same time frame or completing the same work in less time. Progressing exercise difficultly can be accomplished by expanding the range of motion to increase the amount of work performed per repetition or altering the body position to change the lever lengths at certain joints and putting certain muscles in disadvantageous length-tension positions. The mechanism of overload selected is determined by the training objective. Specific examples of how these variables can be leveraged to progressively overload a training stimulus will be outlined in later sections.

ACUTE TRAINING VARIABLES

Whereas training principles provide a general foundation that shapes the training process, acute training variables are the adjustable components of a program that can be manipulated to achieve the desired outcomes. Intensity, volume, rest periods, exercise selection, exercise order, and training frequency can all be fine-tuned to create a training stimulus that nudges an athlete toward a certain physiological adaptation. The success of a training program hinges on the proper management of these training variables in order to apply the optimal stimulus given an individual athlete's needs, desired performance outcomes, and current state of readiness.

Intensity

Exercise **intensity** is the most powerful tool that a strength and conditioning professional has to direct a training stimulus toward a desired adaptation. Intensity describes how the training work is performed. It is a multifactorial variable that involves the interaction between both objective and subjective components of the task execution (40). External load, repetition velocity, and perceived exertion can all be used to prescribe training intensity by setting a standardized scale created from a maximal point of reference. These scales are then used to assign intensity relative to the maximal value. Assigning external load using a percentage of an athlete's one repetition-maximum (% 1RM) is a traditional method to prescribe intensity. This option is suitable for assigning loads in primary resistance training exercises for advanced hockey athletes but has minimal use for low training age athletes as well as most assistance (accessory) exercises.

Repetition **velocity** or **tempo** is a key variable used to determine the challenge an exercise poses to the neuromuscular system. Exercise tempo considers the three phases of a movement: eccentric, isometric, and concentric (42a). **Velocity-based training** (VBT) is a commonly used method to prescribe intensity that uses the mean or peak concentric repetition velocity to assist in determining the external load prescription for an exercise (22, 37). Peak concentric velocity is suitable for ballistic exercises with loads less than 70% of the 1RM, whereas mean concentric velocity can be used for nonballistic or heavy-loaded (>70% 1RM) exercises. When applying VBT to prescribe load, it is best practice to use individual **load-velocity profiles** (LVPs). An LVP is created by performing a standardized, progressively loaded protocol that tracks the mean or peak concentric velocity (exercise-dependent) at three to five increasing loads (38). A sample protocol to create a trap bar deadlift LVP may consist of a hockey athlete performing maximally accelerated concentric repetitions with loads that correspond to 40%, 60%, and 80% of the athlete's 1RM. A complete LVP includes a trend line plotted using the load versus velocity data points to allow for the estimation of loads at various velocities along the line (38). Strength and conditioning professionals can then use the equation of the trend line to estimate the loads an individual athlete may need to achieve the targeted velocity range that has been prescribed based on the intended training adaptations.

The VBT method is valuable because it allows for the daily individualization of external loads to match fluctuations in an athlete's day-to-day readiness (**autoregulation**). Using autoregulation maintains the integrity of the training stimulus under variable conditions. An athlete in a fatigued state may require a reduction of the anticipated exercise load to reach the targeted velocity range, whereas a high state of readiness may necessitate increases in load. This contrasts the percent of 1RM methods, where external load prescriptions tend to be fixed and do not afford the same within-session flexibility as VBT.

The final consideration for exercise intensity is the athlete's perceived effort. How challenging an exercise subjectively feels to an athlete can vary considerably. The **repetitions-in-reserve** (RIR) method uses an athlete's estimation of number of repetitions away from failure to prescribe intensity (72). Similar to VBT, this autoregulatory method allows for load prescriptions to be adjusted to accommodate for an athlete's day-to-day variation in performance. It is advantageous because it does not require testing or technology and so is applicable across many exercises. Its subjective nature may make it difficult for some athletes to accurately determine their RIR, meaning strength and conditioning professionals must work closely with athletes to help them gauge their effort.

All told, there are multiple variables capable of capturing training intensity. Since intensity is a main determinant of the nature of a stimulus, it should be programmed with great purpose, along with a pragmatic approach that considers the athlete population, training goals, and available resources.

Volume

The neuromuscular system is sensitive to overall resistance training volume, meaning it offers a potential option to overload a strength stimulus (32). The volume of resistance training can globally be quantified using the **repetition–load method** (sets × reps) or, more commonly, the **volume–load method** (sets × reps × load). Volume within a session can therefore be altered by changing the number of sets or repetitions, amount of load, or number of exercises within a training session.

There tends to be an inverse relationship between volume and intensity. Training prescriptions that target maximum strength, power, reactive strength, or rate of force development (RFD, see page 66 for a full description) require higher-intensity and lower-volume strategies. This results in repetition assignments that tend to be lower (≤5) with a higher number of sets (≥3). Alternatively, training intended to elicit structural adaptations such as hypertrophy or improvements in muscular endurance requires higher volumes of total work completed with lower loads. This results in higher repetition protocols (≥6) with fewer sets (1 to 4). An athlete's training age may alter these parameters. Low training age athletes tend to require less intensity and fewer sets to elicit strength adaptations. For example, to develop maximal strength, a development athlete may only need 2 to 3 sets of 8 to 10 repetitions at 70% to 75% of the 1RM. A high-performance athlete likely needs 3 to 6 sets using loads above 80% of the 1RM with repetition ranges lower than 5 to create a similar training response.

Since the number of repetitions is strongly dependent on the intensity target and, subsequently, the training goal, there is less flexibility in using repetitions to change total volume. Instead, altering the number of sets permits changes in volume while allowing intensity to be maintained. Controlling training volume is an important area of program design because it is a primary factor in the amount of fatigue an athlete accumulates. There is an upward limit of volume that an athlete is able to effectively tolerate before entering a state of overreaching. **Overreaching** is characterized by short-term decrements in performance caused by excessive training fatigue (30). High-volume protocols that intentionally push athletes toward a state of overreaching are occasionally desirable for advanced athletes who require high training stress to stimulate the target adaptations. Alternatively, reducing training volume while maintaining intensity can promote recovery and result in the intended performance outcomes to be realized. These deloading protocols are often planned for the end of a mesocycle or during training phases where performance is being optimized.

Rest Periods

The rest intervals between resistance training exercises are determined by the training goal and training age of the athlete. Altering the rest duration affects the overall density of a training session. Exercise **density** is a measure of load lifted across a specific time window. It can be increased or decreased depending on the desired adaptations by manipulating the amount of work performed or the time frame it is completed within. When rest periods are minimized, the anaerobic resources that can be replenished are limited. The athlete begins the next set with residual fatigue, creating a potent metabolic and hormonal stimulus (31), but that may compromise the work performed within the set. These shorter rest periods (e.g., less than 30 seconds of rest) that drive up training density are advantageous for creating muscular endurance.

The metabolic stimulus offered with truncated recovery periods presents a trade-off because it decreases acute force production capabilities. Reducing training density by extending rest periods permits closer to full recovery between sets and allows for consistent levels of force generation across each effort. High-load or high-velocity exercises, such as those targeting maximal strength, power, RFD, or reactive strength, should therefore be followed by longer rest periods that are greater than 2 minutes (31). Hockey athletes who have lower training ages and levels of general fitness should generally be provided with longer rest intervals that prevent significant accumulated fatigue before beginning the next set. This ensures that the ability to perform each exercise proficiently continues throughout a session.

Exercise Selection

Exercises serve as a means to apply a training stimulus. There are often multiple options that can achieve the desired outcome, although some may be more suitable for certain athletes than others. Selecting which exercises are included in a program requires several considerations, many of which are dependent on the athlete's current capacity for movement and the training goal. Strength and conditioning professionals must be agile in their ability to draw from their exercise databases and make sound decisions on which exercises to include or eliminate based on the parameters of the situation. Variables that guide exercise selection include the following:

- Training objective: What is the target adaptation and performance outcome? How does overload need to be applied to achieve this (e.g., additional load? higher movement velocity?) How much exercise specificity is needed?

- Training phase: What season is the athlete in? Are there movements that need to be introduced now so they can be an option in later phases? Are there exercises that should be avoided to prevent undesirable muscle soreness or overloading certain sport-specific patterns?

- Technical competency: Which exercises has the athlete mastered? Which level should the athlete begin on the spectrum of progressions for a particular movement?

- Training history: What movements has the athlete successfully used in the past to elicit the target adaptation? Which do the athlete prefer?

- Injury history: Is the athlete currently injured? Are certain movements contraindicated because they cause pain? What injuries have occurred in the past that may limit the athlete's ability to load certain positions due to mobility or stability deficits?

- Anthropometrics: Does the athlete have any congenital joint shapes or limb lengths that may affect how the body moves? For example, an athlete with relatively long femurs and a short torso struggles to squat deeply without a steeper forward torso lean compared to an athlete with shorter femurs and a longer torso.

- Resources and logistics: What equipment and space are available? How many athletes are performing the exercise simultaneously? How will the session flow?

Using these criteria, primary exercises should be selected first. Primary exercises provide the main stimulus to elicit the desired adaptation and move the athlete toward the major performance goal. Secondary exercises can serve to address a secondary training goal or support the primary exercises. For example, a high-performance hockey athlete with a main training goal of maximal strength and a secondary focus on lower body power may have trap bar deadlift and barbell bench press as primary exercises with a power clean from the knee and dumbbell countermovement jumps as secondary exercises. Primary and secondary exercises should be performed with maximal intent, and the outputs (load or velocity) should be tracked across a training phase. Assistance and torso exercises can be selected last. Although they play an important role in building long-term structural tolerance and postural control, they have the least influence on the primary training outcomes.

Exercise Classification

Classifying exercises assists in the organization of exercise libraries and selection of appropriate movements for the targeted training stimulus. The result is a systematic approach that allows for simple selection of alternative options that can accomplish the desired adaptation as well as helping to ensure that programs are reasonably balanced across the different categories. There are several methods of classifying exercises: primary contraction type (i.e., isometric, concentric, eccentric), degree of specificity (i.e., specific development exercises, general development exercises, assistance exercises), joint involvement (e.g., upper versus lower body, compound multijoint versus isolated single-joint, bilateral versus unilateral), and direction of movement (e.g., horizontal, vertical, push, pull). A common system to classify strength exercises uses the following groupings:

- **Loaded power**—Ballistic or near-ballistic exercises with additional external load where the intent is to move as fast as possible
- **Upper body pull**—Upper body pulling movements, posterior-chain emphasis
- **Upper body push**—Upper body pushing movements, anterior-chain emphasis
- **Hip-dominant**—Lower body hinging movements, knee flexion exercises, posterior-chain emphasis
- **Knee-dominant**—Lower body squatting and stepping movements, knee extension exercises, anterior-chain emphasis

Torso and stability exercises can be classified using the following categories:

- **Breathing**—Exercises that encourage proper use of the diaphragm and pelvic floor during respiration
- **Anti-extension**—Exercises that resist spinal extension
- **Anti-rotation and rotation**—Exercises that resist or create torso rotation
- **Anti-lateral flexion**—Exercises that resist lateral spinal flexion (side-bending)
- **Hip stability**—Exercises that challenge hip control and strength across one or multiple planes
- **Shoulder stability**—Exercises that improve scapular rhythm and glenohumeral control across one or multiple planes

Progressions and Regressions

Along with having an exercise classification system, a template of progressions and regressions is a useful tool for strength and conditioning professionals to have in their programming arsenals. This is especially important when working with development-level athletes or those with injuries. Progression and regression options provide a stepwise pathway to achieve proficiency for a target movement pattern that is intended to be overloaded via external load or velocity in future phases. An example progression sequence for a rear foot elevated split squat (RFESS) pattern may look like this:

Body weight split squat →Dumbbell split squat → Dumbbell RFESS
→ Barbell split squat → Barbell RFESS

Using this template, if a barbell RFESS is the eventual target exercise to train lower body maximal strength, a strength and conditioning professional working with a hockey athlete of low training age may begin the program with a bodyweight or dumbbell split squat. The strength and conditioning professional can then work through the higher-level progressions over multiple training phases as the athlete acquires the requisite mobility, stability, coordination, and strength within the pattern.

Loading potential is an additional factor to consider when selecting exercises. There are trade-offs between complexity, stability, and intensity. Exercises that require more coordination or stability restrict the extent to which they can be overloaded with external load or velocity (8). This concept can be seen when comparing a chaos-style barbell bench press (bench press performed with weights hung from bands at either end of the barbell) to a traditional barbell bench press. The former version may be deemed a progression of the latter; however, the added instability requirements decrease its potential for intensification with additional load or velocity. This does not mean that coordinatively challenging exercises or those with higher stability demands are not useful exercises, but it provides a reminder that every exercise choice comes with trade-offs. Navigating the exercise selection process requires choosing exercises appropriately suited for the athlete that provide an effective stimulus to elicit the desired training adaptations.

Exercise Order

Once the training goal, intensity, volume, rest, and exercises have all been determined, the sequence of exercises within a single session must be determined.

Athletes are freshest at the beginning of a session and tend to fatigue as it progresses. Thus, primary and secondary exercises are typically done earlier to maximize the execution quality and desired outputs for the highest priority movements. Placing them toward the end may compromise the potency of the training stimulus and lead to inferior results. General heuristics on exercise order include the following:

- High-velocity to low-velocity movements
- Heavy loads to low loads
- Total body multijoint movements to split movements (upper or lower body emphasis) to single-joint movements
- Neurologically demanding to structurally demanding to metabolically demanding
- Primary and secondary exercises to assistance exercises

Taken together, exercises for most hockey athletes should be arranged in the following sequence of targeted adaptations: speed (low load, high velocity), power (low to moderate load, moderate velocity), maximal strength (high load, low velocity), and structural (low to moderate load, low velocity). It is useful to remember that primary and secondary exercises are selected based on the level of training importance given to each and do not necessarily indicate the order in which they are performed. Using the example outlined in the Exercise Selection section, a hockey athlete would do sets of the power clean (secondary exercise) in the first superset of the session, followed by the trap bar deadlift (primary exercise) in the second superset, and finish with assistance exercises.

Training Frequency

Training **frequency** is the number of times a training stimulus is applied within a given time period. The frequency of resistance training can vary significantly depending on the athlete, time of year, and training goal. Frequency should be selected to allow for adequate recovery between training sessions. It is generally recommended to have 48 to 72 hours of recovery following high-intensity and high-volume training, whereas only 24 to 48 hours may be needed following low or moderate load training. During the off-season, hockey athletes typically resistance train three or four days per week depending on how the other components of the microcycle are planned.

During the regular season and playoffs, the density of the competition schedule dictates the optimal resistance training frequency. For development-level hockey athletes, two days per week should be the goal. Although these athletes are participating in a higher volume of practices and games than in the off-season, the consistent, year-round exposure to physical literacy and resistance training are key aspects of their long-term athletic development. Their lower training ages mean the volume and intensity of the sessions can be moderate and the stimulus still sufficient to drive the intended adaptations. For moderate or high training age athletes, such as those in a university setting who play games on the weekends, two resistance training days per week is common. These athletes require more intensity to create meaningful adaptations. As a result, split strategies, such as a strength-emphasis day and a speed- or power-emphasis day, may be advantageous (table 4.1).

Table 4.1 Regular Season Microcycle Examples

Exercise type	Mon	Tues	Wed	Thurs	Fri	Sat	Sun
Development	Total body STR (60 min)	Off	Total body STR (60 min)		Off		
	Practice		Practice	Practice		Game	Game
High performance	Heavy PWR Lower STR (60 min)		Light PWR Upper STR (60 min)				Off
	Practice	Practice	Practice	Practice	Game	Game	
Elite	STR* (15 min)		PWR* (15 min)	Game	PWR* (15 min)	Game	Off
	Practice	Game	Practice	STR* (15 min)	Practice	STR* (15 min)	

Note: STR = strength. PWR = power. * = microdose strategy.

Microdosing is a strategy commonly implemented for elite athletes who have dense competition schedules with high travel demands (24). In these scenarios, load management is complex and there is a constant risk of excessive overall load on the athlete as well as the detraining of strength qualities. Microdosing can mitigate these challenges by reducing single-session training volumes but applying the stimulus more frequently (daily or near-daily) such that total weekly volumes and intensities can be maintained without the accumulation of excessive fatigue. This approach provides sufficient training inputs to maintain the neural and structural qualities that support force production over the long term without disrupting short-term performance.

SPORT-SPECIFIC GOALS OF A RESISTANCE TRAINING PROGRAM

The SAID principle can sometimes be misinterpreted as the goal of resistance training instead of as a guideline. This has led to an abundance of off-ice "hockey-specific" exercises and training programs that mimic the movements athletes execute on the ice but fall short of delivering meaningful changes to on-ice play. More accurately, the intent of resistance training is to serve the overall hockey performance model by creating physiological adaptations that have positive transference to on-ice preparedness and performance. Gym-based resistance training is general by nature because it is several degrees of separation away from the complex environment of game play. Despite this, multijoint compound exercises that may be considered general are incredibly capable of transferring to a wide variety of on-ice tasks because they overload one or multiple qualities that support sport-specific performance. For example, a development-level athlete who lacks strength may improve skating speed primarily by enhancing lower body maximal strength via general exercises.

Strength and conditioning professionals must determine the primary limiting factors of an athlete's on-ice performance and address them systematically with the appropriate training means. Like a Formula One driver attempting to race in an old minivan, hockey athletes with deficiencies in general strength qualities may have their upper level of performance constrained in certain on-ice tasks. Although extremely skilled drivers can make up for vehicle deficiencies, upgrading to an elite car with excellent components provides more tools to win a race and the opportunity to fully realize performance potential. This race car analogy can be extended to help highlight the positive effects of developing different strength abilities for a hockey athlete:

- Maximal strength places a bigger engine in the car. It provides an athlete with a higher ceiling of force-generating potential.
- Mechanical power adds horsepower to the engine. It improves an athlete's explosive performance.
- Eccentric strength creates a better braking system. It supports an athlete's ability to rapidly stop and change directions.
- Hypertrophy reinforces the frame and exterior of the car. It adds muscle mass to support maximal strength and improve structural tolerance.
- Rate of force development introduces a more reactive gas pedal. It enhances an athlete's ability to produce force quickly when time is constrained.
- Torso and joint stability align the tires and improve the car handling. They aid in force transfer through the kinetic chain and reduce the amount of unfavorable joint loading in certain areas.

Overall, developing the listed strength qualities has potential to transfer to two main areas of hockey performance: enhancing physical abilities that underpin on-ice tasks and improving injury resilience.

Improving the ability to apply force in various manners through resistance training provides more force-generating potential to support the execution of different hockey skills. There are certain considerations that can guide expectations around transfer of resistance training to specific on-ice tasks. Decontextualized skills such as linear skating speed, change of direction (COD) ability, managing physical play, shooting speed, and puck handling demand varying ranges of coordinative skill that require both physical abilities and technical execution. Each skill exists on a physical–technical continuum that represents the proportion for which the performance outcome is determined by the physical elements versus the technical elements. Of the categories listed, linear skating is the least technical and most strongly dictated by general physical abilities, such as maximal strength and power, meaning gym-based training has a high probability of positive transference to faster skating. Puck handling is on the opposite end of the spectrum. Proficiency requires highly technical motor skills, suggesting that task performance can only be minimally influenced by general strength or power improvement. By using this theoretical continuum, strength and conditioning professionals can identify the greatest opportunities for transference, select appropriate training targets, and program accordingly.

In parallel with properly planned on-ice load exposure, resistance training also contributes to a hockey athlete's preparedness by pushing the ceiling of structural tolerance to a level that exceeds a predicted-level of tissue stress exposure. Tissues are injured when the force demands exceed their load-bearing capacity, whether acutely or chronically. As such, stronger athletes tend to get injured less often (25). By increasing the strength of ligaments, tendons, joint cartilage, and fascia, hockey athletes are more likely to be able to withstand the multifaceted structural demands the game places on their bodies. Furthermore, resistance training that addresses movement dysfunctions within certain patterns may lessen the risk or severity of acute and overuse injuries to the lumbo-pelvic-hip complex that are prominently found in hockey athletes.

Long-Term Athletic Development

Program objectives and prescribed training methods are largely driven by a hockey athlete's stage in the **long-term athletic development** (LTAD) pathway. Following the principles of LTAD prepares a hockey athlete for long-term success in the sport without sacrificing physical health and function after the sports career. Strength and conditioning professionals can use these as overarching concepts to ensure that their programming for hockey athletes respects longitudinal performance growth and durability, as opposed to exclusively short-term gains.

The stages of LTAD can be broadly categorized as youth, development, high performance, and elite (table 4.2). Hockey athletes in each stage have different performance needs that require altered programming strategies in order to address them. The magnitude of improvement athletes achieve from resistance training and the extent of transfer to game performance also depend on where they are on the LTAD pathway. There is a direct relationship between trainability and the transfer of training that should be considered when setting training-related

Table 4.2 Long-Term Athletic Development Phases

Descriptor	Youth	Development	High performance	Elite
Age	<13	14-18	19-23	>24
Training age	None	Low	Moderate	High
Competitive level	Local, travel	Travel, prep school, junior	Junior, university, national team	Professional, senior, national team
Trainability	High	High	Moderate	Low
Transfer	High	High	Moderate	Low
Resistance training objectives	Physical literacy	Exercise competency, max strength	Max strength and power	Individual
KPI examples	Movement competency (squat, hinge, push, pull)	Chin-up, CMJ, 30 m sprint	Relative 3RM trap bar deadlift, CMJ, 30 m sprint	Based on individual physical profile
Individual or group programming?	Group	Group	Individualized (group KPIs)	Individualized (personal KPIs)
Progressive overload	Movement progressions	Volume	Load	Speed
Intensity of primary exercises	Low	Low to moderate	Moderate to high	High

Note: KPI = key performance indicators. CMJ = countermovement jump.

goals and expectations. **Trainability** is the athlete's capacity to grow and improve from the training stimulus (11). Athletes in the earliest stages of the LTAD pathway have low training ages and correspondingly low levels of general physical abilities. As a result, their trainability and potential for transfer is at its highest. Improving basic strength levels has a profound impact on their hockey performance; they skate faster, shoot harder, become more effective during physical play, and fatigue less quickly.

As youth athletes progress though the developmental, high performance, and elite levels, their trainability reduces along with the degree that general strength improvement significantly transfers to improvement in on-ice tasks. This does not diminish the importance of resistance training at higher training ages. Instead, high training age hockey athletes require more individually directed programming to continually accumulate marginal gains throughout the latter portions of their careers. Consistent resistance training supports their on-ice performance by optimizing their systems to generate high force outputs at high speeds and builds structural tolerance to create short- and long-term injury resilience.

As a whole, resistance training is a foundational component for LTAD and must be programmed in a manner that considers the relationship between trainability and transference. Resistance training programs and their expected performance outcomes should reflect athletes' LTAD stage. Programs for high performance and elite hockey athletes are more individualized, more intensive, and less variable than those for younger cohorts, who need a more general training stimulus, less intensity, and more exposure to a variety of exercises to build movement competency. Prescribing advanced programming for developmental hockey athletes should be avoided because the athletes do not have the general physical abilities to realize the full potential of the stimulus, future exposures to the stimulus may be less potent, and their future trainability may be reduced prematurely.

Physical Performance Profiling

Physical performance profiling is an effective practice to shape the training goals and subsequent strength programming for athletes who have progressed to the later phases of LTAD. Previously identified KPIs can act as anchors to create simple profiling decision trees that objectively categorize athlete needs. For example, KPIs for a trained hockey athlete may be a relative 3RM trap bar deadlift, countermovement jump, and 30-meter (33 yd) sprint to represent relative strength, lower body power, and speed, respectively. Since maximal strength underpins power, it has the most potential for a trickle-down effect to other physical abilities. Thus, it represents the top layer of the decision tree. High performance or elite hockey athletes who lack maximal strength should address this deficit first. If strength levels are acceptable, the next layer is lower body power, followed by speed. The long-term goal is to have athletes who are above average at each level of the KPI tree, which should eliminate any significant general performance deficits that may be a limiting on-ice outputs such as linear acceleration or change of direction.

At the elite level, many athletes meet these physical performance thresholds, meaning that more in-depth individualized profiling is warranted. Advanced assessments such as load-velocity profiles, reactive strength index tests, sprinting profiles, or skating profiles can provide more granular information on an elite athlete's physical abilities. Load-velocity profiles can be particularly advantageous because they can improve the precision of load prescription during training. Importantly, they also objectively evaluate the unique adaptation response an athlete undergoes as a result of the training stimulus. Exposure to different training regimes affects the line in a manner specific to the stimulus. Case studies displaying the changes in trap bar squat jump load-velocity profiles in response to training for two elite women's hockey athletes are displayed in figure 4.1. Maximal strength improvement tends to move the bottom of the line to the right (figure 4.1*a*), whereas high velocity or RFD training is more likely to move the top of the line to the right (figure 4.1*b*, light gray to dark gray). The longitudinal goal is to shift the line up and to the right such that the athlete is moving each load faster (figure 4.1*b*, light gray to black).

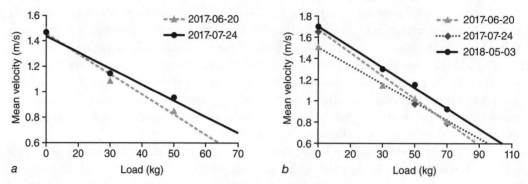

Figure 4.1 Panel *a* and *b* display squat jump load-velocity profiles for two elite women's hockey players. Athlete *a* had a bottom-right shift demonstrating maximal strength adaptations. Athlete *b* had a top-right shift following a single training phase emphasizing high velocity methods. There is an upward-right shift after a full year of periodized strength training.

Lastly, consulting with individual athletes to identify specific areas of game or physical performance that the athlete says are deficient is a highly valuable practice to engage veteran athletes in the programming process. This may potentially help to create targeted programming that can transfer to specific areas of need that may not be captured with most performance assessments.

POSITION-SPECIFIC EXERCISE SELECTION

The considerations for exercise selection outlined in the Acute Training Variables section provided general guidelines that can be applied across all hockey athletes. As hockey athletes progress from development through to high performance, playing position can be more strongly considered in training prescription. The positions in hockey can be broadly separated into skaters and goalies. The expansive overview in chapter 2 showed how the activity profiles between skaters and goalies vary significantly in terms of the locomotor demands and physical engagement with opposing athletes. Although the sport-specific motor tasks performed by skaters and goalies vary, both positions require the ability to express force across a variety of speeds and directions, meaning programs share more commonalities than differences. That said, the distinctions merit a degree of divergence in programming to ensure athletes of both positional groups have the requisite tissue tolerance and physical abilities to excel on the ice. An adaptation-led approach ensures the focus of a program remains on the training goal and recognizes there are several training methods that can be employed to accomplish the desired physiological responses. Table 4.3 provides a comprehensive summary of general loading parameter recommendations to target specific strength abilities relevant to skaters and goalies. It is meant to serve as a programming prescription guide that can be used to assist in prescribing appropriate ranges for sets, repetitions, intensity, and exercise tempo.

Table 4.3 Loading Parameter Table for Various Strength Abilities

Target adaptation	Method	Sets	Intensity (% 1RM)	Reps	Tempo (E:I:C)[a]	Rest (min)
Maximal muscle power	Light power	3-5	20%-60%	3-6	Fast	1.5-2.5
	Heavy power	3-5	60%-80%	5-8	Fast	1.5-3
Concentric early RFD	Light RFD[b]	3-5	20%-60%	5-8	Fast	1.5-2.5
Concentric late RFD	Heavy RFD	3-5	60%-80%	3-5	Fast	1.5-3
Eccentric RFD	Accelerated eccentric loading	3-5	Bodyweight to 60%	3-5	X:1-3:1[c]	1.5-2.5
Maximal muscle strength	Maximal strength	3-5	90-%100% (very heavy)	1-5	2-4:1-3:X	2.5-5
Maximal eccentric muscle strength	Maximal eccentric strength	3-5	90%-110% (very heavy)	3-5	2-10:0:A[d]	2.5-5
Maximal isometric muscle strength	Maximal pushing isometrics	3-5	80%-100% MVIC[e]	2-5	X or 0.5-3 s ramp	2.5-5
Muscle hypertrophy	Heavy load	3-4	70%-85% (heavy)	5-8	2-4:1-3:1-3	2-3
	Moderate load	3-5	50%-70% (moderate)	>8	1-3:1-2:1-3	1-2
Structural balance	Accessory strength	2-4	60%-80% (moderate)	8-15	1-3:1-3:1-3	1-2
Tissue remodeling	Holding isometrics	1-5	30%-60% (light)	1 3-5	1:30-60:1 1:3-5:1	1-2
		3-5	60%-80% (moderate)	1 3-5	1:30-60:1 1:3-5:1	1-2
	Slow tempo eccentrics	2-4	60%-80% (moderate)	5-12	5-10:1:1	1-2
Movement competency	Technical development	3-5	Light	5-10	Controlled	1-1.5

[a] E = eccentric, I = isometric, and C = concentric (42a). [b] RFD = rate of force development. [c] X = movement performed explosively.
[d] A = assist. [e] MVIC = maximum voluntary isometric contraction.
Adapted from Baar (2022); Jandačka and Beremlijski (2011).

Skaters

Skaters can be further classified as forwards and defenders. Although the precise positional demands are different, the fundamental physical and sport-specific requirements of each position are similar. Only athletes at the elite level who require individualized programming precision for transfer will benefit from differentiating between the two skating positions.

Developing the underpinning physical abilities of the various skating skills is particularly important for forwards and defenders. There is no on-ice movement skill that has more influence on how a hockey athlete interacts with the game than skating. How fast hockey athletes accelerate or decelerate is determined by the magnitude and direction of the net impulse they apply into the surface of the ice. Since time is constrained during skating tasks, generating a larger impulse typically requires more force to be applied faster. Creating a more effective angle of application is the second option to positively affect impulse and subsequently movement speed.

Bruce Bennett/Getty Images

How fast hockey athletes decelerate is determined by the magnitude and direction of the net impulse they apply into the ice during floor contact.

Maximal muscle strength, mechanical muscle power, RFD, and reactive strength each have the potential to influence one or more of the factors that affect net impulse while skating. Although they are unique strength abilities, all are inherently interrelated and dictated by specific morphological (muscle fiber type, architecture, and tendon properties) and neural characteristics (motor unit recruitment, synchronization, firing frequency, intermuscular coordination) (20). The exercise and external load can be manipulated to alter the subsequent movement velocity in a manner that creates the conditions for an athlete to express different types of strength abilities. A simple way to understand which resistance training exercises may be the best tool for developing these capabilities is to use a generalized load-velocity continuum (figure 4.2) (48). Whereas the load-velocity profiling described previously provides an objective analysis of performance within a single exercise, a generalized comparison that displays a range of different exercises that lend themselves to a wide range of loads and subsequent velocities helps to align suitable exercises for specific adaptations.

Hockey athletes who need to develop the physical qualities required for skating performance should be exposed to a variety of external loads to challenge their force production abilities under different conditions. One of the most effective approaches to improve a hockey athlete's force production capability across the curve is to use a polarized approach that emphasizes training at both ends of the continuum: maximal muscle strength and speed. Speed and reactive resistance training methodology are outside the scope of this text; however, they play a vital role in the holistic off-ice training model for a hockey athlete, particularly for skating development. Sprinting and plyometrics challenge an athlete's capacity to rapidly apply force in manners that cannot be matched with other modes of training. This does not mean that speed or reactive strength cannot be improved with the modes of resistance training outlined in this chapter, but it serves as a reminder of the SAID principle and that certain training tools are better suited to elicit specific adaptations than others.

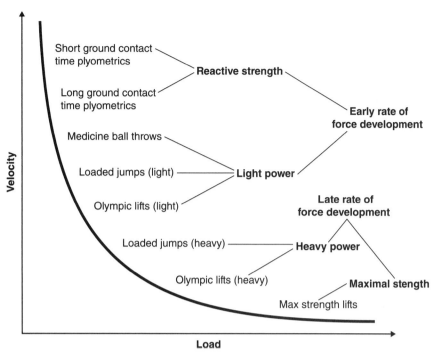

Figure 4.2 A simplified load-velocity continuum that displays corresponding exercise categories. Exercises that use higher external loads limit movement velocity whereas lower external loads lead to higher movement velocities. This general relationship between load and velocity can be used to select exercises that express the specific strength abilities that are being targeted with training.

Maximal Strength

High-load, low-velocity exercises develop an athlete's maximal muscle strength. **Maximal strength** is the amount of force an athlete can voluntarily apply within a given task. Although it is position- and velocity-specific, a robust body of research has demonstrated that maximal force production capacities in isometric and dynamic tasks are related to power, early RFD, and late RFD in athletes (42, 44, 54). A hockey athlete's relative strength level supports the body's impulse-production potential during accelerations, decelerations, and turns. The body's levels of absolute upper and lower body strength are primary contributors to how the athlete manages physical contact and collisions during game play. An underappreciated aspect of physical play is the energetic demand it requires. Stronger athletes who can exert lower levels of relative force output to manage collisions and the struggles for puck possession are more likely to have lower levels of performance fatigability as a game progresses (49). Thus, improving a hockey athlete's total body maximal strength has high transfer potential to several aspects of on-ice performance and long-term health; it should serve as a primary component of most resistance training programs.

Lower body maximal strength can be developed using multijoint, hip-dominant, and knee-dominant exercises. When the demands of the game are considered, hockey athletes need to be able to express extremely high magnitudes of force unsupported on one leg (e.g., early acceleration sprint mechanics), asymmetrically on two legs (e.g., two-foot stopping and turning) and symmetrically on two legs (e.g., physical battles for body position). Because of this diversity in lower body force production on the ice, training maximal strength of the lower

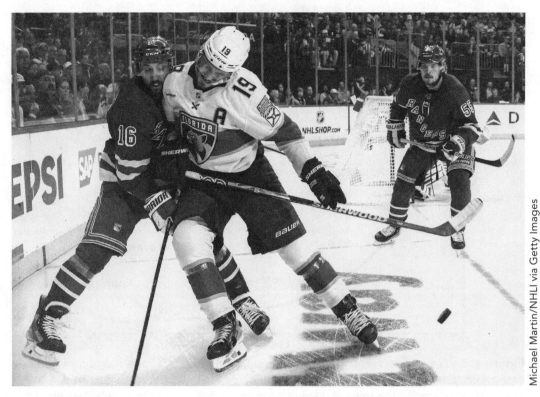

Contact between athletes creates another physical demand beyond skating and shooting.

body using bilateral (e.g., back squat, front squat, trap bar deadlift), partial unilateral (e.g., split squat, lunges, step-up), and fully unilateral (e.g., single-leg squat, single-leg Romanian deadlift) exercises is a sound approach.

Bilateral exercises are characterized by higher levels of stability, which allow for higher absolute loading potential and impulse generation. However, there is a hesitation to prescribe heavy-loaded bilateral exercises for hockey athletes for multiple reasons: They result in higher shear and compressive forces on the lumbar spine (15) and require reasonable levels of lumbo-pelvic control along with hip mobility and stability that some hockey athletes lack. As with any exercise, bilateral options should be selected only if no contraindications exist and the athlete is proficient with the movement. Front squats and trap bar deadlifts are two bilateral options that can be heavily loaded with less demand on the lumbar spine and hip joints than back squats or straight-bar deadlifts. Partial unilateral and fully unilateral lower body exercises have less absolute loading potential but place less compressive and shear force on the lumbar spine. Split squat, rear foot elevated split squat (RFESS), reverse lunge, and single-leg squat variations can be heavily loaded to achieve a maximal strength stimulus. "Hands-free" versions of unilateral exercises use a safety squat bar and are performed with the athlete holding onto the squat rack while executing the movement. Supported split squats or RFESSs significantly reduce the balance challenge and subsequently permit the use of greater external loads or velocities than their traditional counterparts. These are best used with high performance or elite hockey athletes who require more intensification of their maximal strength stimulus to progressively overload their current performance levels.

Upper body pushing and pulling strength affects how a hockey athlete manages physical contact with opponents, the boards, and the ice. They also contribute to how strong athletes are on their sticks, shooting, and face-offs. Similar to lower body exercises, bilateral exercises for the upper body present greater opportunity for absolute loading. Bilateral vertical pulls (e.g., chin-up, neutral grip pull-up), horizontal pulls (e.g., suspension row, bench pull), and horizontal presses (e.g., barbell bench press, low incline barbell bench press) can all be used to develop upper body maximal strength. Bilateral vertical presses require significant thoracic extension and shoulder mobility, which can often be limited due to the chronically flexed postures required in hockey or to previous shoulder injuries. Unilateral versions using landmines or dumbbells are suitable alternatives that have lower mobility requirements but still allow for the pattern to be trained with high intensity.

Mechanical Power

The ability to generate high mechanical power within the context of sport-specific motor skills is frequently cited as one of the keys to athletic success in hockey and other sports (20). **Power** is the rate of completing mechanical work ($P = W/t = (F \times d)/t$), which can be both positive (concentric) and negative (eccentric). Thus, a "powerful" athlete can complete high amounts of mechanical work in a short amount of time. Since **velocity** is equal to distance divided by time ($v = d/t$), the power equation can be rewritten as the product of force and velocity ($P = F \times v$). Power output can therefore be influenced by both the force applied and the velocity reached during movement. Given this, long-term development of power should be supported by longitudinal enhancement and maintenance of high levels of maximal strength. Loads that optimize power output vary by exercise but typically fall between 0% to 50% of the 1RM for ballistic movements and 50% to 90% of the 1RM for Olympic weightlifting derivatives (19). Notably, loads that optimize power output do not necessarily mean they optimally develop power. An athlete who lacks maximal strength or peak force capabilities may increase power output to a greater extent using heavy loads at slow velocities rather than exercises using moderate loads and velocities. A multimodal approach that is founded on maximal strength and integrates a range of exercises, loads, and velocities along the power spectrum is an effective strategy.

Since hockey athletes must move explosively across multiple planes, exercise selection for power development should be multidirectional. Comprehensive programming of power development that details multidirectional training strategies can be found within NSCA's professional resources (48). Vertical power development serves as a foundation for power expression across the other planes. Explosive movement in all planes benefits from forceful hip extension, which can be overloaded effectively with vertical power exercises. The main categories of these exercises include Olympic weightlifting derivatives, loaded jumps, and medicine ball throws. Olympic weightlifting exercises derived from the snatch, clean, and jerk provide a wide range of loading options, making them a useful tool for developing total body power. Catching variations, such as power snatches, split snatches, and power cleans, require the athlete to finish the movement and decelerate the load in the final position. Along with developing concentric power, catch versions challenge an athlete's coordinative ability to rapidly release from maximal tension at the peak of the pull and drop underneath the bar to then quickly self-organize and absorb the load. Pulling options, such as pulls and jump shrugs, eliminate the catch portion of the exercises and have been shown to elicit similar training outcomes to the catch versions (17). These are advantageous for hockey athletes who have chronic wrist or shoulder pathologies that may result in the front-rack or overhead catch positions being painful or restricted. Strength and conditioning professionals who have limited time with their hockey athletes may also gravitate toward pulling options because they can be taught more quickly than the traditional versions.

Loaded jumps provide a versatile option to express power across a range of loading conditions. Their coordinative simplicity minimizes the technical barrier to entry compared to some Olympic weightlifting derivatives. Simple movements also lend themselves to maximal intent and output better than those that require greater coordination. When a countermovement is used, loaded jumps use the **stretch-shortening cycle** (SSC), which challenges an athlete to produce large magnitudes of concentric force following a rapid eccentric contraction. This develops reactive strength qualities as well as eccentric and concentric RFD. Use of the SSC can sometimes be overlooked in hockey athletes because of the concentric-nature of the skating stride. However, improving reactive strength is highly valuable during linear striding because it facilitates the transition from weight acceptance to propulsion, allowing for propulsive impulse to be generated as early as possible following touch down. It also transfers to rapid changes of direction, crossover patterns, and maneuverability in on-ice tasks. Loaded jump exercises can use different types of equipment, including dumbbells, kettlebells, trap bars, and barbells, making them a flexible option that can be implemented with large groups and within most training spaces.

Upper body power for hockey athletes is an additional area of need. Expressions of upper body power on the ice typically originate from the forceful application of force into the ice, meaning a strong and powerful lower body is the foundation for upper body power. Explosive pressing movements (e.g., jerk, push press, bench throw, medicine ball chest pass, shot put, or overhead throw) and pulling movements (e.g., explosive cable row, bench pull, prowler row, medicine ball slam) can be programmed to develop power through the entire kinetic chain.

Concentric Rate of Force Development

Rate of force development describes how fast an athlete can produce force in a defined time span. In other words, it is an athlete's capacity to produce force quickly. It has been referenced in the previous sections because RFD is related to maximal strength, power, and reactive strength abilities. Both eccentric RFD and concentric RFD are relevant to an athlete's skating speed. Early RFD time bands (<100 ms from onset) appear to be more influenced by neural factors and intrinsic muscle properties, whereas later RFD time bands (>100 ms) are more closely related to maximal muscle strength and muscle cross-sectional area (1, 5, 50). Thus, training prescription to enhance early versus late RFD qualities may require different approaches.

For younger hockey athletes with low capacities for peak force production, improving maximal strength and power output with heavier loads is likely to improve the entire slope of the force–time curve from onset to peak force (2, 4). For more trained athletes, this strategy has potential to positively influence RFD, but it would likely manifest in the later portion of the effort (>100 ms). These cohorts require more specific approaches to enhance early concentric RFD. Generally, bodyweight or light-load ballistic exercises such as Olympic lifting derivatives and loaded jumps can be effective in developing early RFD more than heavily loaded options.

High-intensity pushing isometric exercises are additional options to challenge early and late RFD. Pushing and pulling isometric actions are those where the athlete is pushing or pulling against an immovable resistance and are more likely to elicit concentric-based adaptations (58). Alternatively, holding isometric actions require the athlete to resist an applied external load in a static position and create adaptations more closely related to eccentric actions (58). Pushing or pulling isometric exercises to develop RFD should include maximal intent to generate force quickly against the fixed resistance. Multiple repetitions of brief (1- to 3-second) maximal efforts can be prescribed using exercises such as split squat pin pulls for the lower body and bench press pin presses for the upper body.

Eccentric Strength

Hockey athletes need to rapidly express high levels of force in both accelerative and decelerative tasks, which suggests both concentric and eccentric muscular strength and power should be developed over an athlete's career. As previously described, underdeveloped eccentric (ECC) maximal strength and RFD may compromise the performance of linear skating and COD outputs by delaying the application of propulsive impulse in the desired direction of travel. The neuromuscular expression of concentric versus eccentric force relies on different mechanisms; improving concentric outputs does not guarantee improvements in eccentric abilities (and vice versa). The unique properties of ECC muscle contractions, namely that force is not constrained by increasing shortening velocity, mean that targeted ECC training leads to a nuanced adaptive signal. Eccentric training has been shown to positively influence hypertrophy, strength, and power (27, 29). Markedly, it has been suggested that certain methods of ECC training may preferentially target fast-twitch muscle fibers, which have high shortening velocity capabilities and thus high force output potential (29).

Building ECC strength capacities can be done by accentuating the eccentric portion of an exercise. Tempo ECC training uses submaximal loads and slows the descending phase of a movement to increase the duration muscles are lengthening (e.g., greater than 3-second ECC phase). Since the slow tempos limit load and movement velocity, the conditions are not optimal for strength or power improvement. Instead, this method is best used to elicit structural adaptations and improve motor control within the pattern. Tempo ECC training can be programmed during the early phases of the off-season, when the athlete is being prepared for more intensified ECC methods in future phases and speed or power performance is less of a concern.

As opposed to slow ECC actions, accelerated ECC actions typically have greater magnitudes of ECC peak force, ECC impulse, and ECC RFD (3, 33). Thus, accelerated eccentric loading (ACEL) exercises can serve as a potent stimulus for developing eccentric RFD and the ability to manage high force exposures. Athletes should be progressed gradually through rapid ECC exercises. Prior to prescribing loaded ACEL exercises, bodyweight exercises such as snap downs, low amplitude altitude drops, and low amplitude jumps and hops that emphasize a "stick" landing can be introduced to build movement competency and foundational deceleration capacities. Lower body loaded drop catch exercises can then be added to challenge an athlete's vertical deceleration. Both bilateral and unilateral versions are useful for hockey athletes to ensure they can effectively attenuate high peak forces in different limb positions. Examples that can be loaded with bands, dumbbells, a trap bar, or a barbell include squat drop catches, split squat and RFESS drop catches, and single-leg squat drop catches. Olympic lift variations that have the athlete finish the exercise and catch the load can also serve this purpose. Upper body versions can also be implemented such as push-up drop catches and medicine ball catches. Trained athletes may use weight releasers and flywheels to overload the ECC action. General progressions for ACEL exercises include extensive to intensive, bodyweight to loaded, low amplitude to high amplitude, double-leg to single-leg, and "soft" landing strategies where the deceleration impulse is purposefully elongated to attenuate peak force to "strong" or "stiff" landings where the deceleration phase duration is minimized.

Notably, the periodization of ECC training may require more foresight than other training methods. Because ECC training exercises can include high TUT (time under tension), external loads, or contractile velocities, they have a propensity to cause delayed-onset muscle soreness and neural fatigue, which reduce short-term neuromuscular performance. The demanding nature of intensified ECC training may contribute to longer periods of delayed transformation (time interval between training stimulus and realization of performance gains) than traditional training methods (18, 47). This means the training outcomes of an ECC-emphasized mesocycle may take 6 to 8 weeks to emerge, which can make it more challenging to evaluate the extent of training adaptations and subsequent performance benefits derived from the training stimulus.

Hypertrophy

Through a combination of normal growth and maturation, along with consistent exposure to resistance training, most hockey athletes add several kilograms of upper and lower body muscle mass throughout the course of their playing careers. Hypertrophic responses to training lead to greater cross-sectional area of the targeted muscles and create more force-generating potential. The added muscle mass therefore supports maximal strength outputs and potentially relative strength. Whereas mass-specific force application is highly relevant for skating speed and on-ice maneuverability, on-ice collisions play out in absolute terms. Aside from the skill-based contextual elements of delivering or accepting body contact, an 'athlete's mass and absolute levels of maximal strength are the two principal factors that determine how the athlete fares in collisions or struggles for position. Further, muscle mass may also enhance tissue tolerance and joint integrity, which can play a role in reducing the incidence of noncontact and contact injuries.

Despite these positive justifications for hypertrophy-focused resistance training, there are potential trade-offs of increasing mass in a hockey athlete that should be considered. As mentioned, skating tasks are constrained by a bodyweight-dependent ability to apply force. Adding muscle mass has the potential to negatively affect skating performance if an asymmetrical amount of fat mass is gained in parallel, the muscle mass is disproportionately added to the upper body, or the muscle mass is developed in isolation without concurrent exposures to high-force or high-velocity tasks. Hypertrophy training should therefore be approached thoughtfully because not all muscle-building protocols yield the desired performance enhancements.

Muscle protein synthesis signaling pathways can be triggered when the muscle is exposed to significant mechanical tension or metabolic stress (14, 34). High levels of mechanical tension can be created using heavier loads (6RM-12RM) whereas higher repetition protocols with light loads taken to near failure (>12RM) tend to promote metabolic stress (13, 16, 59). Mixed-method approaches that achieve the necessary training volume by using various movements, loads, and tempos within these ranges allow for multiple protein signaling pathways to be leveraged within the same training program. Such an approach also assists in maintaining an athlete's force generation capacity at fast and slow contraction velocities during hypertrophy training phases. Gaining muscle mass should be seen as a long-term, multiyear project that is supported by proper nutritional strategies and close monitoring of body composition, skating speed and power output throughout the process.

Torso and Stability

All movements on the ice rely on a sequence of force transfer from the ice up through the kinetic chain. Building postural control means improving an athlete's ability to create the appropriate amount of trunk stiffness, at the right moment, while maintaining mechanically advantageous positions. Creating too much stiffness, not creating enough, or having a significantly misaligned thorax and pelvis reduces an athlete's ability to sequentially transmit energy between the lower and upper body. In addition to being a significant factor in explosive outputs, chronic postures and individual joint function are key contributors to an athlete's long-term health. Postural positions affect the contractile requirements of the surrounding musculature, the tensile demands on the respective connective tissues, and the orientation of the articular surfaces. Like a car with misaligned tires that wear out asymmetrically, an athlete who has global postural dysfunction overloads certain tissues and joints when compared to more favorable alignments. This is of utmost concern due to the high incidence of structural issues within the hip joint and soft tissue injuries to the adductors, hip flexors, and abdominals seen in hockey athletes across all levels.

Torso training program design is enhanced by having a foundational understanding of the movement limitations that often emerge in hockey athletes and the primary underlying sources that may be creating them. For example, the sustained positions of hip flexion and anterior pelvic tilt associated with skating often result in hockey athletes presenting with muscular facilitation and inhibition patterns that characterize lower and upper cross syndromes (or "crossed" syndromes) (36). Along with these global compensatory postural adaptations, hockey athletes also frequently present with local range of motion (ROM) restrictions, specifically in the hip, across multiple directions (e.g., limited hip flexion and extension, internal rotation, external rotation, adduction, and abduction). Deficits in ROM of the ball-and-socket hip joint can correspond with a loss of appropriate arthrokinematic movement of the femoral head within the acetabulum, which can increase stress in certain areas of the joint. For example, restriction in the posterior hip capsule is a common finding that can prevent the head of the femur from gliding posteriorly during movements that require flexion and internal rotation. This results in an anteriorly positioned femoral head, which may lead to impingement of the anterior soft tissues and labrum.

Addressing postural issues through the thorax and pelvis requires an individualized approach because movement deficiencies can emerge from deficits in multiple qualities including the following:

- **Joint mobility**—Pain-free active ROM (e.g., the athlete's active control of available hip extension ROM in isolated tasks such as a prone flexed-knee hip extension). Mobility is affected by a joint's available passive ROM and its local stabilization system. Passive ROM can be limited for several reasons, including joint morphology (e.g., anteverted or retroverted hip structures), soft tissue restrictions (e.g., muscle shortness, fascial tension, scarring), or neural tone (e.g., muscular guarding to stabilize a lax joint).

- **Local joint stability**—Synergistic muscular contraction around a joint that provides proprioceptive feedback, reactive stiffness, and joint integrity under static and dynamic conditions. These local stabilizer muscles tend to be deep, monoarticular muscles that assist in controlling alignment and ROM at a single local segment but also work to create static tension when multiple joints are involved.

- **Global stability**—Ability to dissociate the movement of separate joints (e.g., an athlete's ability to extend their hip during a bird dog exercise without compensatory movement occurring such as lumbar hyperextension).

- **Motor control**—Coordinated movement patterns emerging from the sequential action of several involved joints that are driven by the central nervous system via feed-forward and feedback processes (e.g., an athlete's ability to perform the hip extension pattern within a linear march exercise in a coordinated manner).

Each of these trainable factors that affect movement quality through the trunk and pelvic regions requires specific approaches in order to address dysfunction; applying the incorrect training intervention may result in transient improvements that quickly revert or, more concerningly, further feed dysfunction. For example, the hip flexors and anterior thigh muscles can often have excessive neural tone that causes athletes to feel tightness. A logical solution may be to prescribe stretching exercises. However, analyzing the potential origins of the tightness may reveal stretching to be a counterproductive strategy, whereas stability exercises may be a more suitable strategy. The body tends to create soft tissue stiffness in areas exposed to repetitive stress or that lack the stability needed to protect the articular surfaces from damage. During skating, the explosive hip extension, abduction, and external rotation of late propulsion bring the head of the femur anteriorly within the hip capsule, pressuring the anterior labrum. The rapid transition into recovery by flexing, adducting, and internally rotating the hip can further stress the area by compressing the tissues anteriorly, especially if the athlete has posterior capsular restrictions. Over time, repeated trauma can contribute to tearing of the anterior labrum that can be minor or significant. Labral damage reduces passive stabilization around the joint, disrupts proprioception, and contributes to a loss of control of the head of the femur within the acetabulum. The muscles surrounding the hip respond by chronically tightening as a protective mechanism to reduce the risk of injury. Consequently, aggressive stretching protocols to alleviate tightness may reduce a proportion of the local protective stiffness the body has developed and potentially expose the anterior anatomical core muscles, hip flexors, adductors, and labrum to additional strain while skating. Instead, along with small doses of targeted mobility exercises, training prescription should include exercises to restore local hip joint stability as well as ones that improve the ability to dissociate hip movement from the surrounding joints.

Overall, a well-planned torso training program for hockey athletes should address static and dynamic stability globally in conjunction with the local stability of primary joints within the thorax and pelvic girdle including the hips, lumbar spine, and shoulders. Several positive outcomes arise by emphasizing the alignment of the thorax and pelvis through exercise, including the restoration of diaphragm and pelvic floor function, reestablishing length–tension relationships of surrounding musculature, regaining ROM of the hip and shoulder, and optimizing central stability for efficient, total body movement.

Global Stability   Fundamental torso training addresses breathing dynamics and an athlete's ability to maintain postural integrity while resisting motion in various positions and directions. Breathing drills from a prone or 90-90 supine position that require a 360-degree full inhalation and exhalation may improve function of the diaphragm and pelvic floor. Executing a full respiration cycle can be included in many of the torso exercises described in this chapter to increase the activation of the deep spinal stabilizers and act as an assessment tool. Athletes who struggle to perform a controlled inhalation and exhalation without excessive effort likely lack the competency to progress to a more difficult variation. Establishing postural control through the sagittal plane should be a primary emphasis to correct lumbo-pelvic compensation patterns. Anti-extension exercises serve this purpose and create the foundation of torso training by encouraging a posterior pelvic tilt (from an anterior tilt position), neutral spine, and internal rotation of the anterior rib cage. Anti-extension exercises include bird dogs, dead bugs, and front plank variations. Most athletes struggle with the most basic level of these exercises and should not be progressed until they have mastered the basic drills.

Anti-rotation, rotation, and anti-lateral flexion exercises comprise the next layer of torso training. On the ice, every movement—linear skating, crossing over, shooting, and passing—involves a rotary component that consists of either moving or resisting movement through the transverse plane. Basic rotary stability can be developed using controlled anti-rotation exercises, such as anti-rotation presses, chops, and lifts, that teach an athlete to maintain postural stability and control against transverse and diagonal forces. Higher levels of rotary stability and strength can be developed with moderate- or heavy-loaded asymmetrical exercises such as split squats, single-leg Romanian deadlifts (RDLs), single-arm presses, and single-arm rows. When the athlete has demonstrated a basic ability to sustain posture under rotational forces, dynamic rotational movements can be added, such as rotational chops, lifts, and landmine rotations. Rotary power can be trained using rotational medicine ball throw variations; however, if a hockey athlete lacks the stability required to execute the rudimentary exercises previously described, that athlete may struggle to efficiently dissociate and transfer energy through the kinetic chain. Anti-lateral flexion exercises such as side planks and asymmetrical loaded carries challenge postural integrity primarily within frontal plane and should be included within a comprehensive torso program.

Local Stability   Hip stability exercises encourage femoral centering within the acetabulum under static and dynamic conditions. Improving hip stability for hockey athletes should be multiplanar, emphasize repatterning basic hip flexion and extension, and address adduction and abduction strength. The sustained positions of anterior pelvic tilt and hip flexion in hockey athletes disrupts the contractile function of the hip flexors and surrounding musculature. Although effective exercise programming should typically emphasize training movements over specific muscles, in some contexts it is important to have an understanding of the functional anatomy that may be feeding a dysfunctional pattern in order to select the appropriate training intervention. Eleven muscles have the potential to assist hip flexion, depending on the positions of the hip and pelvis. The iliacus and psoas are the primary contributors to hip flexion above 90 degrees due to having an advantageous moment arm relative to the other hip flexors. Having athletes work on isolated hip flexion above 90 degrees from lying, seated, and standing positions can challenge a poorly functioning psoas to act as the primary hip flexor as opposed to the tensor fasciae latae, which often can become an overdominant synergist during the movement.

Patterning hip extension while emphasizing posterior pelvic tilt via contraction of the lower abdominals anteriorly, and gluteals and hamstrings posteriorly, can be accomplished using basic drills performed statically or dynamically (e.g., double- and single-leg hip bridges, quadruped single-leg hip extension, wall marches). Hip extension is also a common component of many anti-extension exercises, such as bird dogs and dead bugs, which serves as a reminder that exercises can often address multiple qualities concurrently.

A significantly imbalanced ratio of hip abduction to adduction strength has been identified as a potential risk factor for adductor strains in hockey athletes (63), although more evidence is needed (53). The hip abductors tend to be stronger than the adductors, meaning abduction exercises, including quadruped fire hydrants and mini band lateral walks, can be primarily used as activation work rather than strengthening. Hip abduction is also challenged during many anti-lateral flexion exercises previously described (e.g., side planks) as well as those that require single-leg stances. Isolated hip abduction work using bands or cables may be used as preparation exercises prior to training or in return-to-play scenarios.

Addressing the adductors requires a multifactorial approach that begins with the postural control exercises. During explosive and complex movements when both lower extremities are involved, the adductors are working bilaterally to stabilize the pelvis-on-femur on one side while simultaneously controlling the femur-on-pelvis motion on the other. The adductors are not only responsible for adducting the hip but contribute to hip flexion and hip extension, depending on the position of the joint, and act to stabilize the pelvis in multiple planes. Thus, they are under constant load while skating. Adductor strength should be challenged at different muscle lengths, in multiple planes, and under static and dynamic conditions. Training isolated adduction in short and long positions such as supine flexed knee or straight-leg adductions ensures the muscles have adequate contractile ability at different lengths. These exercises can be progressed to adductor side plank versions beginning with short levers and then advancing to longer lever versions. The adductors can be challenged eccentrically in closed chain conditions using slide board exercises such as half-kneeling lateral slides and slider lateral squats. More dynamic frontal plane strength exercises, including lateral lunges, crossover step-ups, or crossover sled drags, strengthen the adductors in a more integrated manner.

Although not always considered under the umbrella of torso training, the shoulder girdle attaches to the thorax, meaning shoulder function is directly affected by posture. Shoulder stability exercises that enhance scapular control can be included to help address weakness or dysfunction commonly found in the musculature of the posterior shoulder. They can also be used to address chronic shoulder instability issues found in hockey athletes caused by previous injuries such as acromioclavicular (AC) sprains or shoulder dislocations. Rudimentary strengthening exercises such as band external rotations or pull aparts can be implemented as activation work within a warm-up prior to resistance training. More integrated options, such as reaching exercises like wall slides or scapular push-ups, can help to encourage controlled movement of the scapula on the rib cage while maintaining pelvis and rib cage alignment. Crawling and loaded carry exercises provide locomotor-type patterns that can be used to connect movements of the shoulder to those of the lower limb. There are many variations of these exercises that can be implemented, including multiplanar, dynamic, or higher-load options such as bear crawls, unilateral loaded carries, or Turkish get-ups.

Whereas the exercises described address postural control primarily through activation or strengthening of inhibited musculature, exercises to target tissues that have been facilitated or chronically shortened may also be useful. Isometric actions and tempo ECC training can stimulate the remodeling of connective tissue and decrease the neural tone of facilitated muscles (6, 35, 56). Holding isometrics that accumulate approximately 2 minutes of TUT for the facilitated muscles in moderate to lengthened positions can provide the tensile stimulus needed to elicit fascial, tendon, and other connective tissue adaptations (6). These can be done with light to heavy loads broken up across several repetitions of 5 to 60 seconds, depending on the load. Example exercises that can address lower body and upper body facilitation patterns, respectively, are the split squat and push-up exercises held in the bottom positions. To encourage activation of the inhibited muscles, athletes can be encouraged to "pull" themselves into the positions while holding. By doing so, both the facilitated and inhibited muscles are simultaneously being exposed to the needed training stimulus: Facilitated areas are being lengthened and inhibited areas are being activated. These are often programmed during the initial off-season phase following the transition period when on-ice demands are minimal. The timing prevents a tug-of-war between skating reinforcing overly flexed postures and the exercises prescribed to correct them.

Structural Balance and Structural Tolerance

The task requirements of hockey are inherently asymmetrical, which results in anterior-posterior and interlimb strength imbalances. Major muscle strength asymmetries may constrain movement options, predispose an athlete to injury, or limit force production abilities in certain tasks (10, 60). Although determining the optimal bandwidths of agonist-antagonist and interlimb strength ratios is difficult, the concept of having relatively balanced strength outputs across different joints and sides of the body for hockey athletes is sound. Significant differences in upper or lower body strength on the left versus right sides are often a result of previous injury. These cases require an individualized approach to address the specific issue. Anterior-posterior ratios are applicable to all hockey athletes. Hockey athletes tend to have higher levels of strength through the anterior chain muscles due to the flexion-based postures of skating tasks. Subsequently, including a higher ratio of posterior-chain, or pulling, exercises to anterior-chain, or pushing, exercises for both the upper and lower body as assistance exercises can help manage the anterior-chain bias of the sport.

Structural tolerance refers to the capacity of the tissues, including bones, joints, ligaments, tendons, and muscles, to withstand a progressive increase in training load and resist fatigue or injury (71). In other words, it is the athlete's ability to successfully cope with the volume and intensity of training and competition. The development of structural tolerance is not accomplished solely with resistance training, but it is a key training method to promote these capacities. Resistance training can positively affect structural tolerance by improving the load-bearing capacity of the trained tissues. It also contributes to an athlete's total accumulated chronic training load in combination with on-ice work and other training modalities. Thus, resistance training contributes to a hockey athlete's overall robustness and to the ability to tolerate the predicted and unpredicted stressors across a training year without injury or significant decrements in performance.

Advanced Strategies for Skaters

Hockey athletes who have acquired satisfactory levels of movement competency in main exercises and relative strength may have success further developing their RFD and power capabilities with more advanced methods of exercise programming such as velocity-based training (VBT), complex training, and cluster sets.

As described within the Acute Training Variables section, VBT methods use velocity ranges to prescribe exercise intensity. These methods are especially useful for developing RFD and power because they shift focus away from primarily external load toward concentric bar speed, which drives an athlete's intent to accelerate maximally during each repetition. This is a key advantage of VBT because, regardless of the actual movement velocity, it increases the potency of the training stimulus when compared to loads lifted submaximally with controlled tempos (9).

There are several approaches available to integrate VBT within a training program. As with any method, the desired adaptations should guide training prescription—meaning that assigning velocity zone targets should be done intentionally. A simple option that also serves as a suitable introduction to VBT is to prescribe a fixed external load using traditional set and repetition percentage-based schemes while using bar speed solely as a within-set feedback tool to drive maximal concentric intent. This can enhance the quality of each repetition but does not fully leverage the autoregulatory benefits of VBT.

Implementing velocity-loss thresholds involves setting a predetermined limit that the mean concentric velocity of each repetition must stay above. The threshold velocity is typically relative to the maximal speed an athlete can achieve at a given load. For example, if the ceiling velocity is set at 0.7 m/s, prescribing a 15% velocity loss places the lowest allowable speed at 0.6 m/s. When an athlete falls below the threshold, the set is terminated. Once the velocity parameters are established, various velocity-loss protocols can be constructed that either fix or vary the load, the number of repetitions, and the number of sets. Using the same example, a fixed-set, fixed-load protocol that allows for variable repetition numbers may have an athlete complete 5 total sets at 80 kg (176 lb). The number of repetitions per set is variable, meaning the athlete would complete as many repetitions as possible above 0.6 m/s. In these scenarios it is often prudent to outline a maximal repetition per set threshold to control for excessive volume if the load is underestimated. A fixed-repetition, fixed-load protocol that allows for variable set numbers may prescribe 12 total repetitions above 0.6 m/s across as few sets as possible. A fixed-set, fixed-repetition protocol with variable load may prescribe 5 sets of 5 repetitions. If the athlete drops below 0.6 m/s within a set, decrease the load the following set to ensure the velocity is restored to the target range. All of these methods serve to maximize power output across a set at the given load.

Effective execution of these protocols requires a certain amount of finesse by the strength and conditioning professional to select an athlete's initial load and make appropriate within-session adjustments. Load-velocity profiles can assist in estimating starting load selection for those athletes. The target velocity is inserted into the equation of the linear trend line to calculate the predicted load required to elicit the intended bar speed (41). To autoregulate the process and for those athletes who have not completed an LVP, performing incrementally heavier warm-up sets while tracking bar speed converges upon a starting load that matches the athlete's daily level of performance. For example, if the goal is for working sets to be within a velocity range of 0.7 to 0.75 m/s, an athlete may use 3 warm-up sets of increasing weight until finding the load that achieves the target bar speed.

Complex training is an umbrella term that describes methods of training that leverage the acute enhancements of RFD and power in low-load or bodyweight high-velocity exercises (EXP) that follow heavy-load, low-velocity exercises (STR) (21). When performance of a subsequent task is improved because of the potentiating effect of a prior conditioning activity (CA) it is called **postactivation performance enhancement** (PAPE) (23). It is generally suggested that PAPE is best achieved when the CA and target task share similar biomechanical strategies. For example, to improve power output in the vertical direction using a contrast method, an athlete may complete a heavy trap bar deadlift immediately followed by a vertical jump. The intraset rest between the CA and target exercise is largely dependent upon the nature of the CA. Postactivation performance enhancement exists as a balance between fatigue and post-CA potentiation. Immediately following the CA, there are acute fatigue factors that must diminish prior to the enhancement in neuromuscular outputs to be realized (55). Plyometric or lightly loaded ballistic CAs (e.g., tuck jumps or dumbbell countermovement jumps) may be effective in eliciting PAPE after 30 to 60 seconds of rest, whereas heavy-loaded strength CAs (e.g., heavy trap bar deadlifts) may require greater than 5 minutes. It is worth reiterating that these methods are modulated by an athlete's initial strength levels and should only be prescribed for athletes who have accumulated an acceptable level of relative strength. For low training age athletes without a sufficient training base, the high-intensity efforts intended to act as CAs may elicit high levels of neural and metabolic fatigue that may not dissipate within a set or training session.

Cluster sets are an additional advanced training option that include intraset rest periods to maintain high power outputs across the set when compared to traditional sets. For example, instead of assigning 4 repetitions, a cluster set may include two clusters of 2 repetitions separated by 15 seconds of rest. There are various repetition schemes that target different adaptations (66). Prescription should begin with simple cluster set options that align with the desired performance outcome and progress in accordance with the athlete's response to training.

Goalies

There are fundamental differences in how a goalie navigates the ice compared to the other skaters. Like a badminton athlete or boxer, goalies must move reactively in multiple directions, explosively yet controlled, and within a small area. Because their movements are more technical in nature and stopping a puck relies heavily on visual, reactive, and coordinative skills, the success of a goalie is less dependent on general biomotor abilities than for the skaters. A skater with below-average hockey skills and average physical abilities sees a more profound positive impact on game performance as a result of increased strength and power abilities compared to goalie in a similar scenario. This does not suggest resistance training is less important for a goalie's long-term development but can help guide the selection of training objectives and the expected magnitude of transfer.

Like skaters, goalies need to follow LTAD principles and be trained as athletes first, hockey athletes second, and their position third. Positional specificity of exercise selection and training prescription for high training age goalies is more evident in the programming of energy systems, reactive strength, speed, and mobility qualities than resistance training. Most of the program design and exercise selection recommendations for skaters outlined so far hold true for goalies. However, there are certain areas where exercise specificity for higher training age goalies can improve targeted outcomes that are more relevant for their positional needs.

Goalie movements emerge out of two base positions: stance and butterfly. Butterfly-style goaltending results in goalies moving into and out of positions of deep hip flexion, abduction, and internal rotation repeatedly while on the ice. This creates two primary challenges. First, it places significant strain on the hip joint and surrounding musculature, which when done repeatedly can create bony pathology, labral tears, or muscular strains. Second, it requires goalies to perform explosive movements out of positions that place many of the agonist and synergist muscles at unfavorable lengths to produce force. Goalie-specific resistance training programs should consider the long-term structural health of the lumbar spine, pelvis (sacroiliac joints, pubic symphysis), hips (labrum), and knees (medial menisci). Programming should enhance soft tissue tolerance in order to meet the unique on-ice demands and improve a goalie's explosive performance out of the required on-ice positions.

Strength at End Range

Building positional strength for goalies in deeply flexed or fully extended positions can help to increase tissue resilience and address joint stability at these ranges. End range of motion (ROM) isometric exercises are an effective tool for enhancing local stability and proprioception of the involved joint. Although these exercises are useful for skaters, they are particularly important for goalies, who are required to move dynamically through more extreme hip ranges of motion, to maintain long-term joint mobility and stability.

End-ROM isometrics can be performed in many positions. For goalies they are specifically effective in building control and strength in fully abducted, flexed, extended, internally rotated, or externally rotated hip positions. The isometric contractions should be performed on both sides of the target joint, meaning that pushing and holding isometrics may both be included within a sequence. For example, an end-ROM isometric targeting hip adduction and abduction may have a goalie in a quadruped position with one leg abducted, the knee extended, and the foot flat. A pushing isometric that challenges the hip adductors in lengthened positions can be performed by pushing the foot into the floor in a ramp style from 50% to 80% maximal effort over 10 seconds. A holding isometric to address the hip abductors in shortened positions could follow, or be performed separately, where the goalie attempts to unweight the foot. Progression of these exercises can be accomplished by increasing the intensity of the contraction or performing them at deeper joint angles. Low-intensity end-ROM isometrics can be used within the activation portion of on- or off-ice warm-ups. High-intensity versions can be programmed within resistance training sessions and placed in later blocks to ensure the athletes are not fatigued while doing their primary exercises. They can also be used in separate training sessions in combination with more traditional torso training exercises.

Loaded holding isometrics, slow-tempo ECC exercises, and bottoms-up movements can all be used to complement isolated end-ROM isometrics by integrating the improved end-range joint control into total body patterns. Loaded holding isometrics performed in the bottom position of exercises such as split squats, RFESSs, or lateral squats can improve a goalie's strength in low positions. They can also be performed with slow ECC tempos of 4 to 10 seconds to accomplish a similar goal while creating a stronger stimulus for morphological adaptations. Lastly, using bottoms-up exercises that force athletes to initiate loading in the deepest position of the movement improves the ability to self-organize and produce force in a controlled manner without the benefit of an eccentric preload. Split squats, RFESSs, single-leg rack pulls, step-ups, and trap bar deadlifts are all examples of exercises that can be performed in this manner that may be particularly useful for goalies.

Early Rate of Force Development

Goalies must be able to move rapidly in multiple directions through their crease area. Goalie shuffles, pushes, and slides can be broadly categorized into small amplitude or large amplitude efforts. The majority of goalie skating movements are the former. Akin to a boxer's jab, goalies need to be able to rapidly accumulate tension and apply force within a brief window of time. Alternatively, like a boxer's uppercut, where more time is taken to wind up and deliver a forceful blow, larger amplitude movements occur when a goalie uses greater ROM, applies force into the ice for longer, and covers more distance with the push. For both categories, time is constrained, making RFD and power primary underlying strength abilities. Enhancing RFD and power for goalies should follow the same principles described for skaters. That is, they should develop strength abilities across the entire load-velocity spectrum. For developing goalies, building lower body maximal strength serves as a foundation for RFD.

Analyzing the starting position of goalie movements can leave clues on areas where specificity may be warranted. Explosive goalie movements frequently emerge from static or near-static positions such as the butterfly or butterfly derivatives. This is extremely challenging because it negates a goalie's ability to use the SSC to preload the system for concentric force generation. The onset of external force application requires the goalie to take up the slack in the muscle–tendon unit (MTU) before the contractile elements of the muscle can effectively transmit a pulling force through the MTU to its origin and insertion points (70). This rapid tensioning of the muscle–tendon unit has been shown to contribute to an athlete's early RFD ability in explosive actions (62), suggesting that the faster muscle slack is taken up, the sooner effective concentric force can be applied into the ice. A goalie's ability to pretension MTUs via cocontractions can be trained with exercises that have a static start (45). Constraining the starting conditions of the exercise to avoid an eccentric preload via a countermovement or holding isometric can help drive adaptations toward early RFD. Sagittal plane examples that fall within the resistance training spectrum include lightly loaded Olympic lift derivatives from blocks, loaded seated jumps, loaded step-up jumps, and medicine ball granny throws.

Hypertrophy

Having adequate amounts of muscle mass can contribute to overall strength and power performance for goalies. Since goalies are not subject to the same amount of physical contact as skaters, the amount of muscle that optimizes the performance of goalies is comparably less. They do not require the additional armor that may protect them from contact injuries. Additionally, excessive muscle mass, particularly in the upper body, can quickly become a hindrance to their on-ice performance. The ideal amount of upper body mass sufficiently provides the force necessary to accelerate the upper limb rapidly and provide the tensile stability for force transfer. Exceeding this threshold can disrupt limb coordination and speed. Each individual goalie will have a different optimal bandwidth of upper and lower body muscle mass, depending on skeletal structure and playing style. The challenge is to help goalies achieve a body composition that provides the muscular units to maximize force outputs at high speeds without overshooting the target and negatively affecting their quickness.

Total Hip Load

Exercise selection within a resistance training program should work within the goalie's available ROM and be mindful of the total time spent in certain postures. There is a balance that must be struck between preparing a goalie to have the tissue resilience to tolerate the on-ice load and overexposure to unproductive additional load on the joints off the ice in goalie-specific positions. For example, heavy-loaded bilateral squats place significant flexion-based load on the hip joints. Goalies typically have high chronic load on the pelvis and hips, meaning that alternatives that can achieve a similar training stimulus with reduced hip demand, such as trap bar deadlifts or split squats, may be more suitable long-term choices. Since the goalie stance is a knee-dominant position, goalies may generally need higher proportions of posterior chain exercises to create structural balance, particularly within the lower body. Lastly, there has been a move toward off-ice goalie-specific training programs that include high volumes of stance- or butterfly-based movements. Adding significantly more repetitions of goalie movements off the ice may do more harm than good for long-term joint health and career longevity. Instead of using a sledgehammer-like approach, strength and conditioning professionals must be surgical in how they dissect the positional needs and incorporate training specificity that promotes long-term health and performance of goalies.

PROGRAMMING FOR THE INJURED ATHLETE

Despite extensive planning and preparation, acute and chronic musculoskeletal injuries are part of the sport. This section is not intended to be a comprehensive return-to-play manual, but instead it provides general programming strategies for injured athletes. Exercise selection must respect the pathology of the injury and ensure that the area is not being further compromised. All resistance training prescribed for injured athletes should be cleared with medical staff to ensure any contraindicated exercises are communicated. Three strategies for prescribing exercise for injured athletes include regressing the original exercise to a level that can be completed pain-free, leveraging the cross-education effect by selecting exercises that load the uninjured limb while avoiding the injured limb, and using lateralizations to allow the affected limb to be safely involved in the exercise.

Use of Exercise Regressions

Exercise regressions can be useful in guiding exercise selection for significantly injured athletes who may need to fully unload and rebuild movement patterns. For example, a hockey athlete with a moderate medial collateral ligament sprain may regress from a barbell RFESS to a light dumbbell split squat to reduce the loading demand on the injured knee while it heals. Although this is an appropriate option in certain scenarios, regressing exercises can sometimes be a suboptimal strategy because they typically have less loading potential and therefore offer a weaker training stimulus than the original exercise. Exclusively using regressions, especially for athletes with chronic injuries, may result in detraining and risk the athlete losing force capacities over time.

Training the Uninvolved Limbs

Training the uninvolved limbs is extremely useful in maintaining overall strength performance while injured. Not only does this strategy ensure the athlete does not lose strength elsewhere, but training the functional contralateral limb can result in strength improvement or attenuate strength losses on the untrained limb (46). For example, a hockey athlete with an acute AC sprain may be unable to load-bear on the injured side but can likely safely complete heavy resisted pulls and presses on the uninjured arm. Incorporating eccentric training methods while performing these unilateral exercises may be prioritized because they have been shown to be particularly effective in eliciting a cross-education effect (68). Lower body strength could be maintained or enhanced for an athlete with an upper body injury by using exercises that do not require the use of both arms, such as belted sled drags, belted squats, or slider hamstring curls.

Exercise Lateralizations

Lateralizations are exercise substitutes that provide the means to evoke an analogous training stimulus to the original target exercise. These are key to ensuring that athletes with acute injuries or chronic movement limitations can be safely exposed to an intensified stimulus to prevent significant losses in strength while injured. Lateralizations often consist of limiting the ROM, altering the load placement, or changing the equipment that is providing the overload. An example may be a hockey athlete with a wrist injury who is unable to hold a barbell for the RFESS exercise. An appropriate lateralization would be to use a safety bar RFESS to allow the athlete to achieve a similar intensity of stimulus, as opposed to regressing the exercise to a dumbbell RFESS which, although it could also be performed safely, constrains the absolute loading potential of the exercise.

Care for a Common Injury: Femoroacetabular Impingement

There is a high incidence of diagnosed and undiagnosed femoroacetabular impingement (FAI) in hockey athletes, meaning strength and conditioning professionals working in the sport should have specific programming strategies for those athletes affected. Athletes who have been medically diagnosed with CAM-, pincer-, or mixed-hip morphology via imaging and clinical signs and symptoms require programming adjustments to ensure they continue to develop their strength abilities in manners that do not aggravate the area. Knee-dominant movements that include significant amounts of simultaneous hip and knee flexion tend to be more irritating than hip-dominant hinging patterns. These squatting positions require the head of the femur to slide posteriorly while the hip moves through internal rotation and flexion. Hips with FAI are limited in these ranges of motion, which feeds further into their anterior impingement. Exercises that should be avoided or used with caution for athletes with FAI include deep bilateral squatting, full-ROM single-leg squats, full-ROM single-leg step-up variations, crossover step-ups, and cross-under lunges.

Strength and conditioning professionals should use pain or discomfort as a guide to help select appropriate exercises for athletes with FAI on a case-by-case basis, because athletes have differing ranges of function and ROM tolerance. Reducing the ROM to decrease the amount of hip flexion needed for the exercises or moving the load off the shoulders (e.g., using front-rack, goblet, or suitcase positions) may allow athletes to perform typically aggravating exercises pain-free. Athletes can well-tolerate hip-dominant exercises or those that do not require deep hip and knee flexion, such as unilateral and bilateral variations of elevated deadlift patterns (e.g., trap bar deadlift with high handles or rack pulls), RDLs, hamstring curls, hip bridges, hip thrusts, reduced-ROM single-leg squats or step-ups, sagittal plane split squats or lunges where the torso and shin remain vertical, forward sled pushes or drags, and backward sled drags.

PERIODIZATION

Designing resistance training programs for hockey athletes is a part of the more comprehensive planning process that strength and conditioning professionals undertake when preparing athletes for competition. **Periodization** is a planning paradigm that involves the strategic and systematic fluctuations of training in a sequential manner that aims to maximize an athlete's competition performance at specified time points (12). It helps to account for the total stress placed on an athlete at different phases of the year and allows for more strategic implementation of training volume and intensity prescriptions. A periodized plan for hockey athletes is anchored by the competition calendar. Training cycles are planned around those schedule constraints and also consider travel, holidays, and periods of academic stress, if applicable. A certain amount of uncertainty exists within the complex nature of team sport that requires periodization to be viewed as a flexible plan instead of a rigid model. Unexpected schedule or travel changes, individuality of training responses to load, and changes to athlete health or injury status can all disrupt well-intentioned plans and often require altered approaches when they arise.

Long-Term Planning

Periodization involves separating the long-term training cycle, typically called a **macrocycle**, into smaller phases of training that are sequentially ordered in a manner that accounts for short- and long-term performance of general biomotor abilities and sport-specific skills. A periodized plan for hockey athletes may encapsulate multiple years or a single year. Strength and conditioning professionals who work with high school, university, or national team programs may use four-year planning cycles (**quadrennials**) that outline the basic progressions and outcomes across each year (e.g., annual targets in strength and power for each year of college). More commonly, **yearly training plans** (YTPs) are created that consist of three major phases and are further divided into subphases: preparatory (general physical preparation and specific physical preparation), competitive (precompetitive, regular season, and playoffs), and transition (12) (figure 4.3).

Month	May			June	July	August	September	October	November	December	January	Febuary	March	April	
Microcycle	1 2 3 4	5 6	7 8 9	10 11 12 13	14 15 16 17	18 19 20 21	22 23 24 25 26	27 28 29 30 31	32 33 34 35 36	37 38 39 40 41 42	43 44 45	46 47 48	49 50	51 52	
Major phase	Preparatory						Competitive								Transition
Sub-phase	General physical preparation			Specific physical prep.			Pre-competitive	Regular season				Playoffs			Off
Mesocycle	Tissue remodeling/ work capacity	Hypertrophy	Max strength		Power	Reactive strength	Balanced	Balanced							Reconditioning
Volume	Low	Moderate to high	Moderate to high		Moderate to high	Moderate	Moderate to low	Low							
Intensity	Low	Moderate	Moderate to high		High	High	Moderate to high	Moderate to high							
Example methods	Holding ISOs; circuits; technical drills	Tempo ECCs; max reps; exhaustive reps	5 x 5; APRE; pyramid sets		Wave loading; accelerated ECCs	Contrast sets; clusters; accelerated ECCs	French contrast sets	Low volume, max strength sets (e.g., 1-2 x 2-5 @ 78%-85% 1RM); high intensity pushing isometrics							

Figure 4.3 A sample of a yearly training plan that displays general guidelines and examples for each major phase.

The subphases are broken down into smaller training periods called **mesocycles**, often 3 to 6 weeks long, that have a desired training outcome based on the physiological adaptations being targeted. The primary factors involved in planning mesocycles are the integration of motor abilities within a single training phase and the sequencing of consecutive mesocycles. Integration and sequencing can be approached in different manners depending on the athlete cohort and training objectives.

Integration

There are two main approaches to integration: a block approach or a parallel approach. **Block planning** involves overloading a single motor ability while other qualities are trained minimally or not at all. Eliminating other forms of training removes the risk of an interference effect between noncomplementary training stimuli that can diminish the adaptive potential for the main training goal (69). Block structures can therefore be effective for high training age athletes who require significant intensification through concentrated loading to further elicit specific adaptations. However, like the race car that needs several highly functioning components to perform at a high level, the multifactorial nature of hockey requires athletes to excel in a range of general physical qualities. Using a block approach may lead to detraining of certain motor abilities, which may not be desirable.

Instead, a **parallel periodization** approach, also sometimes described as **vertical integration** (28), is likely a more effective choice for most hockey athletes because multiple motor abilities are trained concurrently. The volume load dedicated to each motor ability can by adjusted, depending on the training goal. Loads can be categorized based on the expected response: Excessive loads surpass the adaptive capacity of the athlete and lead to nonfunctional over-reaching, development loads provide an adaptive stimulus that leads to improved performance of the target ability, maintenance loads are insufficient to elicit an adaptation response but prevent detraining, and recovery loads are insufficient to avoid detraining over time but allow for fatigue to dissipate and performance to be realized (67). Importantly, the categorization of these loads is relative for each athlete depending on training age, fitness level, and injury status. For example, a maintaining load for one athlete may be an excessive load for another, meaning strength and conditioning professionals who work in team settings must continually audit how athletes are responding to training and adjust accordingly.

Parallel schemes can either assign equivalent training stress across each motor ability or prioritize specific adaptations by asymmetrically loading different strength qualities within the same phase. For low training age hockey athletes, a parallel scheme with equivalent loads can elicit meaningful improvement in multiple abilities concurrently. Moderate or high training age athletes are likely to see minimal performance improvements with this approach. Equal distribution of training stress may lack the intensification of any single stimulus to elicit a training response or, if several are intensified at once, may push an athlete into a state of overreaching that requires extended periods of recovery to return to baseline. An athlete has a finite reserve of energetic resources available for training and recovery that limits adaptive potential. This must be respected during the training process to optimize long-term gains in performance. Using an emphasis approach within a parallel model combines the benefits of block planning tactics with those of a concurrent scheme. For most hockey athletes, using a parallel mesocycle that has a primary and secondary goal while training other abilities at maintenance loads provides an effective avenue for intensifying a single stimulus, avoids detraining of nonprimary abilities, and reduces the risk of unintentional overreaching. Successfully periodized resistance training programs should also consider the integration of speed and energy systems development across a macrocycle. Aligning strength, speed, and energy system performance goals that are compatible can optimize potential adaptations across each training type by avoiding the interference of one training stimuli by another. For example, performing high volumes of aerobic capacity work during a power training phase may reduce gains in explosive force production because they target dissimilar metabolic pathways (i.e., aerobic capacity versus anaerobic power) and muscle fiber types (i.e., type I slow twitch versus type II fast twitch) (69).

Horizontal Sequencing

Horizontal sequencing describes how mesocycles are ordered or how specific training factors are sequentially prioritized over time. Mesocycles should be sequenced in a manner that creates advantageous conditions—metabolically, structurally, and coordinatively—for the subsequent mesocycles (12, 61). Also called **phase potentiation**, this requires the consideration of the delay between exposure to training load and improved performance (delayed transformation) as well as the rate of detraining (training residuals) of the included motor abilities. Most sequencing strategies follow a cyclic pattern of acquisition, specialization, and realization (65). The acquisition phase addresses general performance factors that support more specific outputs. The specialization phase uses the general qualities previously acquired to tolerate and support the development of specific performance factors that are directly related to sport performance. The realization phase aims to optimize sport performance by reducing resistance training volume to dissipate residual fatigue and allow for more time to be dedicated to sport-specific training and competition.

Planning must always consider short-term (0-7 days), medium-term (7-21 days), and long-term (>21 days) trade-offs when selecting training parameters. Intensive training phases result in acute physiological effects that diminish short-term performance capacity. The purpose of the intensive periods is to overload training to maximize medium- and long-term physiological adaptions that result in performance gains, meaning short-term performance must be willingly sacrificed. For preparatory phases, this is a logical approach given the athletes are not competing in games and on-ice work is significantly reduced. Alternatively, periods of reduced training load may allow for the adaptations initiated during the intensive period to be realized, thereby maximizing short-term performance, but may sacrifice medium- and long-term performance due to eventual detraining if a sufficient stimulus is not reapplied.

Sport-Specific Planning

The **preparatory phase** offers the longest window to acquire physical qualities off the ice and includes the highest volume of resistance training compared to the other major phases. Its length may vary each year, depending on the when the athlete's competitive season ends. Developmental hockey athletes often have club team tryouts following playoffs that may delay the beginning of preparatory training. The initial goals of the general physical preparation (GPP) phase are to reestablish postural control, address movement competency of main exercises, and build general tissue capacity to prepare for training intensification in future phases. As the GPP phase progresses, there is an intensification of the resistance training stimulus. The SPP phase uses the acquired general strength qualities to tolerate and support the development of specific performance factors that directly relate to on-ice performance, including speed, reactive strength, and power.

The **competitive phase** includes a shift in emphasis to the optimization of on-ice performance. Resistance training volume is significantly reduced to match the increase in on-ice volume and intensity. Because of this, losing muscle mass and detraining strength qualities in-season are a common occurrence for hockey athletes. Although maintenance is a logical goal, attempting to preserve strength may inadvertently result in detraining. Instead, the intent should be continual development of strength and power throughout the season by exposing athletes to high-quality resistance training within the constraints of the on-ice and travel schedules. This can be achieved by using low-volume, high-intensity protocols for primary exercises. For example, prescribing 1 to 2 working sets of 3 to 4 repetitions at 80% to 85% of an athlete's 1RM effectively applies a maximal strength stimulus without accumulating meaningful fatigue. Other considerations include reducing the number of assistance exercises and minimizing exercises that may elicit significant muscle soreness, such as those with slow ECC tempos. Instead, concentric-dominant (e.g., trap bar deadlifts, heavy sled exercises, isokinetic devices) or high-intensity pushing isometric options can be implemented more frequently to elicit high force outputs with minimal mechanical stress. Because of the long regular season and uncertainty in the length of playoff participation, tapering and peaking hockey athletes does not follow the traditional model applied to individual sports. Instead, hockey athletes need to be kept at high levels of performance for several months, which further emphasizes the need to avoid the loss of general physical abilities that support on-ice outputs.

The **transition phase** links the end of the competitive phase with the beginning of a new YTP. It is a period of unloading to eliminate the accumulated fatigue from the season, recover from lingering injuries, and reset psychologically after a long season. No formal strength or on-ice training should be scheduled. Instead, the transition phase should emphasize active recovery that may include low-intensity and low-impact activities that can be completed with minimal exertion, such as yoga, swimming, or hiking.

Managing Frontal Plane Load

The volume and intensity of adductor-focused and frontal plane exercises need to be thoughtfully prescribed across a yearly plan. Hockey demands that athletes must have a high capacity to perform explosive movements that partially travel through the frontal plane. Programming should reflect those needs and address lateral movement competency, stability, strength, and power. The challenge is to create the needed tissue capacity and hip muscular strength that can withstand the long-term skating demands an athlete faces while ensuring the total volume of lateral movement performed on and off the ice is not excessive. Adding too much off-ice frontal plane load can fatigue the area or aggravate musculature that may have chronic sensitivity. Since the volume of skating fluctuates through the year, so too should the volume of off-ice exposures. During the competitive season, when skating volume is at its highest, high-volume or high-velocity frontal plane exercises should be used sparingly. Higher velocity frontal plane work off-ice should be done in very small quantities with the intent to prepare for on-ice work (e.g., warm-ups). High-load, low-velocity exercises that are primarily concentric with minimal eccentric work, such as heavy crossover sled drags, can be used in small doses to maintain maximal force output capabilities. Direct isometric adductor exercises can be used regularly at reduced overall volumes to retain length–tension relationships and prevent a reduction in the ratio of adductor to abductor strength.

Following the competitive season, hockey athletes should be given 2 to 4 weeks off from any high-load or high-velocity frontal plane work to allow the musculature to unload prior to building up into full off-season training. Implementing anterior-chain-focused tissue remodeling strategies via holding isometrics and addressing sagittal plane postural control during this initial training phase are effective in resetting hip, lumbo-pelvic, and thoracic function. Frontal plane work can be reintroduced after the unloading phase at low volumes and intensities, isometrically and then eccentrically. Throughout the off-season, the amount of work can increase to improve lateral force output at different velocities. When preseason approaches and athletes begin increasing the volume and intensity of skating, frontal plane work should again decrease accordingly.

Monitoring Load and Strength Performance

Periodized plans are meant to serve as a foundation that permits fluid programming adjustments when unexpected changes due to the schedule, athlete responses to training, or athlete health occur. Comprehensively quantifying the overall training load, the athlete's short-term response to the load, and longer-term changes to strength performance are key components to successfully executing a periodized plan. Doing so provides up-to-date information on the effectiveness of the plan and can be used to determine whether adjustments in planning or programming are required.

Two options that can assist in measuring the trajectory of performance outcomes during resistance training include neuromuscular assessments performed weekly and indicator exercise check-ins completed every 6 to 8 weeks. Tracking neuromuscular performance through a simple test such as a countermovement jump assesses an athlete's acute state of readiness and allows for longitudinal tracking of lower body power. It is worth noting that a low state of readiness caused by residual fatigue is an expected response to intensive training and should generally be accounted for within the periodized plan. When neuromuscular performance is meaningfully compromised following exposure to loads that were predicted to be well-tolerated, there should be further investigation with the individual athlete. These cases often warrant acute adjustments to the proposed plan to ensure training inputs are appropriate for the current scenario.

An indicator exercise acts as a tool to measure medium- and long-term changes in an athlete's force production capabilities. A useful indicator exercise is one that is standardized, easily repeatable, and representative of the target strength ability. Although traditional RM testing can serve this purpose, it may be excessively taxing to perform regularly for high training age athletes, especially in-season, as well as challenging to logistically implement within team settings. Fixed-load repetition out sets are an alternative option that can be performed safely and efficiently and can be integrated within a regular training session. For example, a hockey athlete who had a preseason 1RM bench press of 100 kg (220 lb) may use a maximum repetition set at 85 kg (187 lb) as the upper body maximum strength indicator exercise for the remainder of the season. From this information the strength and conditioning professional can determine whether upper body strength has improved, maintained, or detrained and can adjust programming if required. Another option using VBT technology is to implement a fixed-load velocity test as an indicator exercise. The fixed load could be individualized or consistent across a team to assess the current state of a specific strength ability.

These monitoring strategies are critical in objectively evaluating the effectiveness of the training program and determining the individual adaptation timelines of each athlete. Many strength and conditioning professionals work in team settings, meaning several athletes are completing similar programming simultaneously. Since no two athletes are alike, the dose–response magnitudes and timelines will vary. Being able to capture this variation can help inform short- and long-term programming decisions for both the team and the individuals within it.

CONCLUSION

As a whole, designing effective programs requires a systematic approach that gathers all relevant information regarding the sport, athlete, schedule, and environmental constraints to determine appropriate training goals and subsequent training methods. Training principles help to guide planning and programming. By marrying training principles with an understanding of physiology and physics as well as viewing situational constraints through a pragmatic lens, strength and conditioning professionals can design optimal training programs for hockey athletes of all levels in any environment.

PART II

EXERCISE TECHNIQUE

5

TOTAL BODY EXERCISE TECHNIQUE

CAM DAVIDSON

At the highest levels of competition, successful hockey athletes possess a specific set of qualities. These qualities involve winning battles and races to the puck, a solid net front presence, mastering the ability to dominate space, accurate and repeatable shot mechanics, and speed on a forecheck and backcheck. An athlete who can create space quickly and dominate that space will most likely be successful. Knowing this, the strength and conditioning professional can determine what needs to be trained on and off the ice. These trainable and transferable qualities are explosive speed, power, and strength. There are numerous total body exercises that can be implemented to train and stimulate these qualities.

Total body exercises are a great tool to train these transferable qualities and can be done any time throughout an annual training plan. They can be performed with maximal weights and low speeds (maximal strength), light weights and high speeds (explosive speed), and everywhere in between.

For the exercises listed in this chapter, it is recommended that the athlete properly inhale using **diaphragmatic breathing**, instead of breathing into the neck and shoulder region. This is to ensure the athlete can properly brace the core throughout the movement. To teach how to breathe in this manner, have the athlete follow these instructions: Lie supine on the floor with the feet flat on the floor and the knees flexed at 90 degrees. Place one hand on the belly and the other on the chest. Next, inhale through the nose to feel the belly expand up and the low back settle into the floor. If done properly, the belly rises, the low back pushes into the floor, and the chest rises after the abdomen fills. The shoulders should not move toward the head. Once there is a solid grasp on diaphragmatic breathing in the supine position, the athlete is now ready to practice these exercises.

Exercise Finder

KETTLEBELL SWING

Primary Muscles Trained

Gluteus maximus, erector spinae, biceps femoris, semimembranosus, semitendinosus, rectus femoris, vastus lateralis, vastus medialis, vastus intermedius

Beginning Position

- Begin with the feet shoulder-width apart or slightly wider with the feet pointed slightly outward and with the kettlebell on the floor approximately 12 inches (30 cm) in front of the feet.
- Squat down and grasp the kettlebell with both hands with an overhand grip, making sure to keep the spine in a neutral position (a).
- The eyes should be focused on the kettlebell, not looking up.
- Keep the arms straight.

Movement Phases

1. Move into a hip-hinge position (hips back, knees slightly flexed, torso leaning forward) by moving the kettlebell back between the legs and behind the hips such that the forearms are resting on the thighs (b).
2. Keeping the weight toward the heels, extend the hips forward by squeezing the glutes and quads.
3. Keep the arms straight and relaxed while allowing the kettlebell to swing.
4. The kettlebell will swing forward and up via the force created by extending the hips and knees, not by lifting with the arms (c).
5. As the kettlebell swings back down, move back into the starting hinged position, and repeat for the desired number of repetitions.

Figure 5.1   Kettlebell swing: *(a)* beginning position; *(b-c)* action.

Breathing Guidelines

Inhale before hiking the kettlebell between the legs off the floor. Exhale as the hips extend and the kettlebell swings forward. Inhale as the kettlebell swings downward between the legs, and exhale again as the hips extend and the kettlebell swings upward.

Exercise Modifications and Variations

One-Arm Kettlebell Swing

The beginning position and movement phases are the same here as in the kettlebell swing except that one arm is used instead of two arms. The noninvolved arm should be straight and slightly out at a 45-degree angle away from the body. Keep the noninvolved hand squeezed in a fist during the movement, which limits excessive movement with the arm and prevents placing the hand on the hips.

Coaching Tips

- Maintain a neutral spine throughout the entire movement.
- When extending the hips to swing the kettlebell, do not push the hips too far forward, which places excess stress on the low back during the swing.
- Keep balance biased toward the heels and stay flat-footed throughout the entire movement.
- While performing this movement, try to make the transition from the hinged position to the hips-extended position as quickly and powerfully as possible, maintaining proper technique.
- Do not try to lift the kettlebell with the arms; they are just there to hold the kettlebell and act as a pendulum.
- Keep the chin tucked during the swing to help keep a neutral spine.

TRAP BAR JUMP SQUAT (CONTINUOUS)

Primary Muscles Trained

Gluteus maximus, vastus lateralis, vastus medialis, vastus intermedius, rectus femoris, biceps femoris, semitendinosus, semimembranosus, gastrocnemius, soleus

Beginning Position

- Start with the trap bar on the floor (a).
- Pressure should be evenly distributed throughout the feet, which begin flat on the floor.
- Stand with the feet hip-width apart and slightly pointed outward (not shown).
- The hands should be centered on the trap bar handles.
- Arms straight.
- Latissimus dorsi (lats) engaged.
- Back in a neutral position.

Movement Phases

1. Brace the core, and as forcefully as possible, push the feet into the floor to initiate the drive.
2. Continue to drive, and jump as high as possible (b).

Figure 5.2   Trap bar jump squat (continuous): (a) beginning position; (b) action.

3. Continue to brace through the abdomen during landing so that the chest does not fall forward while returning to the beginning squat position.

4. From here, quickly drive into the floor again and jump as high as possible, continuing for as many repetitions as are prescribed.

5. Set the bar back down after the prescribed number of repetitions.

Breathing Guidelines

Inhale after achieving the beginning position and exhale upon finishing the leg drive. Inhale during the landing and continue to brace.

Exercise Modifications and Variations

Trap Bar Jump Squat (Pause at the Bottom: Dead Stop)

Performed in the same manner as the continuous trap bar jump squat, except the weights are lowered all the way down to the floor and a pause is completed before performing the next jump.

Coaching Tips

- After inhaling and bracing, push the knees out slightly to increase involvement of the glutes. This also makes sure that the knees are not falling toward the center excessively.

- Focus should be driving with the feet and feeling the quads to jump. Doing this as forcefully as possible naturally brings the hips into extension.

- Do not try to push the hips forward during the jump.

- To engage the lats, simply pull the shoulders down toward the hips. Feel the lats flex, which helps brace during the exercise.

BARBELL JUMP SQUAT (CONTINUOUS)

Primary Muscles Trained

Gluteus maximus, vastus lateralis, vastus medialis, vastus intermedius, rectus femoris, biceps femoris, semitendinosus, semimembranosus, gastrocnemius, soleus

Beginning Position

- Place the barbell on the back high up on the traps and shoulders.
- Hands grasp the barbell right outside the shoulders.
- Sternum up and back straight.
- Pressure should be evenly distributed throughout the feet, which begin flat on the floor.
- Feet hip-width apart and slightly pointed outward.
- Eyes facing straight ahead (a).

Movement Phases

1. Brace the core.
2. While staying on a full foot and keeping sternum up, lower down quickly into a quarter-squat position (b).

3. Continue to brace and push the feet forcefully into the floor and drive to jump into the air as high as possible *(c)*.

4. Continue to brace and keep the sternum up, and drop back into a quarter-squat position and proceed to drive and jump again, continuing for as many repetitions as are prescribed.

5. Perform the prescribed number of repetitions and then rack the barbell onto the squat rack (not shown).

Figure 5.3   Barbell jump squat (continuous): *(a)* beginning position; *(b-c)* action.

Breathing Guidelines

Inhale after achieving the beginning position and brace the core. Exhale while driving and jumping into the air. Inhale upon landing and continue to brace the core.

Exercise Modifications and Variations

Barbell Jump Squat (Pause at the Bottom: Dead Stop)

Performed the same way as the continuous barbell jump squat, but separate the repetitions by resetting to the beginning position after each repetition.

Coaching Tips

- When the bar is on the back, pull down with the hands so that the lats activate. Keep pulling in this manner during the set to help keep the sternum up for the entirety of the set.

- Tightly squeeze the quads and glutes before descending into the squat on the first repetition (or each repetition if performing a dead stop).

- Do not inhale into the chest. Instead, inhale using the diaphragm to help brace and keep the sternum up.
- Do not sit the hips too far back during the descent.
- Keep the sternum up and torso vertical.

HANG CLEAN

Primary Muscles Trained

Gluteus maximus, vastus lateralis, vastus medialis, vastus intermedius, rectus femoris, biceps femoris, semitendinosus, semimembranosus, gastrocnemius, soleus, trapezius, deltoids

Beginning Position

- Grasp the bar just outside the leg with knuckles down.
- Pressure should be evenly distributed throughout the feet, which begin flat on the floor.
- Feet hip-width apart and pointed slightly outward.
- Knees slightly flexed so bar is high on the thigh.
- Arms relaxed.
- Sternum up.
- Lats engaged.
- Eyes forward (a).

Movement Phases

1. While remaining flat-footed and keeping the sternum up (to maintain a neutral back position), lower the bar down to just above the kneecaps by hinging at the hips (b).
2. Bring the bar back up to the beginning position by pushing feet forcefully into the floor when standing up.
3. As the knees and hips extend at the top of the push, explosively shrug the shoulders and forcefully pull upward on the bar with the hands while keeping the bar close to the body (c). To help the bar stay close to the body, keep the knuckles facing downward while pulling up on the bar.
4. As the bar travels upward, pull the body under the bar and move both feet outward to hip-to-shoulder-width apart, then "jump" down into a quarter-squat position.
5. Fire the elbows forward and up to catch the bar on the shoulders to complete the repetition (d).

Breathing Guidelines

From the beginning position, inhale deeply and brace before lowering the bar to knee height. Continue to hold that breath until the bar is racked on the shoulders in the quarter-squat position. Exhale while standing to complete the repetition.

Spotting Guidelines

Do not spot the Olympic lifts. It is not safe for the athlete, coach, or surrounding athletes to do so. If the repetition is going to be missed, the athlete needs to dump the bar in front and away from the body and stand clear of the bar.

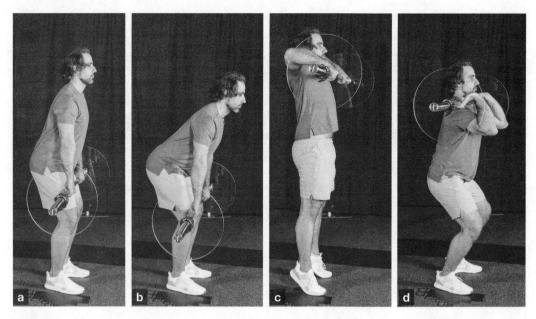

Figure 5.4   Hang clean: *(a)* beginning position; *(b-d)* action.

Exercise Modifications and Variations

Clean Pull from a Hang

From the same beginning position, do the first two movement phases as in the hang clean. At the top of the push, jump up and shrug the shoulders while keeping the arms straight and the bar close to the body. Choose this variation if dealing with any kind of wrist, elbow, or shoulder issue that prevents properly racking a barbell on the shoulders.

Power Clean from Blocks

The only difference in this variation is in the beginning position and the first movement phase. Set the blocks at a height where the bar is right above the knees. The first movement phase is bringing the bar to the high hip position and continuing to the catch position. Perform the rest of the exercise in the same manner. This variation is a great choice for any athlete who is overusing the lower back or not driving the legs properly during a hang clean.

Coaching Tips

- To get the most power and force from the leg drive and to help keep the bar close to the body, try not to rock back to the heels while lowering the bar to the knees; stay on a full foot. This limits the horizontal movement of the barbell away from the body caused by the hips shooting forward.

- Keeping the knuckles down while pulling up on the bar helps keep the bar close to the body. If the knuckles face forward while pulling up, the bar moves away from the body, making it more difficult to achieve a successful lift.

- Push the shoulders forward while shooting the elbows up to catch the bar. This helps to create a better shelf for the bar to rest on the shoulders. Keeping the shoulders back makes the bar land on the collar bone and the throat, which is much more uncomfortable.

- Relaxing the hands during the catch can help bring the shoulders forward and the elbows up, ultimately helping to catch the bar properly.

ONE-ARM DUMBBELL HANG SNATCH

Primary Muscles Trained

Gluteus maximus, vastus lateralis, vastus medialis, vastus intermedius, semitendinosus, semimembranosus, soleus, gastrocnemius, deltoid, trapezius

Beginning Position

- Stand with the feet shoulder-width apart with the toes pointed slightly outward and a dumbbell between the legs.
- Squat down, breaking at the hips first and then the knees.
- Grab the dumbbell with one hand with a pronated (overhand) grip.
- Keep the chest and eyes up while keeping the back straight.
- Hold the dumbbell at (or slightly above) knee height with the elbow fully extended (a).

Movement Phases

1. Inhale and brace the core in the beginning position.
2. Push the feet into the floor forcefully to lift the dumbbell.
3. While keeping the arm straight, drive the upward movement by powerfully extending the hips, knees, and ankles (b).
4. As the hips, knees, and ankles extend, pull hard on the dumbbell, shrug the shoulder, and flex the elbow to bring the dumbbell up overhead while quickly flexing the hips and knees to drop into a quarter squat (c).
5. Pause in this quarter-squat position with the arm locked out with the dumbbell overhead.

Figure 5.5   One-arm dumbbell hang snatch: (a) beginning position; (b-d) action.

6. Stand up (d) and then lower the dumbbell back to the beginning position in a controlled manner. The free hand may be used to help control the weight back down.

7. Perform the prescribed number of repetitions, then repeat for the opposite arm.

Breathing Guidelines

Inhale while squatting down to grab the dumbbell. Brace the core while exploding through the movement. Exhale upon standing with the dumbbell overhead.

Exercise Modifications and Variations

Medicine Ball Side Throw

If a one-arm dumbbell snatch is too challenging, a medicine ball side throw could be a good replacement. Make the medicine ball side throw a total body movement by driving the feet into the floor. Rotate and extend the hips while releasing the medicine ball toward a wall.

Coaching Tips

- Jumping as high as possible during a one-arm dumbbell snatch is not optimal. Once achieving extension of the hips, knees, and ankles, jump down into a quarter squat while pulling the dumbbell overhead. This is more effective for a well-timed catch.
- Keep the knuckles down while pulling the dumbbell overhead. If the fist is turned and the knuckles face outward, the dumbbell will move away from the body, causing it to swing, and making the catch more difficult.
- Flex the elbow up and to the outside, not toward the back.
- Lock out the elbow during the catch. A soft elbow is not recommended.
- Push off the floor by focusing on leg drive using the glutes and the quads, not by pulling with the lower back.

LANDMINE PUSH PRESS

Primary Muscles Trained

Gluteus maximus, biceps femoris, semitendinosus, semimembranosus, vastus lateralis, vastus intermedius, vastus medialis, rectus femoris, soleus, gastrocnemius, deltoids, trapezius

Beginning Position

- Begin standing with one end of the barbell in a landmine device or securely placed in a corner where the end will not move. Hold the other end of the barbell with the hand right in front of the shoulder.
- The feet should be hip- to shoulder-width apart.
- Place the opposite hand to the side away from the barbell.
- Lean the body slightly toward the slant of the barbell (not standing directly vertical; more of a slant than what is seen in photo a), with the ribs down (spine neutral) and eyes looking at the opposite end of the barbell.
- Hold the barbell close to the shoulder. Do not let the barbell move to the side away from the body.

Movement Phases

1. Quickly lower into a quarter-squat position by flexing the hip and knees, making sure to keep the barbell tight to the shoulder (b).
2. From here, push the feet and drive the legs all the way through extension of the hips, knees, and ankles (c).
3. At this extended position, drive the hand into the barbell forcing it overhead (more overhead than what is seen in photo d).
4. While punching the barbell, drop back into a quarter-squat position and hold, making sure the body and barbell are stable (e).
5. Lower the barbell back down to the shoulder, stand up, and repeat for the prescribed number of repetitions.

Breathing Guidelines

Once the beginning position is achieved, breathe in and brace the core. Exhale once the bar is overhead and the body is in a quarter-squat position. Lower the barbell back to the shoulder and repeat.

Exercise Modifications and Variations

Landmine Push Press with a Split Catch

A great variation of the landmine push press is the landmine push press with a split catch. The setup and beginning position are the same. While driving the legs out of the dip (quarter-squat position), instead of keeping the feet hip- to shoulder-width apart, the legs split. Immediately after the drive, the back foot slides back into position on the ball of the foot. This position is roughly 12 to 18 inches (30-46 cm) back from the beginning position. As the back foot slides back and is in position, quickly step the front foot straight forward about 12 to 18 inches. Quickly slide the feet and get into place. This drastically improves the timing of the exercise.

Rotational Landmine Push Press

The rotational landmine push press is similar to the previous variations. Face the side of the hand holding the barbell. If holding with the right hand, face the right side. If holding with the left hand, face the left side. Dip and drive in the same manner as the push press, and when driving the barbell up, turn the body to face forward and catch the barbell overhead with the feet in a split-stance catch. If facing the right, the right foot should be back in the catch. If facing left in the beginning position, the left foot is back in the catch.

This variation can also begin from the floor. Face the barbell and grab the end with the inside arm. If facing right, grab with the left arm; if facing left, grab with the right arm. Drive the legs and pull up on the barbell (keep the sternum up). Close to the end of the leg drive, switch hands and punch the barbell to the finish. If facing right, the right leg is back in a split. If facing left, the left leg is back in a split.

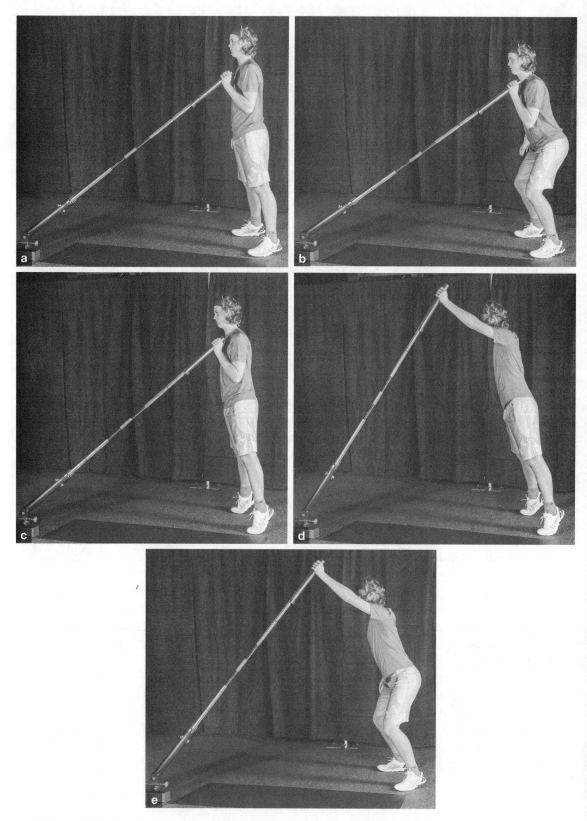

Figure 5.6   Landmine push press: *(a)* beginning position; *(b-e)* action.

Coaching Tips

- Keep the sternum down and the spine at neutral during the entire exercise. Having excessive low back extension can cause discomfort.
- It is not recommended to jump after driving the legs on any variation of the exercise. Drive hard, and immediately jump down or dip down into the catch position.
- Keep the barbell and hand close to the shoulder during the beginning position and the drive phases of the exercise.
- If performing the split catch, slide the back foot back then step out. It is not recommended to step out with the front foot first.
- Always pause in the catch position in any variation of this exercise. This helps balance and lessens the chances of the barbell moving away from the body in any direction.

6

LOWER BODY EXERCISE TECHNIQUE

MIKE POTENZA

Ice hockey is a physically demanding sport that draws upon multiple energy systems and physical performance qualities. Hockey is said to be a game of intermittent acceleration, speed, agility, strength, power, and capacity (3). During a game, a hockey athlete's top speed can reach up to 30 mph (48 km/h) and skaters execute hundreds of short burst accelerations and changes of direction (3). It also has been shown that, depending on position, a hockey athlete can cover 5 kilometers (3.1 miles) during a game (1). From this data it is easy to see the relationship between the unique demands of the game and the importance of lower body resistance training to improve performance qualities like acceleration, speed, agility, strength, and power. Athletes face a physical ceiling when expressing these qualities and that ceiling is dependent on their ability to produce high force and high velocity. These qualities go hand in hand, and the hockey athlete cannot have one without the other. Maximal strength is the foundation for speed because of its relationship to force on the speed–strength continuum (6). The larger the strength foundation of the lower body, the higher the potential for peak speed (6). High levels of lower body strength also allow the athlete to maintain a deep skating stance that is optimal for developing technique and on-ice speed (6).

This chapter provides the reader with a menu of exercises that are ideal for strengthening the lower body of an ice hockey athlete. There are detailed descriptions that coaches and strength and conditioning professionals can use to teach hockey athletes proper technique and execution so they can get the most out of their training and development. There is no substitute for flawless technique. These lower body exercises not only provide gains in performance for the hockey athlete but also act as methods to prevent injury on the ice.

Exercise Finder

FRONT SQUAT

Primary Muscles Trained

Gluteus maximus, semimembranosus, semitendinosus, biceps femoris, vastus lateralis, vastus intermedius, vastus medialis, rectus femoris

Beginning Position

- Set the bar at shoulder height on a squat rack (not shown).
- Step under the bar so that the front of the shoulders and clavicles are in line and in contact with the bar. (Note: The bar should not press against the laryngeal prominence when setting the grip.)
- Position the feet slightly wider than shoulder-width apart, slightly rotated out.
- The grip on the bar can be one of two positions: A crossed-arm position is where the bar rests on top of the anterior shoulder (c). The arms are crossed in front of the chest with the elbows positioned parallel to the floor. A full grip should be used when holding onto the bar to keep it in place during the movement. A parallel-arm position grip is similar to the catch position performed in a hang clean or power clean exercise (d). The bar rests in the same position as the crossed-arm grip, except that now the grip is outside the shoulders with the arms parallel to each other and parallel to the floor. (Ideally, the grip on the bar is with more of a closed hand than what is seen in photo d).
- In a controlled manner, push both feet into the floor to lift the bar off the rack. Take a few small steps backward to set up the beginning position of the exercise (a).
- All repetitions start from this position.

Movement Phases

1. To initiate the descent of the movement, flex at the hips, knees, and ankles, and lower the weight in a controlled manner.
2. During the eccentric phase of the exercise, keep an upright torso, and lower the weight until the top of the thigh is parallel to the floor (b).
3. The concentric portion of the movement requires maintaining the position of the torso and the chosen grip position. To return to the beginning position, drive both feet into the floor and extend the hips, knees, and ankles.

Breathing Guidelines

Inhale prior to the eccentric portion of the movement. Maintain a comfortable intra-abdominal pressure during the descent of the movement. Upon beginning to extend the lower body during the concentric phase of the movement, exhale in a slow and controlled manner.

Figure 6.1   Front squat: *(a)* beginning position; *(b)* action; *(c)* crossed-arm position; *(d)* parallel-arm position.

Spotting Guidelines

- Take a position behind the athlete with feet shoulder-width apart and arms firmly extended under the arms of the athlete. (Note: The positioning of the spotter should not impede the athlete's execution of the exercise.)

- Squat down at the same tempo as the athlete while maintaining a firm arm position close to the athlete's body.

- The spotter can give support to the athlete during this exercise by pushing the athlete's upper body vertically to return to the beginning position.

Exercise Modifications and Variations

Kettlebell Goblet Squat

The kettlebell goblet squat is performed with one kettlebell. The position of the kettlebell during the duration of the movement is even with the sternum. Prior to the movement, use the same breathing technique as in the front squat exercise. Grip the kettlebell on both sides of the handle. Initiate the descent of the movement by flexing at the hips, knees, and ankles to lower the weight. During the eccentric phase and concentric phase of movement, maintain an upright posture in the torso. Squat down until the upper thighs are approximately parallel to the floor. To initiate the upward phase of the exercise, drive the feet into the floor and extend at the hips, knees, and ankles.

Double Kettlebell Squat

The double kettlebell squat requires two kettlebells to be used as resistance. Grip the kettlebells within each hand and align the hands with the shoulders, similar to the front squat position. The kettlebells rest on the outside of the upper arms. Use the same breathing as with the front squat. Maintain an upright posture in the torso during the eccentric and concentric phases of movement.

Safety Bar Squat

The safety bar can be used with both bilateral and unilateral lower body exercises as an alternative to an Olympic bar. Place the safety bar so it sits across the upper trapezius muscles and the base of the posterior neck. This type of training bar is unique because it is counterbalanced and does not need to be held with a grip similar to a back squat. There are two grip options when training with a safety bar. The first option is to hold on to a set of handles that are attached to the interior of the squat rack. Having the arms in this extended position helps maintain an almost completely upright posture throughout the entire movement. The second grip position is holding on to the safety bar handles that extend out from the main portion of bar that rests on the upper trapezius muscles and base of the posterior neck. Manufacturers make these handles long enough where they extend out about 12 to 16 inches (30-40 cm) in front of the body upon setup. The grip (neutral) therefore can be comfortably held in front of the body, which puts the upper and lower arm in a 90-degree position. During the eccentric and concentric phases of movement, maintain an upright posture in the torso. Squat down until the upper thighs are approximately parallel to the floor. To initiate the upward phase of the exercise, drive the feet into the floor and extend at the hips, knees, and ankles.

Landmine Squat

The position of the load during the landmine squat is similar to the kettlebell goblet squat exercise, close to the body and in line with the athlete's sternum. Grip the sleeve of the barbell with a hand-over-hand position. Anchor the opposite end of the barbell securely into a landmine platform or squat rack landmine attachment. Set the feet underneath the hips. Initiate the downward phase of the movement by flexing at the hips, knees, and ankles to lower the weight. During the eccentric phase and concentric phase of movement, maintain an upright posture in the torso and a bar position close to the body. Squat down until the upper thighs are approximately parallel to the floor. To initiate the upward phase of the exercise, drive the feet into the floor and extend at the hips, knees, and ankles.

Coaching Tips

- Ankle mobility is a prerequisite to effective bilateral squatting. Assess the athlete's available ankle range of motion before prescribing any bilateral or unilateral lower body exercise.
- The torso should remain upright in posture throughout the eccentric and concentric phases of the exercise.
- The knees should track in line with the athlete's foot position throughout the entire movement.
- There should be a conscious effort to keep the heels always in contact with the floor throughout the entire movement.

FRONT SPLIT SQUAT

Primary Muscles Trained

Gluteus maximus, gluteus medius, semimembranosus, semitendinosus, biceps femoris, vastus lateralis, vastus intermedius, vastus medialis, rectus femoris, adductor magnus

Beginning Position

- Set the bar at shoulder height on a squat rack (not shown).
- Step under the bar so that the front of the shoulders and clavicles are in line and in contact with the bar. (Note: The bar should not press against the laryngeal prominence when setting the grip.)
- The grip on the bar can be one of two positions: A crossed-arm position is where the bar rests on top of the anterior shoulder. Cross the arms in front of the chest with the elbows positioned parallel to the floor. Use a full grip when holding on to the bar to keep it in place during the movement. A parallel-arm position grip is similar to the catch position performed in a hang clean or power clean exercise. The bar rests in the same position as the crossed-arm grip, only now the grip is outside the shoulders with the arms parallel to each other and parallel to the floor.
- In a controlled manner, push both feet into the floor to lift the bar off the rack.
- Take a few small steps backward to set up the beginning position of the exercise.

Movement Phases

1. To begin the movement, take a large step backward (similar to a reverse lunge) (a). This step back sets up the stance position for the entire movement. Complete all prescribed repetitions on a given side before switching legs.

2. In a controlled manner, flex the knee and hip of the lead leg while lowering the weight to the floor (b). The foot of the lead leg has full contact with the floor and is responsible for controlling the eccentric motion of the weight. The back foot's responsibility is to stabilize the body and maintain balance. Both knees should track in line with the direction of the feet. Keep the feet directed forward during the entire movement. During the eccentric movement, the back knee tracks down toward the floor until it is close to the surface. A 2-inch (5 cm) foam pad can be placed on the floor as a target

for the back knee to touch during the movement (not shown). Maintain an upright posture of the torso throughout the entire split squat movement.

3. During the concentric phase of the movement, drive the front foot into the floor while extending the hips, knees, and ankles in effort to return to the beginning position. Maintain both feet in a fixed split stance position at the top to ensure stability and safety.

Figure 6.2 Front split squat: *(a)* beginning position; *(b)* action.

Breathing Guidelines

Prior to initiating the eccentric portion of the movement, inhale and then lower into position. To initiate the concentric phase of the exercise, drive the foot into the floor and exhale during the upward movement.

Spotting Guidelines

- Stand 1 to 2 feet (30-60 cm) behind the athlete and position the hands under the bar and close to the athlete's torso.
- The spotter's setup should mimic the lower body stance of the athlete. This ensures the spotter is in a position of stability and balance when standing behind the active athlete.
- Offer assistance during the eccentric and concentric phases of movement as well as assisting the athlete with returning weights into the squat rack or stand.

Exercise Modifications and Variations

Rear Foot Elevated Front Split Squat

The split squat can be modified by elevating and propping up the back foot on a padded stand or bench. Technique and execution in the upper and lower body are the same as in the split squat exercise. This variation challenges the athlete through increased demand for greater balance and increases in hip range of motion.

Dumbbell Split Squat

The lower and upper body position and movement patterns of the dumbbell split squat are the same as the front split squat position. The only variation is holding the dumbbells by the sides during the movement.

Kettlebell Goblet Split Squat

The lower and upper body position and movement patterns of the kettlebell goblet split squat are the same as for the front split squat. The only variation is holding the kettlebell at chest height and with a grip on both sides of the handle during the movement.

Safety Bar Split Squat

The lower and upper body position and movement patterns of the safety bar split squat are the same as for the front split squat. The only variation is to have the safety bar in the back position, resting across the upper trapezius muscles. Set the grip on the handles in front of the body.

Front Foot Elevated Front Split Squat

The front foot elevated front split squat position challenges the front leg to squat into a deeper position. The execution of the exercise is the same, both concentrically and eccentrically, as a split squat. Because of the deeper position with the front foot elevated, this exercise increases demand on the quadriceps, glutes, adductors, and hamstring muscles.

Coaching Tips

- The torso should remain upright in posture throughout the eccentric and concentric phases of the exercise.
- The knees should track in line with the athlete's foot position throughout the entire movement.
- During the entire movement, there should be a conscious effort to keep the front heel always in contact with the floor and prevent the front knee from passing over the toes.

BARBELL REVERSE LUNGE

Primary Muscles Trained

Gluteus maximus, semimembranosus, semitendinosus, biceps femoris, vastus lateralis, vastus intermedius, vastus medialis, rectus femoris, iliopsoas

Beginning Position

- Set the bar at shoulder height on a squat rack (not shown).
- Step under the bar so it rests in the back position and across the upper trapezius muscles.
- Grip the bar slightly wider than shoulder-width.
- In a controlled manner, push both feet through the floor to lift the bar off the rack.
- Take a few small steps backward to set up the beginning position of the exercise. Place the feet directly under the hips (a).

Movement Phases

1. To initiate the movement, take a large step back, but not so far as to be unable to return to the beginning position during the concentric phase of the movement. Complete all prescribed repetitions on a given side before switching legs.

2. In a controlled manner, flex the knee and hip of the lead leg while lowering the weight to the floor. The foot of the lead leg has full contact with the floor and is responsible for controlling the eccentric motion of the weight. The back foot's responsibility is to stabilize the body and maintain balance. Both knees must track in line with direction of the feet. Keep the feet directed forward during the entire movement. During the eccentric movement, track the back knee down toward the floor until it is close to the surface *(b)*. Maintain an upright posture of the torso throughout the entire split squat movement.

3. During the concentric phase of the movement, drive the front foot into the floor while extending the hips, knees, and ankles to return to the beginning position. During the concentric phase of this exercise, the torso should remain erect with good posture and not lose stability in the backward-to-forward lunging motion. At the conclusion of the repetition, position the feet directly under the hips.

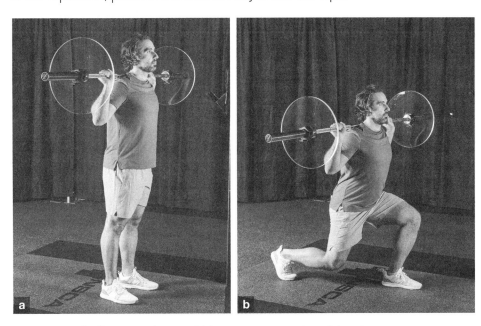

Figure 6.3 Barbell reverse lunge: *(a)* beginning position; *(b)* action.

Breathing Guidelines

Prior to stepping back into the lunge position, inhale, and control the descent to the floor. During the upward phase of the movement, drive the front foot into the floor and exhale in a controlled manner.

Spotting Guidelines

- The spotter should stand 1 to 2 feet (30-60 cm) behind the athlete and be ready to position the hands under the bar and close to the athlete's torso upon the movement of stepping back into the lunge.

- The spotter's setup should mimic the lower body position of the athlete. This ensures the spotter is in a position of stability and balance when standing behind the active athlete.
- The spotter should offer assistance during the eccentric and concentric phases of movement as well as assist the athlete with returning weights into the squat rack or stand.

Exercise Modifications and Variations

Dumbbell Reverse Lunge

The movement patterns for the dumbbell reverse lunge are the same as the barbell reverse lunge. Dumbbells can be used as a variation and held at the sides. Be conscious of upper body posture while holding dumbbells by the sides during this movement to prevent them from swinging (that can happen if the backward-to-forward lunging motion is not controlled).

Barbell Lunge Walk

The barbell lunge walk is a dynamic lunging pattern that can be loaded with several different implements, such as barbells, dumbbells, kettlebells, or body weight. Position the load across the shoulders directly on the upper trapezius muscles. Take a large step forward while maintaining an upright posture of the upper body. The knee of the lead leg should not pass over the line of the toes. Once stabilized in the forward lunge position, lower the hips toward the floor until the thigh is parallel to the floor. Drive the lead foot into the floor to stand up. Once close to the top of the concentric position, there is clearance for the trail leg to step through and return to the standing position. In this exercise, alternate steps to achieve the desired repetition range.

Safety Bar Reverse Lunge

The lower and upper body position and movement patterns of the safety bar reverse lunge are the same as the barbell reverse lunge position. The only variation is to have the safety bar in the back position, resting across the upper trapezius muscles. Set the grip on the handles in front of the body.

Post-Lateral Lunge

The post-lateral lunge begins by standing tall with feet hip-width apart. Initiate the movement by stepping backward and rotating the torso 90 degrees with the arms extended out in front of the body. The lead leg remains in position and points straight ahead. When the stepping leg contacts the floor, begin the eccentric phase of the movement. Lower the hips down until the thigh reaches parallel to the floor. The torso remains tall with good posture throughout each phase of the movement. The knee position of the lunging leg should be in line with the foot and not exceed the toes. Focus on keeping the heel of the lunging leg down and pressed into the floor during the push-off phase of the lunge. Initiate the concentric phase by driving the foot of the lunging leg into the floor to create force that propels the body up and back to the beginning position. During the concentric phase, control rotation while getting back into the beginning position.

Coaching Tips

- The torso should remain upright in posture throughout the eccentric and concentric phases of the exercise.

- The knees should track in line with the athlete's foot position throughout the entire movement.
- The position of the front knee during the initial backward stepping motion should be in line with the midfoot and not exceed the toes. A key indicator of improper knee position is if the heel comes off the floor during the eccentric phase of the movement.

KETTLEBELL GOBLET LATERAL SQUAT

Primary Muscles Trained
Gluteus maximus, gluteus medius, vastus lateralis, vastus intermedius, vastus medialis, rectus femoris, gracilis, adductor longus, adductor magnus, adductor brevis (2)

Beginning Position
- Hold the kettlebell at chest height with a grip on both sides of the handle.
- Position the feet wider than shoulder-width apart and pointed straight ahead.
- The posture of the torso should be upright with the kettlebell in direct line with the sternum.

Movement Phases
1. The first movement is to squat back into the hip on one side of the body. This movement and weight shift creates a squatting pattern on one side and a straight-leg pattern on the other. Maintain a tall torso throughout the entire movement and keep the feet stationary during the exercise.
2. Descend in a controlled manner until the thigh of the squatting leg reaches parallel (or nearly parallel) to the floor and the knee of the opposite leg reaches full extension.
3. During the concentric phase, drive the foot into the floor and extend at the hip and knee of the squatting leg to return to the beginning position.
4. Pause at the beginning position before performing the next repetition.
5. The strength and conditioning professional can prescribe the repetitions to be performed by alternating legs or all with one leg before switching to the other leg.

Breathing Guidelines
Before loading into the lateral squat position, inhale and control the descent in the frontal plane. During the upward phase of the movement, drive the foot into the floor and exhale in a controlled manner.

Exercise Modifications and Variations

One-Arm Dumbbell Lateral Squat

In this exercise, the dumbbell is held in one hand (the opposite hand from the side of the squat). Have the dumbbell hang straight down through the center line of the body. The movement pattern is the same as for the kettlebell goblet lateral squat. While laterally squatting to one side, reach the dumbbell toward the instep of the squatting leg. Keep the torso upright while reaching the dumbbell to the inside of the foot. In the concentric phase of the exercise, drive the foot down into the floor and extend at the hip and knee to return to the top position. The dumbbell should be controlled back to the center line of the body. Distribute body weight equally on both feet at the top of the beginning position between repetitions.

Kettlebell Rack Lateral Squat

When beginning this exercise, grip the kettlebells within each hand and align the hands with the shoulders, similar to the front squat position. Rest the kettlebells on the outside of the upper arms. The movement pattern of this exercise is identical to the kettlebell goblet lateral squat. The challenging part of this exercise is stabilizing the kettlebells with the upper body during the lateral squat movement. During this exercise, focus on two specific areas: engaging the core and maintaining an upright torso throughout the entire movement. Distribute weight equally on both feet at the top of the beginning position between repetitions.

SLIDE LUNGE

Primary Muscles Trained

Gluteus maximus, semimembranosus, semitendinosus, biceps femoris, vastus lateralis, vastus intermedius, vastus medialis, rectus femoris, iliopsoas

Beginning Position

- Stand tall with good posture and position the feet 6 to 8 inches (15-20 cm) apart. Fix one foot on the floor, and place the other foot on a slide board or plastic slider exercise disk.
- Place hands either by the body's sides or on the hips (a).

Movement Phases

1. To initiate the eccentric movement of the slide lunge, flex at the hip and knee, and glide the foot in contact with the slidable surface backward (b). Maintain good posture in the torso during the eccentric and concentric portions of the lunge. The eccentric phase of the lunge movement stops when the knee of the back leg touches the floor. It is critical that the knee of the front leg does not pass over the toes and the heel stays in contact with the floor.

2. During the concentric phase of the movement, drive the front foot into the floor while extending the hip and knee of the front leg to return to the beginning position. During the concentric phase of this exercise, the torso should remain erect with good posture and not lose stability during the lunging motion.

Breathing Guidelines

Prior to lowering into the lunge position, inhale and control the descent to the floor. During the upward phase of the movement, drive the front foot into the floor, and exhale in a controlled manner.

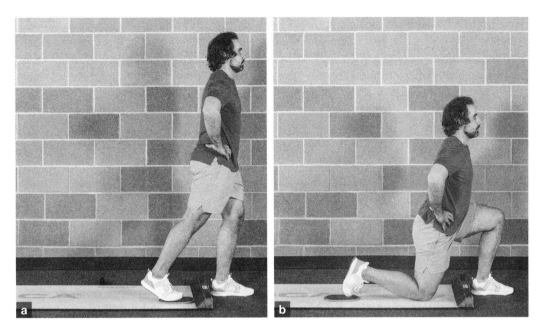

Figure 6.4   Slide lunge: *(a)* beginning position; *(b)* action.

Exercise Modifications and Variations

Lateral Slide Lunge

To begin the lateral slide lunge, stand tall with good posture with the feet positioned 6 to 8 inches (15-20 cm) apart. Fix one foot on the floor, and place the other foot on a slide board or plastic slider exercise disk. Please note that a slide board should be set up lengthwise on the body's side. This setup provides room to glide the foot across the board during the eccentric phase of the exercise.Initiate the eccentric movement by flexing at the hip, knee, and ankle, and focus on sitting back into a squat position on the fixed-foot side. Reach the foot on the slider out with a fully abducted leg while simultaneously squatting down on the other side.Keep the torso upright with good posture during the downward phase of the movement.Distribute weight over the squatting leg during this exercise. Never transfer more than 10% of body weight onto the sliding leg, which would put the adductor muscle group at risk for injury.During the concentric phase of the movement, drive the front foot down and into the floor while adducting the leg on the slide board or slider to the beginning position. Keep the torso erect with good posture, and do not lose stability during the lunging motion. The upper body descends and ascends during the concentric and eccentric phases of this movement.

Cross-Behind Slide Lunge

Begin by standing evenly with a tall posture and the feet 6 to 8 inches (15-20 cm) apart. Position one foot on the floor, and place the other foot on a slide board or plastic slider exercise disk. The eccentric motion of the exercise is similar to the slide lunge, where the sliding leg reaches backward; however, in this movement, the sliding leg reaches back and crosses the centerline of the body and lines up with the outside of the opposite shoulder. Keep the hips square and avoid excessive rotation caused by crossing behind in too wide of a fashion. The knee of the cross-behind leg touches the floor to complete the movement. Keep the torso erect with good posture, and do not lose stability during the lunging motion. During the concentric phase of the movement, push into the floor with the lead leg and ascend as the cross-behind leg travels forward to return to the beginning position.

Coaching Tips

- Repetitions for these exercises should be performed on one side first. It is not ideal to perform these exercises in alternating fashion.
- The upper body descends and ascends during the concentric and eccentric phases of the movement.
- The torso should remain erect with good posture and not lose stability throughout these movements.
- Each of these exercises can be loaded with the following forms of resistance: body weight dumbbells, kettlebells, and bands.

KETTLEBELL ONE-ARM SINGLE-LEG STRAIGHT-LEG DEADLIFT (SLDL)

Primary Muscles Trained

Gluteus maximus, gluteus medius, biceps femoris, semimembranosus, semitendinosus, erector spinae, gastrocnemius, soleus

Beginning Position

- Stand with the feet hip-width apart.
- Hold a kettlebell in the right hand.
- Maintain an upright torso and set the shoulders back to straighten the posture (a).

Movement Phases

1. The first movement is to unweight the right leg and transition onto the left leg in a single-leg stance.
2. Hold the kettlebell in the hand that is opposite to the stance leg (i.e., when standing on the left leg, hold the kettlebell in the right hand).
3. Now, with the kettlebell and stance leg on opposite sides, sit the hips back and begin to lower the kettlebell and raise the back right leg.
4. Maintain perfect posture throughout this movement. The back leg stays extended, and the torso is firmly set in a neutral-back position (b). Pause at the bottom when executing this exercise.
5. For the concentric movement phase of the exercise, drive the stance leg into the floor and return toward the beginning position. The trail leg and upper body need to provide stability to the system and maintain a straight-line posture throughout the exercise.

Figure 6.5   Kettlebell one-arm single-leg SLDL: *(a)* beginning position; *(b)* action.

Breathing Guidelines

Inhale prior to initiating the lowering part of the movement, and maintain balance during the descent. During the upward movement phase, maintain balance and exhale slowly.

Exercise Modifications and Variations

Landmine One-Arm Single-Leg Straight-Leg Deadlift (SLDL)

The movement pattern for this exercise is the same as in the kettlebell one-arm single-leg SLDL. The major differences are the implement and setup. Set up the bar in the landmine attachment. Stand with the feet under the sleeve of the barbell. Squat down with good posture, and grip the bar with the inside hand. Ascend from the squat position and stand tall on the outside leg, holding the barbell in the opposite hand. The inside leg now becomes the leg to extend backward in the descent of the lift. Keep the load close to the shin during the eccentric phase of the movement. Complete all repetitions on one side before switching sides.

Dumbbell One-Arm Single-Leg Straight-Leg Deadlift (SLDL)

The movement pattern and teaching points for this exercise are the same as in the kettlebell one-arm single-leg SLDL. The only variation to this exercise is to use a dumbbell as the form of resistance.

Coaching Tips

- Set the gaze straight ahead before starting the exercise.
- Maintain good posture in the standing position.

- The eyes track down to the floor during the eccentric phase of the movement and track back to standing on the concentric phase. Maintain a controlled tempo and speed of movement, both concentrically and eccentrically.
- Balance and core stability are key factors in executing this exercise properly.
- Maintain a neutral spine and shoulders-back position as the dumbbell is lowered toward the shins.
- Be sure to lower the dumbbell in line with the shin, and do not let it reach forward past the foot of the standing leg. Reaching the dumbbell away from the body puts undue stress on the lumbar vertebrae.

TRAP BAR DEADLIFT

Primary Muscles Trained

Gluteus maximus, gluteus medius, biceps femoris, semimembranosus, semitendinosus, erector spinae, vastus lateralis, vastus intermedius, vastus medialis, rectus femoris, latissimus dorsi, rhomboids, upper and lower trapezius (2)

Beginning Position

- Stand within the trap bar with the feet in line with the handles. Point the feet forward and place them hip- or shoulder-width apart.
- Flex at the hips and knees slightly so that the torso descends downward to grip the bar.
- From a side view, the chest and shoulders are positioned higher than the hips, the hips are positioned higher than the knees, the shin angle is vertical (more than what is seen in photo a), and the spine is in a neutral position (4).
- Extend the arms completely, perpendicular to the floor, while gripping the bar.
- Keep the head position neutral, and set a line of sight about 2 feet (60 cm) in front of the bar.
- Grip the bar with maximal effort, and brace the core for the liftoff.

Movement Phases

1. To initiate the concentric phase of the movement, drive the feet into the floor and begin extending at the knees and hips.
2. At the conclusion of the concentric phase, the knees and hips are fully extended. Reach a standing position with an upright torso (b).
3. To initiate the eccentric lowering phase of the movement, flex at the hips, knees, and ankles in a controlled manner while maintaining intra-abdominal pressure.
4. Throughout the movement, control trunk flexion and back extension posture. Trunk flexion, which occurs during the eccentric phase of the movement, and back extension, which occurs during the concentric phase of the movement, happen because of proper hip, knee, and ankle flexion and extension.

Figure 6.6   Trap bar deadlift: *(a)* beginning position; *(b)* action.

Breathing Guidelines

Prior to lifting the weight off the floor, inhale to create intra-abdominal pressure. Drive the feet into the floor and exhale slowly past the sticking point of the movement. At the top of the movement, before the descent, inhale slowly to re-create intra-abdominal pressure for the eccentric phase of the movement and in preparation for the next concentric phase.

Exercise Modifications and Variations

Deadlift (Conventional)

The beginning position of the bar is on the floor with no obstructions to the training space. Begin the conventional deadlift by standing behind the bar with feet hip-width apart and the bar touching the shins. Flex at the hips, knees, and ankles to address the bar in the beginning position. Maintain good posture when descending into the beginning position. Upon arriving in this low position, take a pronated or alternating grip on the bar with the hands positioned outside the shins. The chest should be over the bar. Brace the back and core for the initial liftoff. During the concentric phase of the movement, drive the feet into the floor and maintain a neutral spine while rising to reach full extension in the standing position. The bar path during the concentric phase should not travel away from the body and should remain aligned with the midfoot. During the eccentric phase of the movement, the bar's path should travel straight down to the floor and not away from the body. Flex at the hips, knees, and ankles in a controlled manner to initiate the eccentric phase of the exercise. The torso should remain upright and firmly braced during the downward phase of the movement until the weight reaches the floor.

Sumo Deadlift

The main difference between the sumo deadlift and the conventional deadlift is the position of the feet and placement of the grip. The foot position is just outside shoulder-width, and the position of the grip is now on the inside of the legs with the arms extended down toward the bar at full length. The width of the grip should be 6 to 8 inches (15-20 cm) apart. The foot position and the grip strategy in the sumo deadlift make it easier to maintain a more upright torso during each phase of the movement. Sumo deadlift employs more of a squat strategy, as opposed to a hinge strategy like in the conventional deadlift. Begin the exercise by standing behind the bar with feet slightly wider than shoulder-width apart. Flex at the hips, knees, and ankles to address the bar in the low starting position. Maintain posture when descending into the beginning position. After getting set in this low position, take a pronated grip or alternating grip on the bar with the hands positioned on the inside of the shins. During the concentric phase of the movement, drive the feet into the floor and maintain a neutral spine while rising to reach full extension at the standing position. The bar path during the concentric phase should not travel away from the body and should remain aligned with the midfoot. During the eccentric phase of the movement, the bar's path should travel straight down to the floor and not away from the body. Flex at the hips, knees, and ankles in a controlled manner to initiate the eccentric motion. The torso should remain upright and firmly braced during the downward phase of the movement until the weight reaches the floor.

Landmine Deadlift

Set up the bar for the landmine deadlift on the floor and secured in a landmine attachment or squat station landmine attachment. Stand over the plate-loaded side of the bar with the feet on either side of the sleeve of the bar. Keep the foot position between hip- and shoulder-width apart. To initiate the movement, squat down with good posture and knee position. Extend the arms straight down to grip the bar on the sleeve. Once set in the position with a neutral spine, braced core, and a strong grip on the bar, drive the feet into the floor and extend at the hips and knees, reaching full extension at the top position. During the eccentric phase of the movement, the bar path travels straight down to the floor and does not shift to the left or right. Flex at the hips, knees, and ankles in a controlled manner to initiate the eccentric motion. The torso should have good posture and remain firmly braced during the downward phase of the movement and until the weight reaches the floor.

Coaching Tips

- Always maintain good posture, spinal alignment, and a firm core throughout the movement.
- Do not allow the spine to be compromised during the eccentric and concentric phase of the exercise.
- If needed to accommodate long limbs, use an elevated surface or blocks to raise the trap bar or conventional training bar off the floor slightly. This position may fit the hip, knee, ankle, and spinal position better.

ONE-LEG SQUAT OFF A BOX

Primary Muscles Trained

Gluteus maximus, gluteus medius, biceps femoris, semimembranosus, semitendinosus, vastus lateralis, vastus intermedius, vastus medialis, rectus femoris, anterior and posterior tibialis (2)

Beginning Position

- Stand on one leg on top of a 12- to 18-inch (30-45 cm) plyometric box. (Increase the height of the box for taller athletes if needed.) Hold the other leg out to the side, off the side of the box (a).
- Begin with the hands by the body's sides.
- Keep the torso standing tall, with a braced core.

Movement Phases

1. During the eccentric phase of the movement, flex the standing leg's hip, knee, and ankle.
2. While eccentrically loading, raise the arms in front of the body as a counterbalance. This also helps with sitting back into the glute and prevents the knee from passing over the toe during the lowering phase. Squat down until the thigh reaches approximately parallel to the floor (b). The foot of the off leg should not touch the floor fully or act as a break in the bottom position.

Figure 6.7   One-leg squat off a box: (a) beginning position; (b) action.

3. For the concentric phase of the exercise, drive the foot into the box forcefully and extend at the hip and knee. Keep the arms out in front of the body until reaching the beginning position. Maintain torso posture during this upward phase of movement.

4. After a brief pause in the beginning position, perform the remaining repetitions, then switch legs.

Breathing Guidelines

Inhale before initiating the eccentric portion of the movement, then lower into position. In the concentric phase of the exercise, drive the foot into the box and exhale during the upward movement.

Exercise Modifications and Variations

Kettlebell Goblet Single-Leg Squat Off a Box

The execution and technique of the kettlebell goblet single-leg squat off a box is same as the single-leg squat off a box. The only difference is where the load is positioned during the exercise. A kettlebell can be used for resistance and held in the goblet position with two hands, in line with the sternum. The weight is stationary throughout the exercise. Kettlebells offer a challenging form of resistance to lower body strength and the ability to hold good posture during the movement.

Dumbbell Single-Leg Squat Off a Box

The execution and technique of the dumbbell single-leg squat off a box is the same as the single-leg squat off a box. Hold two dumbbells in the hands, positioned by the body's sides. Raise them up with straight arms while squatting down. The dumbbells act as a counterbalance and resistance. Dumbbells aid in the ability to hold upright posture on the descending motion of the squat. While coming out of the bottom position, slowly lower the dumbbells to the sides.

One-Arm Kettlebell Rack Single-Leg Squat Off a Box

The execution and technique of the one-arm kettlebell rack single-leg squat off a box is same as the kettlebell goblet single-leg squat off a box exercise. The only difference is that the kettlebell is held on the non-squatting-leg side of the body at the shoulder. The position of the kettlebell challenges the stability of the core. The weight is stationary throughout the exercise.

Coaching Tips

- The strength and conditioning professional can set a higher box behind the athlete as a target to help measure the depth of the squat. The athlete should not pause on this box during the exercise. Because of the varying heights of athletes and their squatting abilities, an appropriate-sized spacer can be used to fit the targeted depth for the athlete.

- During both the eccentric phase and the concentric phase of the exercise, the athlete should maintain alignment of the hip, knee, and foot. The position of knee valgus during squatting activities increases the risk of injury to the athlete.

- Athletes can use sandbags, aqua bags, or weight vests as additional forms of resistance for these exercises.

- Single-leg squat exercises off a box are great lower body strength-building exercises. These types of patterns are also demanding mechanically, specifically in the area of ankle range of motion. The strength and conditioning professional should assess the athlete's ankle mobility prior to prescribing any of these exercise variations. The athlete must have the prerequisite ankle mobility to perform these exercises efficiently.

SLIDE BOARD LEG CURL

Primary Muscles Trained

Gluteus maximus, biceps femoris, semimembranosus, semitendinosus, obliques, erector spinae (2)

Beginning Position

- Begin in a supine lying position on top of a slide board with the knees flexed and the feet flat on the board (not shown). Place the arms on the floor to the sides of the body for stability.
- The feet can be on top of a towel or wearing slide board booties to help with the gliding motion of the exercise.

Movement Phases

1. The movement is initiated with proper breathing and core activation. Inhale slowly to fill the lower torso and the upper torso with air. This inhalation is key to preparing the stability of the core during the exercise and ensures proper recruitment of the posterior chain musculature during the movement.

2. The second step in breathing preparation for this exercise is the exhalation. During exhalation, forcefully breathe air out of the mouth and tighten the core. Maintain this level of core activation throughout the exercise. Do not stop breathing during the execution of this exercise.

3. Once the core is set, drive the heels into the slide board (a) and lift the hips up into extension. This is the beginning position for every repetition.

4. To begin the eccentric phase of the exercise, slowly glide the feet down the slide board while maintaining hip extension. The movement stops when the knees are fully extended (more than what is seen in photo b).

5. The concentric phase of the exercise begins by pulling the heels back toward the glutes while maintaining hip extension.

6. Keep the thighs parallel to each other with no external hip rotation during any portion of the exercise. External hip rotation minimizes the proper use of the glutes and hamstrings.

Breathing Guidelines

Start supine with flexed-knee hip extension. Inhale as the lower body lengthens into a straight-line position of hip extension. Then exhale during the leg curl phase of the movement.

Figure 6.8   Slide board leg curl: *(a)* beginning position; *(b)* action.

Exercise Modifications and Variations

Stability Ball Leg Curl

The stability ball leg curl variation begins in a supine lying position on the floor with the knees extended and the heels on top of a stability ball. The sequence to set the core is the same as the slide board leg curl. After the core is set, initiate the movement by extending the hips up to create a straight line with the torso. The concentric motion is performed by flexing the knees to roll the ball toward the glutes. Extend the knees to return the ball to the beginning position during the eccentric phase of the exercise. Maintain hip extension (i.e., lifted hips) throughout the exercise, and do not let the glutes touch the floor between repetitions.

Valslide Leg Curl

The execution and technique of the Valslide leg curl is the same as the slider leg curl exercise. The major difference is the implement used, the Valslide, which consists of thin plastic disks that are made of a material that can slide very easily on virtually any surface. In the beginning position, each foot should be on a Valslide. The setting of the core and the beginning position, eccentric phase, and concentric phase of the movement are the same as the slider leg curl. Valslides provide independent use of each limb during exercise, which adds to the functionality of training and the variety of unilateral exercise programming.

Single-Leg Eccentric Slider Leg Curl

In this variation, set up in the position described in slider leg curl exercise. The difference in execution and technique is that, from the beginning position, one leg extends out during the eccentric phase of the movement. Return to the beginning position by using both legs during the concentric phase of the movement. The eccentric demand on the musculature is the focal point of the exercise. Two legs are used concentrically to limit fatigue in the musculature during that phase of the exercise.

One-Leg Slider Leg Curl

The single-leg slider leg curl exercise is probably the most demanding of these variations on the hamstrings and glutes. This exercise variation's technique and execution are similar to the slider leg curl with the only difference being that it is performed unilaterally. The off leg should be held off the floor and flexed at the hip and knee during the movement. Perform all repetitions on one side before switching.

Coaching Tips

- Set the core with a strict sequence of inhalation and exhalation prior to initiating the movement.
- External hip rotation should be prevented during the entire exercise regardless of whether the exercise is performed bilaterally or unilaterally.

GLUTE-HAM RAISE

Primary Muscles Trained

Gluteus maximus, semimembranosus, semitendinosus, biceps femoris, erector spinae, gastrocnemius

Beginning Position

- For the setup position, kneel vertically on the glute-ham bench. Create a 90-degree angle at the knee such that the shoulders, hips, and thighs are aligned and perpendicular to the floor and the lower legs are parallel to the floor. Note that some glute-ham benches create a knee angle less than 90 degrees (a).
- The ankles should fit securely under the heel pads with the feet on the support platform pointing straight down to the floor.
- Cross the arms in front of the body.

Movement Phases

1. Initiate the eccentric phase of the movement by pushing the feet into the support plate, and begin to descend downward, with the upper body and lower body moving as one unit. A common mistake is to hinge at the hips during the eccentric phase of the movement; this results in an unsafe flexed position on the machine.
2. Continue downward at a controlled tempo until the upper body is parallel to the floor (b) and then perpendicular to the floor (not shown).
3. To initiate the concentric phase of the exercise, engage the glutes, hamstrings, and erector spinae to bring the body up into a horizontal position from the feet to the head.
4. At this point of the movement the knees flex into the pads of the machine, and the torso and upper leg rise as one unit returning to the beginning position.

Breathing Guidelines

Inhale before initiating the eccentric portion of the movement, then lower into position. To initiate the concentric phase of the exercise, engage the posterior chain musculature, and exhale during the upward movement phase.

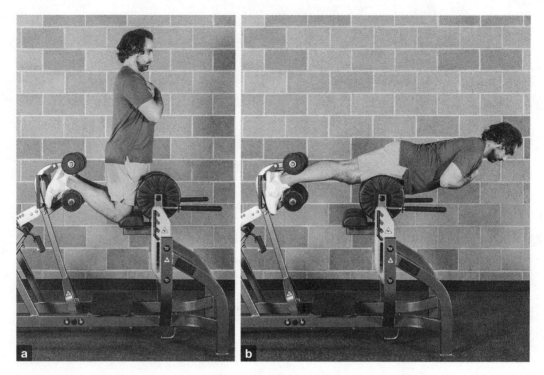

Figure 6.9 Glute-ham raise: *(a)* beginning position; *(b)* action.

Exercise Modifications and Variations

Partner Nordic Glute-Ham Raise

Kneel on the floor with a pad under the knees. From the side, the body will create a 90-degree angle at the knee such that the shoulders, hips, and thighs are aligned and perpendicular to the floor and the lower legs are parallel to the floor. This exercise requires a partner to kneel behind the body and hold the feet down firmly for safe lowering to the floor. Keep the foot dorsiflexed throughout the exercise. To initiate the eccentric movement, keep the torso rigid while extending the knees to slowly lower down to the floor. Extend the arms out in front in preparation to catch the body in a push-up position when the descent can no longer be controlled by the hamstrings and glutes. To initiate the concentric phase of the movement, provide just enough push off the floor using the arms to get the torso to the point where the hamstrings and glutes can engage and pull the body back to the beginning position. A common fault during this portion of the exercise is to kick the hips back during the push-up or hyperextend at the low back, thus compromising the alignment of the torso. It is critical to maintain alignment of the torso and upper leg during the eccentric and concentric phases of the exercise.

Coaching Tips

- Keep the torso stable throughout the movement.
- During the concentric phase, the athlete should not hyperextend at the spine in efforts to return to the beginning position.
- Point the feet straight down to the floor throughout the movement.
- The athlete should always control the tempo during the exercise.

STEP-UP

Primary Muscles Trained

Gluteus maximus, gluteus medius, semimembranosus, semitendinosus, biceps femoris, vastus lateralis, vastus intermedius, vastus medialis, rectus femoris, adductor magnus

Beginning Position

- Set the bar at shoulder height on a squat rack (not shown).
- Step under the bar so it rests in the back position and across the upper trapezius muscles.
- Grip the bar slightly wider than shoulder-width.
- In a controlled manner, push both feet through the floor to lift the bar off the rack.
- Take a few small steps forward to address the step-up box and set up the beginning position of the exercise (a).
- Begin each repetition with both feet on the floor prior to taking a step up.

Movement Phases

1. From the beginning position, lift one leg up and step onto the center of the box. Maintain the posture of the upper body during this leg-lifting phase of the movement.

2. With the lead foot firmly positioned on the box, drive the foot down to extend the hip and knee. While pushing into the box, transfer the weight onto the lead leg, causing the rear leg to come off the floor (b). Continue with hip and knee extension of the lead leg, and bring the trailing leg up to a standing position on the box (c). Maintain upright posture during step-up through the range of motion.

Figure 6.10 Step-up: (a) beginning position; (b-c) action.

3. To initiate the eccentric phase of the exercise, unweight the trail leg off the box. Use the drive leg to lower the body eccentrically to the floor. During this motion, maintain balance, keep an upright posture, and support the load with an activated core.

4. Once the rear foot is planted on the floor, return to the beginning position, where both feet are in contact with the floor and body weight is distributed evenly.

Breathing Guidelines

Before initiating the concentric portion of the movement, inhale to set the intra-abdominal pressure of the trunk. During the concentric phase of the exercise, drive the foot into the box, and exhale during the upward movement phase. Inhale during the eccentric portion of the exercise.

7

UPPER BODY
EXERCISE TECHNIQUE

TIM LEBBOSSIERE

While it does not get as much credit as lower body training, upper body training is important for the hockey athlete. Whether it is a skater taking a slapshot, engaging in a battle, or taking contact; or a goalie reaching across the crease to make a save, upper body musculature and force production play an important role.

From a performance standpoint, being able to produce more force over a shorter time period is vital. When taking a stride the arms, flexing and extending, work in conjunction with the legs, flexing and extending, to propel the body forward. When taking a shot or making a pass, the upper body takes the power generated by the lower body that is transferred through the core and releases that power into the stick. And when engaging in a battle or protecting the puck from an opponent, the upper body can resist the opposing athlete to gain or maintain possession.

The upper body also plays a role in injury reduction. When giving and accepting contact, having a greater muscle volume can create armor (or padding) for the joints and bones. The forces that the upper body can produce can also prevent the joints from getting into positions that the athlete's range of motion does not allow for.

Lastly, when training the upper body, strength and conditioning professionals want to ensure that imbalances are being addressed to maintain optimal length–tension relationships to promote structural balance. This may include a variety of movements, such as horizontal and vertical pressing and pulling exercises, as well as movements that isolate individual muscles at specific joints. This helps the hockey athlete produce and resist high levels of force.

ONE-ARM LANDMINE PRESS (HALF-KNEELING)

Primary Muscles Trained

Anterior deltoid, trapezius, triceps brachii

Beginning Position

- Place a barbell in a landmine attachment.
- Stand with the back leg's quadriceps muscle up against the end of the barbell (not shown). This is the optimal distance away from the lever arm of the landmine.
- Assume a half-kneeling position, with one knee down and the other knee flexed in front of the body so that both knees are at a 90-degree angle.
- Pick up the barbell by the collar and position it about 2 inches (5 cm) in front of the shoulder. Hold the barbell with the same-side hand as the knee that is down (a).

Movement Phases

1. Maintain an upright posture throughout the exercise. Resist leaning back to counter-balance the weight in front of the body.
2. Press the barbell upward until the elbow is fully extended (b).
3. At the top, there should be a tiny shrug of the shoulder up toward the ear to upwardly rotate the scapula.

4. At the top, the biceps should be in line with the head between the eyes and the ear, depending on the athlete's mobility.
5. Flex the elbow, returning the barbell to the beginning position.

Figure 7.1 One-arm landmine press (half-kneeling): *(a)* beginning position; *(b)* action.

Breathing Guidelines

Prior to the first repetition, inhale to create tension throughout the body. As the barbell is being pressed upward, exhale. Then, inhale again as the barbell is lowering back to the beginning position.

Spotting Guidelines

Stand behind the athlete at an arm's distance. If assistance is needed, grasp the athlete's wrist, and help finish the repetition, keeping the hand there while lowering the barbell back to the beginning position. Do not provide spotting unless assistance is needed because it could interfere with the movement or distract the athlete.

Exercise Modifications and Variations

This exercise can be completed in various stances, such as a staggered stance or parallel stance. Not only can this make the exercise easier because of the change in angle off the landmine attachment but, depending on the goal of the movement, leg drive can be incorporated to make it more of a total body movement.

Coaching Tips

Ensure that the torso stays upright, or even slightly forward, to avoid the body cheating to handle more weight.

MULTI-GRIP BENCH PRESS

Primary Muscles Trained

Pectoralis major, anterior deltoid, triceps brachii

Beginning Position

- Lie supine on a bench with the head, shoulders, and hips all in contact with the bench and both feet fully on the floor.
- Retract the shoulders and create a small arch in the lower back so that it is not in contact with the bench.
- Position the body on the bench so that the eyes are directly under the barbell when it is on the rack.
- Using 45-degree, slightly pronated handles, lift the barbell from the rack with thumbs around the handles so the barbell is directly above the chest with the elbows extended and the wrists locked (a). This can be performed either unassisted or with help from a spotter.

Movement Phases

1. Lower the barbell to the chest so the bar is in line with the nipples (b).
2. The lowering should be under control so that the barbell lightly touches the chest without bouncing.
3. Without excessively arching the back or losing any contact points with the floor or the bench, press the bar back toward the ceiling until the elbows are fully extended.
4. The elbows should be at a 45-degree angle off the body during the lowering and lifting phases.

Breathing Guidelines

Prior to the beginning of a repetition, start to inhale and continue inhaling throughout the whole eccentric phase. As the barbell touches the chest and changes direction, exhale, continuing to exhale throughout the concentric portion of the movement until the beginning position is reached.

Spotting Guidelines

Take a staggered stance behind the athlete and the bar. If the athlete requires assistance to lift the barbell out of the rack, grab the neutral grip handles between the athlete's hands

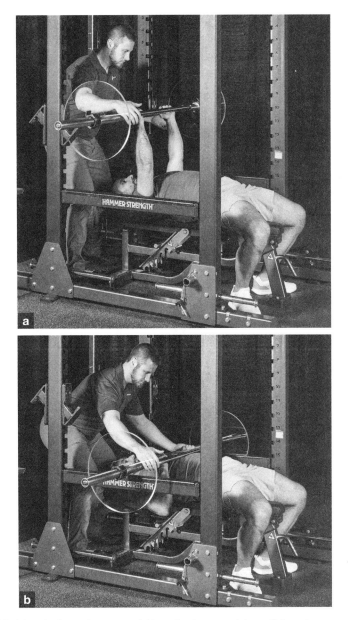

Figure 7.2 Multi-grip bench press: *(a)* beginning position; *(b)* action.

(rather than what is shown in the photos). Have the athlete give a 3-second countdown before assisting to lift the barbell out of the rack until it is above the athlete's chest with the arms fully extended. During the exercise, keep close by but never put the hands on the barbell in a way that interferes with performance. If assistance is needed, grab the barbell again on the neutral grip handles between the athlete's hands (rather than what is shown in the photos) and assist in lifting the barbell back to the beginning position or guide the barbell back to the racked position.

Exercise Modifications and Variations

A multi-grip barbell can create a safer shoulder position than a standard barbell, but dumb-bells can also be a modification. Dumbbells allow the athlete to stabilize each arm individually and choose any movement pattern. With dumbbells, the exercise can be modified by alternating arms or just doing one arm at a time. This integrates the core more than the two-arm variations because there is now a rotary component that requires the body to stabilize.

Coaching Tips

It can become tempting to lift more weight by lifting the hips off the bench, arching the back more, or bouncing the barbell off the chest. Maintaining proper form throughout the entirety of the exercise is crucial to reduce injury risk.

STANDING CHEST PRESS (CABLE)

Primary Muscles Trained

Pectoralis major, anterior deltoid, triceps brachii

Beginning Position

- Set the height of the cable column at chest height with a double-handle attachment.
- Facing away from the cable column, stand with a parallel stance and knees slightly flexed.
- Grab the handles so they begin under the armpits between the arms and the lats.
- Start with the hands 1 to 2 inches (3-5 cm) in front of the body at the nipple line, with the elbows at a 45-degree angle off the body.

Movement Phases

1. Maintain an upright posture throughout the exercise. Resist the urge to lean forward to counterbalance the weight.
2. Press the handles out in front of the chest until the elbows are fully extended.
3. At the fully extended position, there should be a slight protraction of the shoulder so that the scapulae wrap around the rib cage.
4. Flex the elbows, returning to the beginning position.

Breathing Guidelines

Prior to the first repetition, inhale to create tension throughout the body. Exhale as the handles are pressed forward. Then, inhale as the arms and the hands return to the beginning position.

Exercise Modifications and Variations

Cable columns are common in many facilities, but if one is not available, this exercise can be performed just as easily with bands. All that is needed is an anchor point to attach the bands to. As the resistance becomes greater, it is more difficult to balance against the band's backward pull, so this is a great time to introduce a staggered stance rather than a parallel stance. Not only does this stance provide more stability by having a wider base of support but it also integrates a small rotational component to the exercise. Another way to introduce a rotational component is to perform the exercise with a single arm or in an alternating arm fashion. To introduce a new stimulus, this exercise can be done at many different angles, depending on the desired results. To perform an inclined pressing movement that activates the upper pectoralis major, set the cable column at the bottom position. To perform a declined pressing movement that activates the lower pectoralis major, set the cable column at a higher position.

Coaching Tips

Allowing the scapulae to move around the rib cage at the end of the movement is an often-overlooked piece of the puzzle. In other movements, like a bench press, the scapulae are locked in retraction against a bench. Allowing the scapulae to move through full retraction and protraction in a cable chest press increases movement variability for the upper body.

PULL-UP

Primary Muscles Trained

Latissimus dorsi, posterior deltoid, rhomboids, trapezius, biceps brachii

Beginning Position

- Grasp a pull-up bar with a pronated grip with thumbs around the bar.
- Hang at an arm's length with the elbows extended and the shoulders slightly engaged (a).

Movement Phases

1. Pull the body upward until the chin is over the level of the bar (b).
2. The head should remain retracted in a neutral position to avoid cheating the range of motion by pushing the head forward.
3. Lower the body in a controlled manner back to the beginning position.

Figure 7.3   Pull-up: (a) beginning position; (b) action.

Breathing Guidelines

Prior to the first repetition, inhale to create tension throughout the body. As the elbow flex to lift the body, exhale. Then, inhale as the elbows extend and the body is lowered back to the beginning position.

Exercise Modifications and Variations

All variations of this exercise are based on grip position. Supinating the grip puts the biceps in an advantageous position, which is where most athletes are strongest. Having the palms facing each other in a neutral grip is another variation that may be stronger than the pronated grip.

Lat Pulldown

If a pull-up is too challenging, a great substitution exercise is the lat pulldown. Set a load on a cable column that is lighter than body weight and pull the bar attachment down to the body, rather than pulling the body up to the bar. This exercise can be done in a variety of ways: two arms, one arm, standing, staggered stance, half-kneeling, or any combination of these positions.

Coaching Tips

An athlete achieving a first pull-up can be a challenging feat. Many strength and conditioning professionals have adopted using a band as an assistance technique to reduce an athlete's body weight during the movement. When using band assistance, the range of motion where an athlete is the weakest, the bottom, is where the band has the most tension and is assisting the most. Another alternative approach for athletes who cannot complete a full pull-up is the eccentric-only pull-up. Athletes are stronger during the eccentric action and can still train through the full range of motion. If an athlete can perform multiple unassisted pull-ups, the next logical progression is to attach weight to the body via a weight vest, a weight belt, or a similar apparatus.

ONE-ARM DUMBBELL ROW

Primary Muscles Trained

Latissimus dorsi, posterior deltoid, rhomboids, trapezius, biceps brachii

Beginning Position

- Standing approximately 2 feet (61 cm) away from a bench, place a dumbbell between the feet and the bench.
- Unlock the knees and push the hips backward with a neutral spine to perform a hip hinge pattern until the torso is parallel to the floor.
- Placing one hand on the bench for support, grab the dumbbell with a neutral grip using the free hand (a).
- The bench height should allow the torso to remain approximately parallel to the floor while being supported by the hand.

Movement Phases

1. Keep the spine neutral and the shoulders square to the floor throughout the whole movement.
2. Pull the dumbbell up and back so the hand finishes at the bottom of the rib cage and the elbow finishes behind the body *(b)*.
3. Lower the weight, under control, back to the beginning position.

Figure 7.4 One-arm dumbbell row: *(a)* beginning position; *(b)* action.

Breathing Guidelines

Before the first repetition, inhale to create tension throughout the body. As the elbow flexes to lift the dumbbell, exhale. Then, inhale as the elbow is extended to lower the dumbbell back to the beginning position.

Exercise Modifications and Variations

Alternative apparatuses can be used rather than a dumbbell for this exercise. Using a kettlebell can be a great option to reduce stress to the wrist. The kettlebell may make it easier to obtain a neutral wrist position and avoid radial and ulnar deviation, which might make it easier to row more weight. Using a landmine is also a great option to provide more weight than a dumbbell or kettlebell may be able to. When using the landmine, it should be set perpendicular to the body, and the working hand starts more toward the midline than other variations due to the arcing motion of the landmine.

Renegade Row

The bench-supported one-arm dumbbell row can also be performed from a plank position, thereby creating a large rotary stability component. By having the hands on the handles of the dumbbells rather than resting on the floor, it is possible to row one dumbbell at a time to challenge the ability to stay square to the floor. This variation is challenging and requires a lower weight than other variations.

Coaching Tips

Maintaining the proper torso angle is key to using the correct musculature. If the athlete is more upright, the upper trapezius becomes a prime mover over the latissimus dorsi and rhomboids.

ONE-ARM CABLE ROW

Primary Muscles Trained

Latissimus dorsi, posterior deltoid, rhomboids, trapezius, biceps brachii

Beginning Position

- Set the cable column at chest height with a single-handle attachment.
- Facing toward the cable column, stand with a parallel stance and knees slightly flexed.
- Grab the handle with one arm with the elbow fully extended (a).

Movement Phases

1. Keep the shoulders square to the cable column throughout the whole movement.
2. Pull the cable back so the hand finishes at the bottom of the rib cage and the elbow finishes behind the body (b).
3. Extend the elbow, returning to the beginning position.
4. Repeat for the required number of repetitions.

Figure 7.5   One-arm cable row: (a) beginning position; (b) action.

Breathing Guidelines

Prior to the first repetition, inhale to create tension throughout the body. As the elbow flexes to pull the cable toward the body, exhale. Then, inhale as the elbow extends to return the handle back to the beginning position.

Exercise Modifications and Variations

This exercise has a wide array of variations to change the stimulus. The grip can be changed to supinated, pronated, or neutral. The stance can be changed from a parallel stance to a staggered, half-kneeling, or one-leg stance. The height can be adjusted from chest height to various high and low settings. All these variables can be combined in different ways to reduce monotony as well as introduce a new stimulus.

Another variation is to stand perpendicular to the cable column, holding the handle with the outside arm to perform a rotational cable row. With the inside leg stable, rotate the hips and shoulders toward the cable column to load the musculature of the inside leg. Then, using the inside leg to generate power, rotate away from the cable column while simultaneously rowing to produce a total body powerful exercise. This variation may be more akin to the rotational nature of the hockey stride.

Coaching Tips

Due to the many different variations available, make sure that the goal of the exercise is clear to everyone involved. The goal of the exercise should determine which variation is used.

EXTERNAL ROTATION

Primary Muscles Trained

Infraspinatus, teres minor, posterior deltoid

Beginning Position

- Seated on the floor or a flat bench, flex one knee in a hook-lying position so that the foot is flat and the calf and hamstring are touching.
- With the same-side arm holding a dumbbell with a pronated grip, position the elbow on the vastus medialis by the same-side knee at a 90-degree angle.

Movement Phases

1. Maintain a pronated grip throughout the entirety of the movement.
2. Maintaining the 90-degree angle of the elbow, internally rotate the shoulder so the dumbbell lowers toward the pelvis (a).
3. Upon reaching maximum internal rotation without compensation, externally rotate the shoulder so the dumbbell moves away from the pelvis and back to the beginning position (b).
4. Repeat for the required number of repetitions.

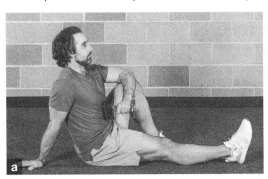

Figure 7.6   External rotation: (a) beginning position; (b) action.

Breathing Guidelines

As the weight is lowered toward the pelvis, inhale. As the weight is being lifted away from the pelvis, exhale. Another option is to start the inhalation during the beginning position of each repetition and continue the inhalation during the eccentric portion of the movement.

Exercise Modifications and Variations

90-90 External Rotation

The seated position for external rotation can be helpful because the elbow can rest on the leg, but many variations exist. One variation can be done by lying supine on a flat or slightly inclined bench. Start by rowing the weight with a 90-degree angle of the shoulders and elbows. While maintaining the height of the elbows and the angle of both the shoulders and elbows, externally rotate the shoulder until the hands are in line with the ears. This type of external rotation is known as 90-90 external rotation. Instead of using a dumbbell, the exercise can be done on a cable column with a double or single handle. Like with the lying version, row the elbow(s) back to the 90-90 position before externally rotating the shoulder(s) so the hand(s) finish in line with the ears. Similar to other cable exercises, this exercise can be done at varying heights and stances, such as staggered and half-kneeling.

Coaching Tips

The rotator cuff muscles cannot handle as much weight as can be used in other multijoint exercises. Focus on movement quality overload, because trying to move excess weight leads to compensation from other muscles.

INCLINE Y

Primary Muscles Trained

Rhomboids, trapezius, posterior deltoid, infraspinatus, teres minor

Beginning Position

- Adjust a bench to create a low incline (less than 45 degrees).
- Putting one leg on each side of the bench, support the chest on the inclined portion of the bench so that the head is at the top of the pad.
- Maintain a neutral spine so that the head does not protract forward.
- Fully extend the arms on each side of the bench so they are reaching toward the floor (a).

Movement Phases

1. Maintain a neutral grip throughout the entirety of the movement.
2. While keeping the elbows extended, flex the shoulders until the dumbbells are level with the head (b).
3. The arms should create a "Y" position with the body.
4. Lower the arms, staying under control, back to the beginning position.
5. Repeat for the required number of repetitions.

Figure 7.7   Incline Y: *(a)* beginning position; *(b)* action.

Breathing Guidelines

As the shoulder is flexed and the weight is lifted away from the floor, exhale. As the weight is being lowered and returned to the beginning position, inhale.

Exercise Modifications and Variations

If a bench is not available, this exercise can also be substituted by performing it in a bent-over, hip-hinged position, on a stability ball, or with a cable column. In the bent-over variation, unlock the knees and maintain a neutral spine throughout the movement to ensure good movement quality and reduce the chance of injury. With the stability ball variation, use the ball to support the chest. The knees can rest on the floor, if needed, so the arms can be extended toward the floor on the other side of the ball.

Coaching Tips

This exercise is similar to the external rotation exercise in the fact that this musculature cannot handle as much weight as other compound exercises. Focus on movement quality rather than load, because trying to move excess weight leads to compensation from other muscles.

REAR DELT RAISE (INCLINE T)

Primary Muscles Trained

Rhomboids, trapezius, posterior deltoid, infraspinatus, teres minor

Beginning Position

- Adjust a bench to create a low incline (less than 45 degrees).
- Putting one leg on each side of the bench, support the chest on the inclined portion of the bench so that the head is at the top of the pad.
- Maintain a neutral spine so that the head does not protract forward.
- Fully extend the arms on each side of the bench so they are reaching toward the floor *(a)*.

Movement Phases

1. Maintain a neutral grip throughout the entirety of the movement.
2. While keeping the elbows extended, flex the shoulders until the dumbbells are level with the head *(b)*.
3. The arms should create a "T" position with the body.
4. Lower the arms, under control, back to the beginning position.
5. Repeat for the required number of repetitions.

Figure 7.8 Rear delt raise (incline T): *(a)* beginning position; *(b)* action.

Breathing Guidelines

As the shoulder is horizontally abducted and the weight is lifted away from the floor, exhale. As the weight is being lowered and returned to the beginning position, inhale.

Exercise Modifications and Variations

One way to progress this movement to make it more challenging is to perform it side-lying with one arm at a time. In this variation, lie sideways on a flat or slightly inclined bench. With the top arm only, begin this exercise with the elbow extended and shoulder horizontally adducted so it requires a large range of motion. Even though the original exercise requires lower loads than many other compound exercises, this variation requires even less weight.

If a bench is not available, this exercise can also be performed in a bent-over, hip-hinged position on a stability ball or with a cable column. In the bent-over variation, it is key to unlock the knees and maintain a neutral spine throughout the movement to ensure movement quality and reduce the chance of injury.

With the stability ball variation, use the ball to support the chest. If needed, the knees can rest on the floor so the arms can be extended toward the floor on the other side of the ball.

Alternating arms in any of these variations and performing a band pull apart are other ways to provide a new stimulus and reduce monotony.

Coaching Tips

The latissimus dorsi is a strong, powerful muscle that wants to perform all the movements for the posterior shoulder. Making sure that the arm stays in line with the shoulder, rather than below the shoulder, reduces the activation of the latissimus dorsi and allows for the correct musculature to perform this exercise.

INVERTED ROW

Primary Muscles Trained

Latissimus dorsi, posterior deltoid, rhomboids, trapezius, biceps brachii

Beginning Position

- Set a barbell on a rack at belly button height.
- Sitting on the floor under the barbell, grasp the bar with a pronated grip.
- Fully extend the hips and knees so that the body is in a straight line from the top of the head through the bottom of the feet.
- The chest should be directly under the bar so that the arms are perpendicular to the floor *(a)*.

Movement Phases

1. Maintain a rigid torso throughout the entirety of the movement.
2. Pull the body upward until the chest touches the barbell *(b)*.
3. Lower the body in a controlled manner back to the beginning position.

Figure 7.9   Inverted row: *(a)* beginning position; *(b)* action.

Breathing Guidelines

Prior to the first repetition, inhale to create tension throughout the body. As the elbows flex to lift the body, exhale. Then, inhale as the elbows extend and the body is lowered back to the beginning position.

Exercise Modifications and Variations

Most of the variations of this exercise are based on grip position. Supinating the grip puts the biceps in an advantageous position, which is where most athletes are strongest. Having the hands in an alternated grip can be less challenging on the hand and forearm musculature but creates a rotary stability component with the exercise. If a barbell and rack are not available, a suspension strap or apparatus is a common piece of equipment used in many facilities. This exercise is performed the same way but now can also be done with a rotating grip.

Coaching Tips

For some athletes, this variation with the legs fully extended can be too challenging. In this case, the knees can be flexed at a 90-degree angle so they can push against the floor to provide assistance to the upper body. Keep the hips extended during this modification to make sure momentum is not used by flexing and extending the hips.

PUSH-UP

Primary Muscles Trained

Pectoralis major, anterior deltoid, triceps brachii

Beginning Position

- Position the hands on the floor slightly wider than shoulder-width directly under the shoulders and fully extend the elbows.
- Fully extend the hips and knees so that the body is in a straight line from the top of the head through the bottom of the feet (a).
- Slightly protract the shoulders so the scapulae wrap around the rib cage and the upper back is pushed upward.
- Slightly tilt the pelvis posteriorly to engage the abdominals.
- Maintain most of the body's weight over the hands so the arms are approximately perpendicular to the floor.

Movement Phases

1. Maintain a rigid torso throughout the entirety of the movement.
2. Maintain a neutral, packed-chin position.
3. Lower the body in a controlled manner until the chest is a fist's distance away from the floor (b).
4. Press the body upward, returning to the beginning position.

Breathing Guidelines

As the body begins to lower, inhale until the bottom position is reached. Then, exhale as the elbows extend and the body is pressed back to the beginning position. Inhalation can start at the beginning position but should be continued throughout the eccentric portion of the movement.

Figure 7.10   Push-up: *(a)* beginning position; *(b)* action.

Exercise Modifications and Variations

Similar to a bench being inclined or declined for bench press, the hands or feet can be elevated in a push-up to target slightly different musculature.

Elevating the hands also makes this exercise easier by changing the percentage of body weight to press. If there is no equipment available to elevate the hands, a simple work-around is to perform a kneeling push-up, where the knees are the point of contact with the floor, rather than the feet.

Elevating the feet is a challenging variation but allows a higher percentage of body weight to be loaded throughout the movement. Due to the different angle, the head can potentially interfere with reaching full range of motion at the bottom of the movement. To avoid this, the hands can also be slightly elevated (less than the feet) with handles to allow for the proper range of motion.

Coaching Tips

The push-up is a well-known exercise because no equipment is needed. To ensure proper length–tension relationships so the correct musculature is being used, a proper setup is very important. By slightly protracting the shoulders and posteriorly tilting the pelvis, the athlete creates a plank position that should be maintained throughout the entirety of the movement, making this more than just an upper body exercise.

8

ANATOMICAL CORE EXERCISE TECHNIQUE

MARIA MOUNTAIN

A strong and stable anatomical core is essential for a hockey athlete's success. It is easy to see the value of a strong core in winning puck battles along the board. For example, the core is what allows the best athletes to move the puck with their feet while fending off an opponent with their upper body.

Kibler and colleagues described anatomical core stability as the "ability to control the position and motion of the trunk over the pelvis to allow optimum production, transfer and control of force and motion to the terminal segment in integrated activities" (1). For the hockey athlete, the terminal segment could be the skates applying force to the ice, the upper body applying force to an opponent or the stick applying force to the puck.

Throughout this text the hockey athlete experiences different types of muscle action. In addition to concentric and eccentric loading, this chapter includes the use of isometrics. For clarity, **yielding isometrics** are actions where the hockey athlete holds a segment stable against an external load. The roll out exercise provides an example of this type of muscle action where the athlete contracts the anterior abdominals to maintain a neutral spine position throughout the range of motion.

Overcoming isometrics are muscle actions where the athlete voluntarily pushes against an immovable object. The Pilates ring adductor squeeze exercise is an example of this type of action when there is no visible compression of the ring.

Exercise Finder

CHOP

Primary Muscles Trained

The primary muscles trained with the chop are the stabilizers of the torso (transversus abdominis, internal obliques, external obliques, multifidi, and quadratus lumborum). The rotary force is initiated through the upper extremities (pectoralis major, pectoralis minor, latissimus dorsi, trapezius, rhomboids, anterior deltoid, posterior deltoid, biceps, and triceps).

Throughout the repetition, focus on stabilizing the torso against the diagonal force of the chop. Muscles of the hip are used to stabilize the pelvis (gluteus maximus, gluteus medius, adductor magnus, adductor longus). The specific muscles recruited vary based on the progression.

Beginning Position

- Begin in a tall kneeling position with the knees flexed to 90 degrees.
- Keep the hips in neutral extension (with the thighs in line with the long axis of the torso), and have a neutral spine (i.e., a normal erect position of the torso with natural lordosis and kyphosis).
- Grasp the resistance with both hands by reaching up and across diagonally at approximately 45 degrees above parallel *(a)*.

Movement Phases

1. Maintain a tall torso, and brace lightly with the abdominals in preparation for the chop.
2. Using the arms as prime movers, pull the resistance toward the midchest.
3. When the hands reach the midchest, push the resistance down toward the floor while maintaining a neutral pelvis. A small degree of rotation of the torso on the pelvis is acceptable, but the focus is on maintaining the overall stability.
4. At the end of the downward movement, the arms should make a 45-degree angle with the floor (b).
5. Complete the repetition by eccentrically controlling the load as the hands return to the midchest and then up to the beginning position.
6. Repeat for the required number of repetitions, then switch sides.

Figure 8.1   Chop: (a) beginning position; (b) action.

Breathing Guidelines

Use the abdominal muscles to create intra-abdominal pressure (brace lightly). As the loads get heavier, take in a normal breath at the beginning position and hold that breath while bracing through the **sticking point** (the most difficult point in the exercise's range of motion) of the movement, followed by an exhale.

Exercise Modifications and Variations

Once the tall kneeling version is mastered, change the stimulus by progressing to a bilateral standing position, and then increase the complexity by going to a staggered stance, either standing or half-kneeling.

Coaching Tips

Monitor the athlete for trunk position and stability, and watch for flexion and extension of the lumbar spine while doing the movement. Some rotation between the pelvis in the rib cage is acceptable. If the athlete cannot execute the movement without lumbar flexion or extension, lighten the load until the athlete can demonstrate proficiency.

LIFT

Primary Muscles Trained

The lift is another rotary stabilization exercise using similar muscle chains as the chop, but in an opposite manner. The muscles of the torso work to stabilize (transversus abdominis, internal obliques, external obliques, multifidi, and quadratus lumborum). The muscles of the upper extremity are responsible for the lifting movement (pectoralis major, pectoralis minor, latissimus dorsi, trapezius, rhomboids, anterior deltoid, posterior deltoid, biceps, and triceps). Muscles of the hip are used to stabilize the pelvis (gluteus maximus, gluteus medius, adductor magnus, adductor longus). The specific muscles recruited vary based on the progression.

Beginning Position

- Begin in a tall kneeling position with the knees flexed to 90 degrees.
- Keep the hips in neutral extension, and have a neutral spine.
- Grasp the resistance with both hands by reaching down and across diagonally at approximately 45 degrees below parallel (a).

Movement Phases

1. Maintain a tall torso and brace lightly with the abdominals in preparation.
2. Using the arms as the prime movers, pull the resistance from the outside of the hip toward the midchest.
3. When the hands reach the midchest, push the resistance up toward the ceiling at a 45-degree angle while maintaining a neutral pelvis.
4. A small rotation of the torso on the pelvis is acceptable, but the focus is on maintaining overall stability.
5. At the end of the upward movement, the arms should make a 45-degree angle with the ceiling (b).

Figure 8.2 Lift: (a) beginning position; (b) action.

6. Complete the repetition by eccentrically controlling the load as the hands return to the midchest and then proceed down to the beginning position toward the outside of the hip.

7. Repeat for the required number of repetitions, then switch sides.

Breathing Guidelines

Use the abdominal muscles to create intra-abdominal pressure (brace lightly). As the loads get heavier, take in a normal breath at the beginning position and hold that breath, bracing through the sticking point of the movement, then exhale.

Exercise Modifications and Variations

Once the tall kneeling version is mastered, change the stimulus by progressing to a bilateral standing position, and then increase the complexity by going to a staggered stance, either standing or half-kneeling.

Coaching Tips

Monitor the athlete for trunk position and stability, and watch for flexion and extension of the lumbar spine during the movements. Some rotation between the pelvis and the rib cage is acceptable. If the athlete cannot execute the movement without lumbar flexion or extension, then lighten the load until the athlete can maintain a stable torso.

PALLOF PRESS

Primary Muscles Trained

The Pallof press is a rotary stabilization exercise. The muscles of the torso work to stabilize (transversus abdominis, internal obliques, external obliques, multifidi, and quadratus lumborum). The muscles of the upper extremity are responsible for the pressing movement (pectoralis major, pectoralis minor, latissimus dorsi, trapezius, rhomboids, anterior deltoid, posterior deltoid, biceps, and triceps). Muscles of the hip are used to stabilize the pelvis (gluteus maximus, gluteus medius, adductor magnus, adductor longus). The specific muscles recruited vary based on the progression.

Beginning Position

- Begin in a tall kneeling position with the knees flexed to 90 degrees.
- Keep the hips in neutral extension, and have a neutral spine.
- Grasp the resistance with both hands at touching the midchest (a).

Movement Phases

1. Maintain a tall torso, and brace lightly with the abdominals in preparation.
2. Using the arms as the prime movers, press the resistance straight out from the midchest until the arms are fully extended straight in front of the chest (b).
3. Flex at the elbows and extend at the shoulders to return to the beginning position with the hands at the midchest.
4. Throughout the repetition, maintain a stable torso and pelvis; there should not be any rotation.

5. At the midpoint of the repetition, the arms should be parallel to the floor.
6. Repeat for the required number of repetitions, then switch sides.

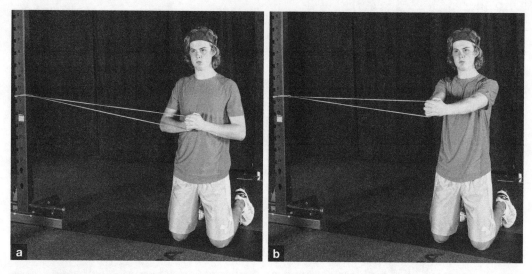

Figure 8.3 Pallof press: *(a)* beginning position; *(b)* action.

Breathing Guidelines

Use the abdominal muscles to create intra-abdominal pressure (brace lightly). As the loads get heavier, take in a normal breath at the beginning position and hold that breath, bracing through the sticking point of the movement, then exhale.

Exercise Modifications and Variations

Once the tall kneeling version is mastered, change the stimulus by progressing to a bilateral standing position, and then increase the complexity by going to a staggered stance, either standing or half-kneeling.

Coaching Tips

Monitor the athlete for trunk position and stability, and watch for rotation of the torso during the movement. If the athlete cannot execute the movement while maintaining a stable torso, then lighten the load until the athlete can.

LANDMINE RAINBOW

Primary Muscles Trained

The landmine rainbow helps develop rotary anatomical core stability with a high muscular demand for both prime movers and stabilizers. This exercise requires stabilizing the pelvis and torso (serratus anterior, internal and external obliques, rectus abdominis, quadratus lumborum, multifidi, and erector spinae), while generating force through the upper body (pectoralis major and minor, rhomboids, trapezius, deltoids, biceps, and triceps).

The muscles of the hip and lower extremities also contribute to the stabilization, to varying degrees, based on the progression (gluteus maximus, gluteus medius, adductor magnus, adductor longus).

Beginning Position

- Begin in a tall kneeling position in front of a landmine with the knees flexed to 90 degrees.
- Keep the hips in neutral extension and maintain a neutral spine.
- Grasp the barbell with both hands at midchest level (not shown), then press it up and away from the chest and shoulders by extending the elbows (a).

Movement Phases

1. Maintain a tall torso, and brace lightly with the abdominals in preparation.
2. Alternately lift and lower the bar from side (b) to side (c), following the path of an arc.
3. As the bar is rotated from side to side, the elbow of the arm doing the eccentric action (the top arm) stays relatively straight. The arm doing the concentric action (the bottom arm) flexes slightly at the elbow.
4. A small degree of dissociation between the pelvis and the rib cage is acceptable, but the emphasis is on maintaining stability of the torso and pelvis; it is not intended to be a rotary power exercise.

Breathing Guidelines

Use the abdominal muscles to create intra-abdominal pressure (brace). As the loads get heavier, take in a normal breath at the beginning position with the elbows extended and the bar centered on the chest. Hold that breath and brace through the sticking point of the movement, then exhale while returning to the beginning position.

Exercise Modifications and Variations

Once the tall kneeling version is mastered, change the stimulus by progressing to a bilateral standing position, and then increase the complexity by going to a staggered stance, either standing or half-kneeling. If a landmine attachment is not available, the end of the Olympic barbell can be placed in a corner of the gym. The walls may need to be cushioned to protect the surface. Alternatively, two Olympic plates can be placed flat on the floor, with one against each wall or side by side. The end of the bar can be placed where the two plates meet.

Coaching Tips

Monitor the athlete for trunk position and stability. Watch for flexion, extension, or excessive rotation of the lumbar spine as the athlete goes through the movement. A small amount of rotation between the pelvis in the rib cage is acceptable. If the athlete cannot execute the movement without lumbar flexion, extension, or excessive rotation, then lighten the load until the athlete can maintain a stable torso, or consider using a training bar instead of an Olympic barbell.

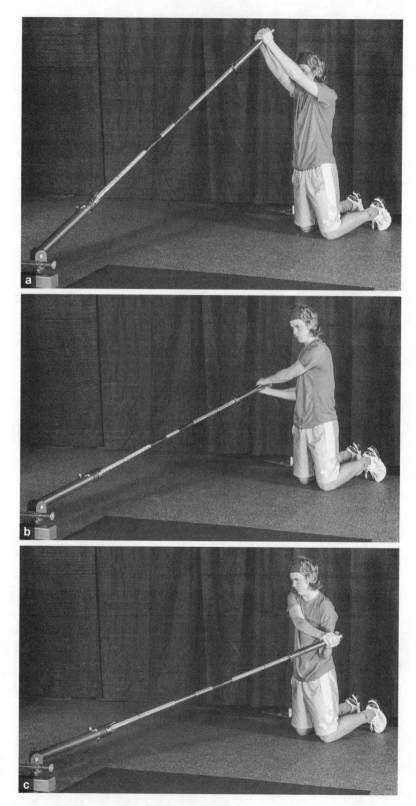

Figure 8.4 Landmine rainbow: *(a)* beginning position; *(b)* action to one side; *(c)* action to the other side.

PULLOVER

Primary Muscles Trained

When performing the pullover, generate the movement using the upper extremities (latissimus dorsi, triceps, teres major, and anterior deltoid). To create a stable base for the upper body action, actively stabilize the anatomical core (rectus abdominis, internal and external obliques).

Beginning Position

- Lie supine on a flat bench with the knees flexed and the feet flat on the floor. If a neutral back position with feet on the floor cannot be attained, elevate the feet on a box (or two) placed at the foot of the bench.
- Grasp one dumbbell with both hands, and while cupping one end of the dumbbell, hold it straight above the chest with the elbows flexed to approximately 10 degrees (a).

Movement Phases

1. Brace lightly with the abdominals in preparation.
2. Maintaining the approximately 10 degrees of elbow flexion throughout the movement, flex the shoulder lowering the load overhead.
3. At the bottom of the movement, when feeling a stretch through the latissimus dorsi, maintain a neutral spine by using the abdominals to resist extension through the lumbar spine (b).
4. Extend through the shoulder joint, bringing the arms back to the beginning position.

Figure 8.5   Pullover: (a) beginning position; (b) action.

Breathing Guidelines

In the beginning position, take in a breath and hold that breath to create some intra-abdominal pressure through the eccentric phase of the repetition, exhaling through the sticking point of the concentric phase.

Spotting Guidelines

Help the athlete grasp the dumbbell or kettlebell with both hands by holding the weight securely; wait for a clear verbal command from the athlete to let go of the load. As the athlete lowers and lifts the weight, keep the hands close to the load throughout the range. If the athlete requires assistance, assist at the load (dumbbell or kettlebell), not by supporting the athlete's arms.

Exercise Modifications and Variations

The pullover can be modified to accommodate equipment availability by using a kettlebell. If the goal is regressing or progressing the demand on the abdominals to stabilize the anatomical core, there are several variations. To regress the anatomical core stabilization demand, start in a supine position on the floor rather than a flat bench. To add more demand to the abdominals from the floor-based variation, position the feet off the floor with the knees and hips flexed to 90 degrees. Even more challenge can be applied to the abdominals by extending the knees with the hips positioned in 45 to 90 degrees of flexion (the less flexion, the more load on the abdominals). To add posterior chain activation (glutes, hamstrings, erector spinae) while challenging anatomical core stabilization, consider the cross-bench technique. Position the body perpendicular to the long axis of a weight bench. The posterior shoulder and upper thoracic are supported by the bench, but the rest of the torso is self-supported in a bridge position. The hips are in neutral and the knees flexed to 90 degrees and feet flat on the floor.

Coaching Tips

Place fingertips under the athlete's lower back in the beginning position to make sure the back is neutral. Cue by saying "keep the ribs stable" through the range. Feel for any change in the pressure as the athlete goes through the repetition. If the pressure on the fingertips decreases, the athlete is extending the lumbar spine and not stabilizing the torso.

DEAD BUG

Primary Muscles Trained

The dead bug trains the many parts of the abdominals (rectus abdominis, transversus abdominis, internal oblique, and external oblique).

Beginning Position

- Lie supine on the floor with the hips and knees flexed to 90 degrees and the ankles dorsiflexed.
- Flex the shoulders to 90 degrees with the elbows in full extension, actively reaching toward the ceiling (a).
- Keep the arms and thighs perpendicular to the floor.
- The lower back should be in a neutral position, without a visible gap between the back and the floor.

Movement Phases

1. Contract the abdominals to brace the torso and resist lumbar extension throughout the repetition.

2. Aggressively reach the arms toward the ceiling throughout the repetition.

3. Extend the hip and knee of one leg while continuing to use the abdominals to resist lumbar extension until the leg is almost parallel to but not touching the floor (b).

4. Flex the hip and knee to return to the beginning position without any loss in torso position.

5. Repeat the action with the other leg.

Figure 8.6   Dead bug: (a) beginning position; (b) action.

Breathing Guidelines

In the beginning position, take in a breath and hold that breath to create some intra-abdominal pressure through the eccentric phase of the repetition as the extremities are lowered toward the floor. Then exhale through the sticking point while returning to the beginning position.

Exercise Modifications and Variations

Once stabilizing the torso while moving one leg at a time is achieved, the dead bug can be progressed by adding in simultaneous flexion of the contralateral shoulder to the extension of the hip. In other words, if extending the right leg, continue to aggressively reach the right arm toward the ceiling, while flexing the left shoulder until the right leg and left shoulder are almost parallel to the floor. A variation that adds significant challenge to the rectus abdominis is the double-leg dead bug. Aggressively reach both arms toward the ceiling while extending both legs simultaneously until they are almost parallel to but not touching the floor.

Coaching Tips

Kneel beside the athlete and place the fingertips between the floor and the lumbar spine to monitor stability of the torso throughout the range of motion. If the pressure in the fingertips decreases as the athlete goes through the repetition (typically during the eccentric phase), cue the athlete to better control the torso using the abdominals, or regress the exercise by reducing the range of motion.

LEG LOWER

Primary Muscles Trained

This anatomical core exercise challenges stability using muscles of the anterior chain including the rectus abdominis, rectus femoris, and iliopsoas; with assistance from the internal oblique, external oblique, and transversus abdominis.

Beginning Position

- Lie supine on the floor with both knees extended and the hips flexed to 90 degrees, such that the legs are perpendicular to the floor.
- Dorsiflex the ankles.
- Flex the shoulders to 90 degrees and aggressively reach toward the ceiling (a).
- The lower back should be in a neutral position without a visible gap between the athlete and the floor.

Movement Phases

1. Contract the abdominals to brace the torso and resist lumbar extension throughout the repetition.
2. Aggressively reach the arms toward the ceiling throughout the repetition.
3. Aggressively reach through the heels throughout the repetition.
4. Slowly lower one leg—keeping the knee fully extended—while continuing to reach with the other leg and both arms still reaching toward the ceiling. Use the abdominals to resist lumbar extension as the leg lowers.
5. Lower the leg until it is parallel to the floor, but not touching the floor (b). Continue reaching through the heel of that leg as though trying to actively lengthen it.
6. Flex at the hip to raise the leg to return to the beginning position without any loss in torso position.
7. Repeat with the other leg.

Figure 8.7 Leg lower: (a) beginning position; (b) action.

Breathing Guidelines

In the beginning position, take in a breath and hold that breath, creating and maintaining intra-abdominal pressure through the eccentric phase of the repetition as the leg is lowered toward the floor. Then exhale while returning to the beginning position.

Exercise Modifications and Variations

Once torso stability while lowering one leg at a time is established, the leg lower exercise can be progressed by simultaneously lowering both legs while keeping the shoulders flexed to 90 degrees and the arms aggressively reaching toward the ceiling. Another way to add challenge to a leg lower is by moving the arms from a position of being perpendicular to the floor to an overhead reach for either the single-leg or double-leg version.

Coaching Tips

Kneel beside the athlete and place the fingertips between the floor and the lumbar spine to monitor the stability of the torso throughout the range of motion. If the pressure in the fingertips decreases as the athlete goes through the repetition (typically during the eccentric phase), cue the athlete to better control the torso using the abdominals, or reduce the range of motion.

CABLE HIP FLEXION

Primary Muscles Trained

The flexors of the hip, including the rectus femoris and iliopsoas, are the prime movers, but other muscles contribute to the stabilization of the movement based on the beginning position, including the rectus abdominis, internal obliques, external obliques, transversus abdominis, gluteus maximus, gluteus medius, quadratus lumborum, lumbar extensors.

Beginning Position

- Lie supine on the floor with both legs extended on the floor.
- Place the arms on the floor at the body's sides.
- Place a cable attachment on one foot.
- Dorsiflex both ankles *(a)*.

Movement Phases

1. Brace with the abdominals to stabilize the torso and maintain the contraction throughout the set.
2. Isometrically extend the hip of the nonactive leg (the leg without the cable attachment) by lightly pressing the straight leg into the floor.
3. Concentrically flex the hip and knee with the cable attachment to bring the knee as high as possible without losing the neutral torso position. The goal is to flex the hip to more than 90 degrees (to get the thigh beyond perpendicular to the floor) *(b)*.
4. Maintain the dorsiflexed ankle throughout the repetition.
5. Eccentrically extend the hip and knee to return to the beginning position without losing torso position.
6. Maintain the light isometric extension of the nonactive leg throughout the repetition.
7. Repeat for the required number of repetitions, then switch legs.

Breathing Guidelines

Use the abdominal muscles to create intra-abdominal pressure (brace lightly). As the loads get heavier, take in a normal breath at the beginning position and hold that breath, bracing through the sticking point of the movement, then exhale.

Figure 8.8 Cable hip flexion: *(a)* beginning position; *(b)* action.

Exercise Modifications and Variations

Increase the challenge of cable hip flexion by progressing from supine to standing to a plank position. The first progression from the single-leg supine hip flexion is moving to supine double-leg hip flexion—working both legs, attached to the cable, at the same time, rather than individually. For single-leg standing cable hip flexion, face away from the cable attachment on the low pulley and stabilize through the hip, back, and abdominals while lifting the resistance by flexing at the hip and knee. Again, dorsiflexion is maintained throughout the repetition. Try to lift the thigh above parallel to the floor. Finally, get into an extended front plank position (push-up position) facing away from a low pulley and with a Valslide under one or both feet. Maintaining a neutral back position throughout the movement, perform either a single- or double-leg cable hip flexion.

Coaching Tips

Place the fingers or hand on the athlete's lower back to monitor for any flexion or extension. Does the athlete flex the lumbar spine while flexing the hip? This is a compensation pattern where the athlete is likely using the rectus abdominis to posteriorly tilt the pelvis and assist with the apparent hip flexion.

Ensure that the athlete can flex the hip beyond 90 degrees. If that is not possible with an external load, then assess whether the athlete can do it using body weight. If not, then it is time to assess whether it is an activation or strength issue or a mobility issue.

ROLL OUT

Primary Muscles Trained

The roll out is an anterior anatomical core exercise targeting the rectus abdominis, internal obliques, external obliques, and transversus abdominis as the primary stabilizers of the torso. The latissimus dorsi, triceps, and posterior deltoid are the prime movers for upper body action, and the rectus femoris and iliopsoas stabilize the hip joint.

Beginning Position

- Kneel in front of a stability ball and place the forearms parallel to one another on top of the ball.
- Assume a front plank position with toes on the floor and forearms on the ball.
- The body should be in a straight line from the top of the head to the ankles (a).

Movement Phases

1. Brace with the abdominals, and flex the quadriceps to maintain a straight-line body position.
2. Press forearms into the ball, protracting slightly at the shoulders.
3. While maintaining a straight-line body position, flex at the shoulder joints to roll the forearms and the stability ball upward (away from the center of mass) as far as possible without losing body position and without feeling a strain in the lower back (b).
4. Return to the beginning position.
5. Do the required number of repetitions.

Figure 8.9   Roll out: (a) beginning position; (b) action.

Breathing Guidelines

In the beginning position, take in a breath and hold that breath, creating and maintaining intra-abdominal pressure through the eccentric phase of the repetition. Then exhale while returning to the beginning position.

Exercise Modifications and Variations

The roll out can be progressed by adjusting the beginning position to an extended plank or push-up position with the hands on the ball rather than the forearms. If the athlete requires a regression, start from a tall kneeling position with the forearms on the stability ball.

Coaching Tips

Roll out with the ball to the point where the athlete feels the abdominals working but before the point of feeling any straining in the lower back.

Also watch that the shoulders stay in a strong and slightly protracted position, rather than letting them retract or elevate during the exercise.

BALL HIP FLEXION

Primary Muscles Trained

The movers for ball hip flexion are the rectus femoris and iliopsoas, but this exercise requires a lot of stabilization, too. Stabilization of the torso requires the work of the rectus abdominis, internal obliques, external obliques, and transversus abdominis. Stabilization across the knee and ankle is facilitated by the vastus medialis, vastus intermedius, vastus lateralis, and tibialis anterior. Stabilization at the shoulders relies on the pectoralis minor, pectoralis major, serratus anterior, anterior deltoid, and triceps.

Beginning Position

- Assume a quadruped position on the floor with a stability ball on the floor behind the feet.
- Brace with the abdominals to stabilize the torso. Place one foot on the ball and then the other (not shown) to move into a push-up position with the hands on the floor and both feet on the stability ball (a).

Movement Phases

1. While maintaining a neutral torso, flex the hips and knees to draw the knees up toward the chest without rounding the back (b).
2. Reverse the movement, extending the hips and knees to return to the beginning position.

Breathing Guidelines

Use the abdominal muscles to create intra-abdominal pressure (brace lightly). Take in a normal breath at the beginning position and hold that breath, bracing through the sticking point of the movement, then exhale.

Exercise Modifications and Variations

From the basic bilateral version, ball hip flexion can be progressed to a single-leg version, starting with only one foot on the ball and the other leg extended parallel to the

Figure 8.10 Ball hip flexion: *(a)* beginning position; *(b)* action.

weight-bearing leg. Then perform the hip and knee flexion, drawing only the weight-bearing knee up toward the chest. The non-weight-bearing leg remains extended in line with the torso. Ball hip flexion can also be done as a pike movement where the knees stay in full extension. Rather than flexing the knees and the hips to draw the knees toward the chest, flex at the hips only. In this version the knees stay fully extended and the hips elevate as the feet are drawn up toward the arms. The pike version can also be performed bilaterally or unilaterally.

Coaching Tips
Emphasize movement at the hip and watch for accessory motion at the lumbar spine. If the athlete is combining hip flexion with lumbar flexion, provide cues to maintain a stable torso while using the hip joints.

LATERAL MINI BAND WALK

Primary Muscles Trained
This exercise is used to target the primary hip abductors, including the gluteus medius and gluteus minimus, with assistance from the tensor fasciae latae. The gluteus maximus is involved as a secondary abductor of the hip.

Beginning Position
- Position a mini band around both legs on the upper tibia, just below the knees.
- Stand with a hip-width stance.

Movement Phases

1. Without allowing either knee to fall inward and maintaining a level pelvis and level shoulders, step laterally by abducting at the lead hip.

2. Stabilize over the lead leg, maintain a level pelvis and level shoulders, and eccentrically control the adduction of the trailing hip, returning to the beginning position.

3. Repeat for the required number of repetitions or distance in each direction.

Figure 8.11   Lateral mini band walk: action.

Breathing Guidelines

Use the abdominal muscles to create intra-abdominal pressure (brace lightly). Take in a normal breath at the beginning position and hold that breath, bracing through the sticking point of the movement, then exhale.

Exercise Modifications and Variations

Start with a light or medium mini band. When the movement can be performed without compensation (like rocking side to side), increase the challenge by using the next heavier mini band.

Coaching Tips

Cue the athlete to maintain a level pelvis and level shoulders. One effective cue is "Try not to teeter-totter the shoulders."

MINI BAND EXTERNAL ROTATION

Primary Muscles Trained

This external rotation exercise targets the deep lateral rotators of the hip, including the piriformis, gemelli, obturators, and quadratus femoris.

Beginning Position

- Position a mini band around both legs on the upper tibia, just below the knees.
- Stand with a hip-width stance in a semi-squat position with knees in 70 to 80 degrees of flexion (a).

Movement Phases

1. Maintain a stable pelvis and torso through the set.
2. Keep one leg stable as the other leg rolls into hip internal rotation as far as is comfortable (b). Pause, and then externally rotate the working leg as far as possible against the resistance of the mini band (c).
3. The ankle will go through closed chain eversion and inversion, but the foot should remain in contact with the floor throughout.
4. Repeat for the required number of repetitions, then switch sides.

Figure 8.12   Mini band external rotation: (a) beginning position; (b-c) action.

Breathing Guidelines

Use the abdominal muscles to create intra-abdominal pressure (brace lightly). Take in a normal breath at the beginning position and hold that breath, bracing through the sticking point of the movement, then exhale.

Exercise Modifications and Variations

To increase the challenge, use the next heavier resistance mini band. To increase the neural complexity, alternate from one side to the other, rather than repeating all repetitions on one side and then the other.

Coaching Tips

Have the athlete place the hands on the hips at the top of the pelvis to monitor the stability of the pelvis and isolate the movement to the hip joint. It is also a good opportunity to monitor the alignment of the athlete's spine while performing a discrete hip movement from a semi-squat.

90-DEGREE MINI BAND STEP OUT

Primary Muscles Trained

This version of the step out exercise uses the gluteus medius, tensor fasciae latae, and gluteus minimus. With the hip in a flexed position, there is also a load on the piriformis, gemelli, obturators, and quadratus femoris.

Beginning Position

- Position a mini band around both legs on the upper tibia, just below the knees.
- Stand with a hip-width stance in a semi-squat position with knees in 70 to 80 degrees of flexion *(a)*.

Movement Phases

1. Anchor with one leg while performing a 90-degree opening step with the other leg by rotating the pelvis on the femur of the anchor leg against the resistance of the mini band *(b)*.
2. The head, torso, and pelvis move together throughout the 90-degree opening step.
3. Do not let the knee of the anchor leg fall inward.
4. At the end of the opening step, place the stepping leg on the floor for a pause *(c)* and then perform a controlled return to the beginning position.
5. Throughout the entire movement, keep the pelvis centered between both feet.
6. Perform all repetitions on one side and then the other.

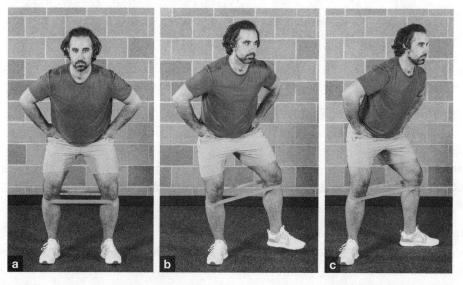

Figure 8.13 90-degree mini band step out: *(a)* beginning position; *(b-c)* action.

Breathing Guidelines

Use the abdominal muscles to create intra-abdominal pressure (brace lightly). Take in a normal breath at the beginning position and hold that breath, bracing through the sticking point of the movement, then exhale.

Exercise Modifications and Variations

To increase the challenge, use the next heavier resistance mini band. To increase the neural complexity, alternate from one side to the other, rather than repeating all repetitions on one side and then the other.

Coaching Tips

Instruct the athlete to actively work against the band with the stepping leg. Bring the athlete's attention to the feeling in the lateral hip of both the anchor leg and the stepping leg to learn to identify how the muscles control the hip work.

PILATES RING ADDUCTOR SQUEEZE

Primary Muscles Trained

The adductor squeeze is used to develop the adductor magnus, adductor longus, adductor brevis, gracilis, and pectineus. Each muscle's contribution varies based on hip position.

Beginning Position

- Lie supine with the knees flexed to approximately 90 degrees with both feet flat on the floor (hook-lying) and spaced hip-width apart.
- Assume a neutral pelvis and spine position.
- Place a Pilates ring between both thighs, just above the knee joint.

Movement Phases

1. While maintaining the neutral pelvis position, squeeze both thighs into the Pilates ring, compressing the ring with an adduction and internal rotation force.
2. Eccentrically control the abduction and external rotation while return to the beginning position.

Breathing Guidelines

Use the abdominal muscles to create intra-abdominal pressure (brace lightly). Take in a normal breath at the beginning position and hold that breath, bracing through the sticking point of the movement, then exhale.

Exercise Modifications and Variations

The position of the hip changes the contribution of force from the different hip adductors and internal rotators; as a result there are many variations to challenge the adductors. From the supine hook-lying position, flex at the hips into a supine 90-90 position with the knees stacked above the hips (with the hips and knees flexed to 90 degrees). Still lying on the floor, the Pilates ring can be moved to the ankles for a straight-line (neutral hip and knee position) adductor squeeze from both prone and supine positions. Then stand to perform the Pilates ring adductor squeeze exercise.

LATERAL KNEELING ABDUCTOR LIFTOFF

Primary Muscles Trained

The lateral kneeling abductor liftoff is an end-range horizontal abduction strengthening exercise from the hip that also requires trunk stabilization. The primary muscles used to complete the action include the gluteus medius, the gluteus minimus, and the tensor fasciae latae. This exercise helps athletes use their entire active range of motion.

Beginning Position

- Assume a quadruped position on the floor with a neutral pelvis and spine.
- The athlete extends one leg straight out to the side with the hip flexed (60-90 degrees) and horizontally abducted (a).

Movement Phases

1. Maintaining a level pelvis and neutral spine, lift the straight leg slightly off the floor using only the lateral hip muscles (b).
2. Pause, then return to the beginning position.
3. Perform all repetitions on one side and then the other.

Figure 8.14 Lateral kneeling abductor liftoff: (a) beginning position; (b) action.

Breathing Guidelines

Use the abdominal muscles to create intra-abdominal pressure (brace lightly). Take in a normal breath at the beginning position and hold that breath, bracing through the sticking point of the movement, then exhale.

Exercise Modifications and Variations

To increase the challenge of both the abduction and anatomical core stabilization, horizontally abduct at both hips into a half-kneeling groin-stretch position. This results in a stretch in the adductors in the beginning position and through the liftoff.

Coaching Tips

Place one hand on the athlete's lower back to monitor and provide sensory feedback to the athlete, indicating how stable the pelvis and torso are.

SIDE PLANK WITH BOTTOM LEG SUPPORT OR TOP LEG SUPPORT

Primary Muscles Trained

The muscles trained depend on which version is performed. When doing a side plank with bottom leg support, the primary muscles trained are the gluteus medius, gluteus minimus, and tensor fasciae latae. When side planking with top leg support, the adductor magnus, adductor brevis, adductor longus, gracilis, and pectineus are the primary targets. Both versions also place a high demand on the muscles of the torso, including the internal and external obliques, quadratus lumborum, and longissimus thoracis.

Beginning Position

- Lie propped up on one elbow on one side, with the elbow aligned below the shoulder joint.
- Abduct the shoulder to approximately 70 to 80 degrees, and lightly brace the muscles of the torso while lifting the hips off the floor to bring the body into neutral spine alignment. This is the side plank beginning position (*a*).

Movement Phases

1. When performing the bottom-leg-supported side plank, abduct the hip of the non-weight-bearing leg (the top leg) to lift it approximately 6 to 8 inches (15-20 cm) off the bottom supporting leg.
2. When performing the top-leg-supported side plank, flex the hip and knee of the bottom leg while placing the top leg, which becomes the new weight-bearing leg, on the floor (not shown).
3. Hold this position for the required duration and number of repetitions.

Breathing Guidelines

Breathe with a natural rhythm throughout the exercise.

Exercise Modifications and Variations

In one variation of the bottom-leg-supported side plank, place a small stability ball between the ankles. This removes the active abduction of holding the top leg elevated, but squeezing the ball with the feet provides some isometric adduction. The intensity of top-leg-supported side plank can be increased by placing the top leg on a bench (*b*) or box (this version is known as the **Copenhagen plank**).

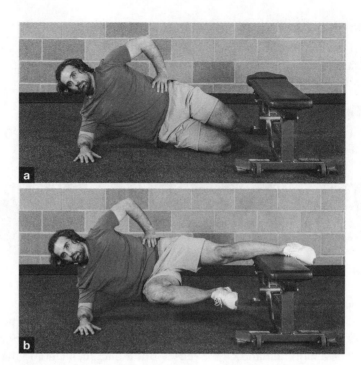

Figure 8.15 Side plank with bottom leg support: *(a)* beginning position; *(b)* Copenhagen plank version.

Coaching Tips

It is a big step for the athlete to go from a floor-based foot placement to the elevated version. Micro-adjust the intensity by positioning the athlete with more or with less of the lower leg supported by the box or bench. Also, help the athlete maintain a position where the frontal plane remains perpendicular to the floor. Subconsciously, athletes often roll the body forward slightly to gain more assistance from the rectus abdominis.

PART III

PROGRAM DESIGN GUIDELINES AND SAMPLE PROGRAMS

9

OFF-SEASON PROGRAMMING

**MARK FITZGERALD (HIGH SCHOOL), MATT SHAW (COLLEGE),
MATT NICHOL (PROFESSIONAL)**

Off-season training can almost be thought of as the "in-season" for the hockey strength and conditioning professional. The off-season is the period where the hockey strength and conditioning professional has the most contact time with the athletes. This is when many physical capabilities can be addressed and improved upon.

GOALS AND OBJECTIVES

The off-season is the most valuable time for hockey athletes to improve physical development without the stress of academics and on-ice performance. The off-season can vary in length depending on the level the athlete is playing. High school and college athletes often have three to four months of uninterrupted training, while a professional athlete can have two to four months, depending upon the length of playoffs. Regardless of the length, the primary goal of the off-season period is to improve specific physical outputs in alignment with on-ice physical demands and prepare athletes for preseason training stress. The off-season should specifically intensify training stress from postseason and focus on the development and transferability of the force–velocity curve within applied motor patterns.

To complicate the issue, due to the violent nature of the sport many athletes need to begin their off-season period actively rehabilitating various injuries or subsequent compensation patterns that have accumulated during the season. Some even require surgical interventions to address these issues that could drastically change their off-season training schedules.

This chapter and the sample programs provided are written with the assumption that the athlete following this guidance has successfully completed the postseason phase and is healthy and fully able to participate in any off-season strength and conditioning program suggested.

Hockey is unique in that impulse during skating is much longer than the elastic nature of running-based sports. Strength and power development become even more influential in developing on-ice speed and force expression. A large emphasis should be placed on the three-dimensional aspects of the hockey stride and each force vector's relative contributions to force production on the ice. Hip extension, abduction, and external rotation all contribute to the development of on-ice power and speed. Likewise, strengthening the adductors in the off-season is important because they are constantly lengthened and weakened across the in-season period without proper maintenance (4). The strength and conditioning professional should keep these goals in mind and use the off-season to leverage physical performance changes in alignment with on-ice performance demand.

Strength and conditioning professionals are faced with challenges related to maximizing results across a team with varying ranges of ability. Flexibility of program methodology, exercise selection, and progression of stress become critical in managing individual differences in programming. With off-season training completed primarily during the summer, athletes may be at home, traveling on vacation, or on-site and overseen by the strength and conditioning professional. The best off-season program is the one that is organized and scaled to maximize consistency, logistics, and coaching effectiveness across team integration.

LENGTH, STRUCTURE, AND ORGANIZATION

Early off-season mesocycles are largely dependent on the length of the hockey team's off-season schedule and the goal orientation of physical development. Teams that make it deep into playoffs may deprioritize specific hypertrophy mesocycles in the off-season. When this occurs, hypertrophy methods of training can be shifted to accessory work within shorter off-seasons. However, teams that do have longer off-seasons or have individuals with lower training ages may find it valuable to include hypertrophy phases to develop a larger foundational volume of training. It is recommended that these phases account for six weeks or less of total time in the off-season (two three-week mesocycles). Hypertrophy training can serve as a linear increase in training intensity between general physical preparation (i.e., bodyweight up to 65% of an athlete's estimated 1RM) and later strength-based mesocycles (>80% of an athlete's estimated 1RM). Jump, throwing, and speed training should still be present in hypertrophy phases to continue progressions from the general preparatory phase. Jump or sprint movements can parallel hypertrophy methods by selecting loaded variations with longer impulse times and higher time under tension. Examples include dumbbell-loaded jumps, moderately loaded medicine ball throw variations (6-10 lb; 2.5-4.5 kg), and sled marches or sprints. Exercises during this phase should include a mix of large complex foundational movements and more isolated exercises to develop supporting agonists. The hypertrophy phase (see table 9.2) illustrates a four-day split that uses a combination of autoregulated progressive resistance exercise (APRE), accessory work, and tempo training methods. The benefit of using APRE during hypertrophy training is the inclusion of sets to fatigue (or technical failure) and being able to derive estimations of an athlete's 1RM for later mesocycles. Accessory work can use higher repetition methods or include tempo sets to force the athlete to control full range of motion and increase time under tension.

Mid off-season transitions programming toward higher intensity training and neuromuscular adaptations. As athletes have progressed across the early off-season training period, they should have established a large base of training that has created technical proficiency using light to moderate loads. Athletes should also have a foundational base of jumping, plyometrics, throwing, and sprinting. Mid off-season training should include three three-week mesocycles using concurrent training to develop high intensity strength, power, speed, and work capacity. Within the concurrent mesocycle example (see table 9.3), athletes are exposed to two days of high intensity strength work with unique focuses, one day of power or speed-based training, and one day to maintain exposure to higher-repetition-based training methods. An example of this structure would be day 1, eccentric or isometric strength; day 2, power and speed; day 3, concentric strength (with or without preceding eccentric movement); and day 4, hypertrophy or escalating density circuits. The advantage to using a concurrent training split is that it maintains exposure to multiple physical qualities within each week. Within this format, 50%

of the training days still prioritize higher intensity resistance training, while the other half of training maintains exposure to dynamic effort training and the maintenance of work capacity. Having consistent weekly exposure to speed and power training in the off-season allows athletes periods of time to develop a technical base under higher velocity training and longer high-quality exposure across the summer. This can be more advantageous than block training, where athletes may only be prescribed a single three-week power and speed mesocycle later in the summer. The final day of the week allows flexibility for individual developmental goals within the team. This repetition effort day can be oriented toward aerobic endurance circuits to promote recovery and blood flow (older training ages), continued hypertrophy training for athletes needing to increase lean mass (younger training ages), or density circuits to help athletes improve body composition and general work capacity. Even though training is voluntary during the summer, the last training session of the week may be missed at times due to travel and vacations. Athletes can do these sessions while traveling, with minimal equipment and interruption to their schedules.

Within each mid off-season mesocycle, the resistance training days can be divided by specific qualities. Day 1 focuses on the development of eccentric or isometric strength, while the second resistance training day within the week focuses on concentric force production, either with or without an eccentric movement preceding it. This is important because resistance training intensity and methodology should account for the specificity of each muscle action. For instance, eccentric and isometric strength can be significantly higher than concentric-based strength levels within well-trained athletes. The intensities and training methods to improve upon each specific muscle action should be relative to the force capacity and training age of the athlete. Using day 1 of each mesocycle to focus on specific muscle-action-based resistance training allows athletes to develop higher levels of eccentric and isometric force, improving upon the potential of the muscle to handle higher loads during deceleration and strength within joint angles specific to hockey performance. Both eccentric and isometric muscle actions are prevalent in how a hockey athlete maintains skating depth, rapidly decelerates, and changes direction on the ice. The second resistance training day then focuses only on the concentric propulsive action of the muscle. Improving upon concentric force production is where athletes can make the largest change within stride force output outside of technical aspects of skating.

The concurrent training program is easy to scale by training age and reflects the development of the entire force–velocity curve. Scaling stress according to training age may mean using lower-intensity eccentric strength (80%-90% of an estimated 1RM) for younger athletes, and it could mean including weight releasers for above 100% of the concentric 1RM for supramaximal eccentrics among athletes of advanced training ages. Younger-training-aged athletes also benefit from submaximal loads with eccentric and isometric tempo to improve the coordination and technique of a movement. The intensity of tempo-based training should be progressed linearly over time and in each year's off-season because inappropriate prescription can create high levels of muscle damage. Additionally, the dynamic effort day can be scaled across mesocycles and according to individual athlete training age. For younger athletes it is important to select exercises that fit their training age and technical abilities while allowing them to create intent behind power and speed training. Loaded sprinting, throwing, and jumping variations may be safer alternatives than more advanced exercises until they can illustrate proper technique under higher velocities. As the training age of an athlete progresses, methods such as using a linear positional transducer (LPT) for autoregulating bar speed, and band- or cord-resisted exercises can be useful for improving power and speed. Unlike higher-intensity resistance training, which is almost always done within the sagittal plane, power and speed work should be trained three-dimensionally for the greatest transfer to hockey. Higher percentages of exercises should focus on linear, frontal, and transverse training. Specific power and speed adaptations, such as eccentric and concentric rate of force development, should be a focus during each mesocycle. Exercise variations can include dynamic reversals, where athletes decelerate into joint-specific angles of the stride and accelerate out as quickly as possible. This can be done within traditional exercises or using jump variations.

The late off-season period serves as the bridge between off-season training and the preparation of the athlete toward preseason training volumes. It is important that off-ice and on-ice training volumes assist athletes in preparing for the stress and demand that they will encounter on the ice during the preseason. If athletes have ice access, the resistance training frequency should begin to taper in the late off-season as the frequency and volume of on-ice training increases. This period is generally six to eight weeks in length and is composed of two to three mesocycles, with each of them two to three weeks long. An athlete's resistance training program may decrease to three days per week during this period to account for increases in on-ice or off-ice conditioning volume. With the increase in training volume directed toward conditioning, the day 4 repetition methods from mid off-season training are eliminated from the weekly structure. The program should prioritize higher percentages of training time toward speed and power development while decreasing strength exposure to one day per week. The week should be organized so that day 1 focuses on power work, day 2 on speed, and day 3 on strength development (see table 9.5). Athletes should be exposed to two to three days of on- or off-ice sprinting (4-12 s) to develop training frequency and weekly volume of high-speed exposure. An additional two to three days should be organized for interval-based training methods, varying from short to long durations (10 s to 2 min) to directly condition the athletes in preparation for preseason practice demands. Athletes who lack access to ice need to supplement with off-ice fitness methods (running and biking) in preparation for preseason training volumes. One of the biggest injury risks in the preseason period is lack of high-speed skating exposure on the hip flexors and adductors. Athletes can never replace the specificity of on-ice skating with off-ice methods such as sprinting; however, sprinting still maintains the cyclical gait and high-velocity hip flexion and extension. When athletes do not have access to ice, it becomes imperative to find the next closest modality, which in this case is off-ice sprinting and shuffling. It may be advantageous for athletes without ice access at home to return to institutional resources early, prior to preseason, to avoid an acute increase in on-ice stress beyond what they can physically handle.

High School

Off-season training for the high school hockey athlete should be focused on building strength and power. Ideally, the athlete has dedicated time away from the ice and can focus on resistance training and participating in other sports and activities. Typically, the high school athlete needs an increased focus during the off-season not only for effort and intensity but also for the education around basic exercise technique. Learning each movement phase of an exercise and why it is important is crucial for understanding what each phase means, which is incredibly valuable to young athletes as they progress through their careers.

Ideally, the off-season program for the high school athlete would be 8 to 12 weeks in length. This allows time for some complete rest after the hockey season as well as a two- to four-week postseason training block. The athlete may do a three-day or a four-day per week program, depending on activity level. This 8- to 12-week program is heavily focused on managing load and having the athlete learn how to control and execute each repetition of each movement with intent and purpose.

Option 1: Four Days per Week

The four-day program, for individuals not participating in other sports during the hockey off-season, is broken up in the following ways: Days 1 and 3 are focused on upper body movements, and days 2 and 4 are focused on lower body movements. The upper body movements are structured around horizontal and vertical motions, with the lower body movements focused on knee-dominant and hip-dominant actions. Ideally this is divided over a week in a way that allows the athlete to have some rest between days.

Monday: day 1

Tuesday: day 2

Wednesday: complete rest

Thursday: day 3

Friday: day 4

Saturday and Sunday: other activities and rest

Option 2: Three Days per Week

The three-day program is designed for the athlete who participates in a more rigorous off-season sport but is still looking to improve performance on the ice. Ideally, the three-day program is performed with a day off between sessions (e.g., Monday, Wednesday, and Friday). These sessions have a total body focus and aim to cover all the needs of the athlete regarding upper and lower body movements—hence the need for spacing out the training days. This option also allows the athlete to participate in off-season sports and activities.

College

College hockey is unique in that it has the longest in-season competition period across all NCAA sports. This creates difficulties among strength and conditioning professionals because off-season training takes place almost entirely during the NCAA's voluntary training periods and outside of the academic year. Therefore, team maturity and investment in voluntary off-season training are critical for developmental success. For many institutions, the college off-season process begins immediately following the postseason general physical preparation phase and near the conclusion of the academic year. Therefore, the off-season training period can range from four to six months until the next year's preseason period begins around September 1. As noted earlier, voluntary training may necessitate variations in program design because many athletes may not be training under a collegiate strength and conditioning professional's supervision or with equal equipment resources. Having variations in programs based upon training age, developmental goals, and equipment resources can improve training adherence and outcomes.

With such a long period of time to focus on physical development, it is easier to conceptualize off-season training in three main stages: early off-season, mid off-season, and late off-season. Early off-season is an ideal time to focus on developing a strong generalized foundation of hypertrophy and foundational resistance training. Hockey athletes must unload from significant on-ice training during this time while tissue stress is very high. In the mid off-season the athletes progress to the highest intensities of training, and the focus is on the development of the force–velocity curve and neuromuscular adaptations to training. During this time, voluntary on-ice training should be reestablished as athletes focus on power skating and skill development. It is important to consider both off-ice physical development and on-ice skill development because they may occur in parallel across the remainder of off-season training for those that have ice access. Finally, in late off-season the athletes should begin to taper lifting frequency and volume while simultaneously increasing exercise task intensity and specificity as close to skating demand as possible. Voluntary on-ice training during this period should begin reintroducing hockey athletes to small group skills and drills. This should take place in the final six to eight weeks prior to the start of preseason and should prepare them for the tissue demand and on-ice workload of preseason practices.

Professional

The NHL off-season can be anywhere from two to four months, depending upon whether athletes were on teams that qualified for the playoffs and how deep into the playoffs those teams went. To further complicate the issue, due to the violent nature of the sport, many athletes need to begin their off-season period actively rehabilitating various injuries or subsequent compensation patterns that have accumulated during the season. Some even require surgical interventions to address these issues, which could drastically change their off-season training schedules.

This chapter and the sample programs provided are written with the assumption that the athlete who would be following this guidance has successfully completed the postseason phase and is healthy and fully able to participate in any off-season strength and conditioning program suggested.

Successful hockey performance relies heavily on speed and power. The off-season is the time when improvements in these areas are made. As will be discussed in later chapters, the in-season training phase of the year is a challenging time to follow a regimented resistance training schedule, and consistently training for maximum strength or hypertrophy can be unsafe. Therefore, use the relatively short time of the off-season to make those qualities a priority and train for them. For most of the off-season phase, training takes place four days per week, typically occurring Monday, Tuesday, Thursday, and Friday. Any on-ice training should be scheduled around the resistance training. In the early off-season, any work done on the ice is typically skill-based technical training and is done on day 1 and day 3. The off-ice resistance training work is of slightly lower volume and intensity on these days. It is not advisable to do any tactical or on-ice conditioning work until the late off-season.

Goaltenders carry out a significantly lower volume of weight room work (approximately 25% less on average per phase). This is certainly not to suggest that resistance training is any less important for goaltenders; in fact, the opposite argument could be made. The reason is that a large percentage of the off-ice training performed by goaltenders comes in the form of training methods outside of the weight room (e.g., Pilates, yoga, ELDOA stretching) that are hard to capture with traditional programming conventions. It should also be noted that in the late off-season, goaltenders need to do very specialized technical training on ice for their own benefit but are also often called upon to practice with the rest of the athletes to create a high-quality training session, with the net result being a larger overall volume of on-ice work that must be accounted for from a recovery standpoint. The professional goaltender is a highly skilled athlete that needs less resistance training volume than skaters do.

RECOMMENDED EXERCISES

The key to maximizing off-season development is making subtle changes across mesocycles. Progressions can take the form of the dynamics of the exercise (tempo), the intensity of loading, or increased exercise complexity. Drastic changes in exercise selection should be avoided because they can lead to significant soreness. Creating consistency within movement patterns across mesocycles allows athletes to master muscle dynamics and sustain a longer period of positive adaptation. Therefore, select exercises that can be trained across the force–velocity curve and challenge the individual athlete appropriately based on orthopedics and technical ability. Exercise variations should be selected based upon training age and the individual athlete's ability to stabilize posture against external load. Core exercise variations for younger training ages should assist the athlete in maintaining stability and posture, while progressions of exercises for older training ages may increase demand to stabilize or the absolute loading potential of the exercise.

Exercises across the off-season should progress from general to specific. The fundamental pattern of movement may be the same, but the intensification of loading, range of motion, plane of motion, and velocity should all trend toward on-ice performance demand. Strength exercises should prioritize unilateral movements to improve the transfer of single-leg force output, stability, and proprioception involved within skating. Unilateral strength exercise selections should follow progressions of split squats, rear foot elevated split squats, reverse lunging, and off-box single-leg squats. This progression starts with higher floor contact and stability, then transitions into fully unilateral loading. Loading types such as dumbbells, barbell, or safety bar can create differences in center of mass; axial loading and stability and must be considered. The highest absolute loading unilaterally would be the hands-assisted safety bar split squat or reverse lunge variation, reserved for highly trained athletes. The inclusion of hands-assisted safety bar training allows athletes to increase stability (controlled through hand assistance as necessary) with lower orthopedic prerequisites to perform the movement, giving athletes the highest absolute unilateral training loads. Bilateral exercises such as the trap bar deadlift and front squat are still important to include because they improve postural strength and force production, and they can induce a significant hormonal response. For younger training-age athletes, postural strength and stability can drastically improve kinetic force transfer into the ice and decrease energy leaks within the trunk and pelvis. Older training-age athletes can progress the intensity of resistance training via the inclusion of accommodating resistance. Chains and bands can create additional stimuli to increase force output near end-range hip extension, increasing the demand within training.

Power and speed training should transition from heavier power training during the mid off-season to explosive or ballistic training in late off-season. Early establishment of foundational exercises such as the hex bar deadlift allows for late off-season progressions to higher velocity power clean pulls or loaded hex bar jumps. Strength and conditioning professionals can make use of velocity-based training (VBT; see chapter 4 for more detail). VBT refers to a system of training where the movement velocity of an exercise is measured using a specific device (e.g., a linear power transducer) for the sake of measuring exercise intensity and providing real-time feedback to the user (5). Research has shown that VBT can enhance neuromuscular performance and reduce neuromuscular fatigue associated with strength and power training (8). It has also been suggested that the real-time feedback during training sessions provided with VBT devices is more effective in increasing performance in sport-specific parameters when compared to traditional resistance training (6).

The use of LPTs during this type of training can give athletes access to programming based upon velocity ranges instead of inaccurate estimated training percentages. To improve upon stride outputs on-ice, athletes should focus their power training on improving long-impulse force production. However, exercises with short force impulse or plyometrics that are highly elastic should still be done for tendon health and overall athletic development. Movement dynamics and training tempo can be effective methods behind power and speed training. Maintaining normal exercises but altering the movement dynamics can create higher velocity variations behind almost any movement pattern. For instance, a dumbbell rear foot elevated split squat dynamic reversal can be a strong stimulus to improve eccentric rate of force production and deceleration capabilities of an athlete (see table 9.7, day 2). The athlete should be cued to rapidly pull into flexion and then explosively extend as quickly as possible against load. Within hockey, both the skate and skating mechanics remove significant aid from the muscles' stretch-shortening cycle and the elastic contributions of the Achilles tendon. The use of noncountermovement or concentric-only variations can be effective at teaching athletes to improve rate of force development with greater on-ice transfer. Exercises and jump variations from skating depth and concentric-only contraction are highly transferable constraints.

Complex training is another training strategy that can be useful in the off-season. **Complex training** refers to the combination of heavy resisted-strength exercises paired with a plyometric movement, such as a set of heavy barbell squats followed by a set of bodyweight jumps (1, 3).

Research has suggested that this method of training is superior to heavy load maximal resistance training or unloaded high velocity plyometrics in isolation (1, 3, 7). In addition to being a potentially superior method of developing power, it is certainly a more efficient method of training for the professional team sport athletes who have many other demands on their time and resources from technical and tactical sport training.

Previous studies have suggested that it might be maximally beneficial to allow for as much as two to six minutes of rest between the loaded and unloaded exercises (2). This is largely impractical in the world of strength and conditioning for professional team sport athletes. In our personal experiences of implementing this style of training with a wide age range of athletes, we have found that 60 seconds of rest may be sufficient to elicit a beneficial response. Although this is less than the full postactivation potentiation benefit that might be found by waiting three minutes longer, the trade-off effect is greater training density, a greater overall conditioning effect, and most importantly, greater buy-in and greater intention during training among the athletes.

For the sake of this book, we have made some suggestions as to what the unresisted or the plyometric movements might be, but coaches should choose options that best suit their own specific training environments and the needs of their individual athletes.

With traditional resistance training movements all predominantly conducted in the sagittal plane, it is important to intentionally select exercises that expand into other planes of motion. The ankle, hip, thoracic spine, shoulder, and neck should be challenged consistently in multiple planes of motion. Exercises can be arranged as a matrix, where the athlete moves through sagittal, frontal, and transverse plane repetitions within a single set of an exercise. For example, a lunge matrix has the athlete completing a forward lunge, lateral lunge, and rotational lunge in sequence within a set. It is also important to include isolated work with key stabilizers and smaller agonists of the hip, shoulder, and scapula. This can assist in cleaning up asymmetries and compensation patterns present from the season. Additionally, the intensification of yielding isometric exercises within accessory work linearly progresses from the general preparatory phase and continues to increase strength within weaker ranges of motion. Yielding isometric exercises such as Copenhagen variations, split squats, and posterior chain exercises can all assist in improving tissue that is generally overlengthened and weakened during the in-season phase because of skating posture.

The adductors and hip flexors should be properly progressed across off-season training by following the same general-to-specific progression of training. Early off-season training for both the adductors and hip flexors should include exercises that develop isometric strength in a shortened state. The inclusion of Copenhagen isometrics and ball squeezes can assist in establishing adduction strength at midline. Hip flexor training should begin with banded psoas holds and isolated hip flexion toward end-range-of-motion flexion. As athletes transition into mid off-season, exercise variations should progress to strengthen the tissue eccentrically and concentrically across the tissues' full range of motion. Isolated cable hip exercises, dynamic Copenhagen variations (see chapter 8), and banded slide lunges can be used across different tempo methods. In the late off-season, these tissues need to be exposed to the specific velocities within sprinting on-ice and progressive volume associated with preseason practice. On-ice sprints, supplementary off-ice sprinting and shuffling, and isolated banded speed exercises can assist in preparing these tissues appropriately. Across the off-season, the placement of adductor and hip flexor training should be on days that do not include high-intensity skating stress—and directly before an off day, when possible, to decrease risk of soft-tissue injury.

Anatomical core training (see chapter 8) should be a mainstay in preparing athletes for the rigors of on-ice stress. The ability of the hockey athlete to stabilize the trunk and pelvis and generate force through the lower body creates effective force transfer within the ice. The main priority should be teaching athletes to stabilize the trunk against multidirectional external force. Programming should expose athletes to anti-extension, anti-lateral flexion, and anti-rotational-based exercises. Early off-season should reinforce postural position of the pelvis and rib cage while exposing the athlete to lighter intensity endurance-based training. As athletes reestablish fundamental posture and endurance, intensity can progress by increasing loading and expanding the complexity of exercise. Early off-season progressions may be more ground-based and shorter lever (kneeling) exercises. By mid off-season, exercise selection should progress to standing variations with much higher intensity of loading. The use of cable machines and landmines can allow for the redirection of load in positions more applicable to the sport. Late off-season methods can progress the athlete into lower body dynamic movement and upper body stabilization. Exercises such as a sliding lateral lunge Pallof press (see table 9.8, day 3) can teach athletes to stabilize the trunk and pelvis under dynamic motion of the lower body.

Although stabilizing the trunk should be the priority, the use of medicine ball throwing is an effective method to improve active trunk and pelvic rotation. Medicine ball training can follow the same ground-based to dynamic-stance progression. Starting athletes in kneeling stances where the trunk is taught to rotate against a stable pelvis and then progressing to standing or dynamic-step throwing variations increases the complexity of movement. Athletes should be taught to create rotation proximally from the pelvis and then continue acceleration distally through the trunk and arms. This helps the athlete to achieve higher force output with the proper dispersion of force from central to peripheral.

Training goalies during the off-season can predominantly follow the same developmental approaches as skaters, with a few considerations. Goalies, unlike skaters, may move into extreme end ranges of motion due to the nature of their positional demands. Importantly, training should assist in the development of increasing mobility and strengthening end ranges. It is common to find structural changes to the hip within many hockey athletes, such as femoroacetabular impingement (FAI; see chapters 2 and 4 for more detail). Be careful not to force end ranges beyond the comfort and orthopedic limitations of the athlete. Strength and conditioning professionals should be mindful of the volume of hip stress that goalies receive at all times of the year. On-ice skills, off-ice training, recreational activity, and lifestyle should all be considered so that the hips are not subject to excessive acute and chronic load. As on-ice skill development and skating volume increases in the off-season in preparation for the preseason period, the total volume of training on the hip musculature should decrease. Within late off-season training, goalies should transition lower body stress toward knee-dominant exercises or limit the range of motion of hip-dominant exercises. Knee-dominant exercises such as split squat variations or front squats would be appropriate major exercises for goalies. An exercise like the hex bar deadlift can be adjusted to use higher handle height or by lifting the beginning position of the bar with blocks to reduce hip flexion and maintain loading intensity.

INTENSITY

The intensity of the off-season training period should be progressive within each specific training goal during the concurrent program. As athletes progress into three to six weeks of hypertrophy training, intensities can range from 65% to 85% of an athlete's estimated 1RM. The use of sets to technical failure or mechanical failure should be reserved for athletes that demonstrate maturity in knowing reasonable stopping points and can maintain safety within the environment. The mid to late off-season concurrent mesocycles have daily intensities of a range dependent on the day's training goal, the training age of the athlete, and methodologies. Concentric resistance training can range from 80% to 95% of an athlete's estimated 1RM. Eccentric and isometric-based strength can range from 80% to 130% of an athlete's estimated 1RM. However, the use of supramaximal training should be reserved for trained athletes that have been properly progressed in higher intensity training, taught how to safely use weight releasers, and are directly under on-site supervision. Slowly progressing athletes through progressive linear changes in intensity allows the athletes to technically master both the exercise and the associated neuromuscular demand of higher intensity training.

Power and speed training within the mid to late off-season period can range from nonresisted exercise to as high as 80% of an athlete's estimated 1RM. Mid off-season dynamic effort training should start at higher intensities (65%-80%) and slower velocities and then progress toward explosive power and speed (30%-65%) within late off-season. The main difference within training is the intent of eccentrically and concentrically moving as quickly as possible. The addition of bands and cords can be a powerful tool to eliminate momentum within concentric training and allow acceleration through end-range extension. Likewise, bands can be used to pull athletes into flexion and increase the rate of eccentric deceleration. The availability of LPTs within power and speed training can assist both athletes and coaches in properly identifying appropriate loads within training. Programming intensity through mean velocity ranges gives athletes and coaches greater accuracy behind individual output than basing training off estimated maximal strength. There can be significant differences in biomechanics and neuromuscular performance between athletes with similar estimated maximal strength. As athletes progress into higher velocity speed training in the late off-season, intensity continues to decrease to below 35% of an athlete's estimated 1RM. Training should include explosive strength, ballistic methods, and exercises that allow for maximal velocity. Exercise selection would include throws, light to unloaded jumps, and lightly loaded explosive exercises.

VOLUME

Off-season training volume should be based upon the training age of individual athletes, their training status, and the goal orientation of stress. Training volume can be conceptualized as the sum of all repetitions, time under tension, and sets performed within an individual day along with the weekly total accumulated stress upon isolated tissue within a week. Programming stress should consider both the acute volume and chronic volume on specific tissue. The strength and conditioning professional should be mindful of the volumes of stress programmed within both an individual session and training frequency across a week to properly prepare the hockey athlete's tissue for sport demands. As athletes transition from postseason training to hypertrophy, one of the main goals is to establish tissue resiliency and work capacity. Establishing high frequencies of training through four total body sessions yet deviating methods and types of tissue stress within each day helps athletes establish tolerance behind training frequency and volume. As athletes transition into mid and late off-season mesocycles, the volume of off-ice training descends and training intensity becomes the priority. Within each mesocycle, individual differences in athlete training age may require different volumes of stress. For instance, younger athletes may require relatively low training frequency and total chronic volume to show positive adaptation. Inversely, higher training-aged athletes may require higher volumes of specific training intensities to continue long-term development. The specific adaptation goal also dictates training volume. Although it is not the focus of this text, coaches should use loading parameter tables for further information regarding optimum training volume ranges. Late off-season training frequency and total chronic volume should decrease as on-ice training volumes begin to rise in preparation for preseason skating. As mentioned before, strength and conditioning professionals should take special consideration of both the hip flexor and adductor volume athletes are exposed to across all environments.

Interpreting the Sample Program Tables

+ = *Do the two exercises back-to-back*

AA = Anatomical adaptation

Alt = Alternated

AMRAP = As many as possible (but quality repetitions)

APRE = Autoregulatory progressive resistance exercise

Asst = Assisted

BB = Barbell

BW = Body weight

Cont = Continuous

DB = Dumbbell

DL = Deadlift

Ea = Each side (arm or leg), direction, or exercise

ECC = Eccentric

Exp = Explosive

Ext = External

FFE = Front foot elevated

Fwd = Forward

Goblet = Holding DB or KB with both hands below the chin and elbows pointed out to the side in the midline of the body

(continued)

Interpreting the Sample Program Tables *(continued)*

GPP = General preparation phase

ISO = Isometric

KB = Kettlebell

Kn = Kneeling

Lat = Lateral

LB = Lower body

LPT = Linear position transducer

MB = Medicine ball

m/s = meters per second

OH = Overhead

Order = Performing one set of each exercise (1a, 1b, 1c) in the group one after the other. After the first set is completed, go back to the first exercise in the group and do the second set of each exercise. If certain exercises call for fewer sets than others in the group, perform those sets on the back end of the grouping. For example, if exercise 1a calls for 4 sets and exercise 1b calls for 3 sets, perform exercise 1b during sets 2 through 4 of exercises 1a.

Plyo = plyometric

Pos = Position

RDL = Romanian deadlift

Rev = Reverse

RFE = Rear foot elevated

RFESS = Rear foot elevated split squat

RM = Repetition maximum

Rot = Rotation

RPE = Rating of perceived exertion (intensity based on level of perceived difficulty)

SA = Single arm

SB = Stability ball

SL = Single leg

SLDL = Single-leg deadlift

Tempo = The time, in seconds, for each phase or portion of the exercise, written as "eccentric phase: top (or bottom) position: concentric phase" (King, I., How to write strength training programs. In *Speed of Movement*, p. 123, 1998). For example, a tempo of "1:5:1" for the back squat means 1 second to lower, 5 seconds held at the bottom position, and 1 second to stand back up. *Note*: "Exp" means that the athlete should explode during the movement. A tempo of "Exp" is associated with power exercises because there is not a prescriptive time allotted to each portion of the movement. *Note*: All tempos are written with the first number referring to the movement that is performed first (either eccentric or concentric).

Tib = Tibialis

UB = Upper body

CONCLUSION

The off-season training period is the most important time for the strength and conditioning professional to improve both individual athlete and team physical development. Through proper progression of stress, athletes can increase on-ice speed, strength, muscular endurance, and tissue resiliency. The programming of physical stress in the off-season should account for individual training age and training status, environmental stressors, on-ice skating volume, and proper progression of stress throughout the off-season. The off-season should physically prepare hockey athletes for on-ice stress and furthering their general physical abilities.

Table 9.1   High School: Early Off-Season (Three Days)

Monday (day 1): strength

Order	Exercise	Tempo	RPE	Sets × reps or time	Sets × reps or time	Sets × reps or time	Sets × reps or time
			1-10	Week 1	Week 2	Week 3	Week 4
1a	DB goblet split squat	3:1:1	5-6	3 × 8 ea	3 × 10 ea	4 × 8 ea	4 × 10 ea
1b	DB bench press	5:1:1	7-8	3 × 8	3 × 8	4 × 8	4 × 8
1c	Lateral band walk	Cont		2 × 10 ea	2 × 10 ea	3 × 10 ea	3 × 10 ea
2a	DB SLDL	3:1:1	7-8	3 × 10	3 × 10	3 × 12	3 × 12
2b	One-arm DB row	1:2:2	6-7	3 × 10 ea	3 × 10 ea	3 × 12 ea	3 × 12 ea
2c	Front plank	ISO		2 × 30 s	2 × 30 s	2 × 30 s	2 × 30 s
3a	Split squat ISO	ISO	5-6	2 × 25 s ea	2 × 30 s ea	3 × 25 s ea	3 × 30 s ea
3b	Band face pull	1:2:2		2 × 12	2 × 15	3 × 12	3 × 15

Wednesday (day 2): strength

Order	Exercise	Tempo	RPE	Sets × reps or time	Sets × reps or time	Sets × reps or time	Sets × reps or time
			1-10	Week 1	Week 2	Week 3	Week 4
1a	DB goblet squat	5:1:1	7-8	3 × 8	3 × 8	4 × 6	4 × 6
1b	Half-kneeling one-arm pulldown	1:1:3	5-6	3 × 10 ea	3 × 10 ea	3 × 12 ea	3 × 12 ea
1c	Pallof press	Cont		2 × 10 ea	2 × 10 ea	2 × 10 ea	2 × 10 ea
2a	One-arm DB incline press	3:1:1	6-7	3 × 8 ea	3 × 8 ea	4 × 8 ea	4 × 8 ea
2b	DB SLDL	2:1:1	5-6	3 × 6 ea	3 × 6 ea	3 × 8 ea	3 × 8 ea
2c	Side plank	ISO		2 × 30 s ea	2 × 30 s ea	2 × 30 s ea	2 × 30 s ea
3a	Landmine squat	2:1:1	5-6	3 × 8	3 × 8	3 × 8	3 × 8
3b	Glute bridge	ISO		2 × 30 s	2 × 30 s	2 × 30 s	2 × 30 s

(continued)

Table 9.1 High School: Early Off-Season (Three Days) *(continued)*

Friday (day 3): strength

Order	Exercise	Tempo	RPE	Sets × reps or time	Sets × reps or time	Sets × reps or time	Sets × reps or time
			1-10	**Week 1**	**Week 2**	**Week 3**	**Week 4**
1a	DB RFE split squat	3:1:1	6-7	3 × 8 ea	3 × 6 ea	4 × 8 ea	4 × 6 ea
1b	Half-kneeling DB overhead one-arm press	3:1:1	5-6	3 × 8 ea	3 × 8 ea	3 × 10 ea	3 × 10 ea
1c	Kettlebell goblet single-leg squat off a box ISO	ISO		2 × 20 s ea	2 × 20 s ea	2 × 20 s ea	2 × 20 s ea
2a	DB hip thrust	1:1:3	6-7	3 × 10	3 × 10	3 × 12	3 × 15
2b	BB inverted row	1:1:3	6-7	3 × 8	3 × 8	3 × 8	3 × 8
2c	Half-kneeling cable chop	Cont		2 × 8 ea	2 × 8 ea	2 × 8 ea	2 × 8 ea
3a	Tempo push-up ECC:ISO	3:3:1	7-8	3 × 8	3 × 10	3 × 12	3 × 15
3b	Band pull apart	Cont		2 × 12	2 × 12	2 × 15	2 × 15

Table 9.2 High School: Early Off-Season (Four Days)

Monday (day 1): upper body—strength

Order	Exercise	Tempo	RPE	Sets × reps or time	Sets × reps or time	Sets × reps or time	Sets × reps or time
			1-10	**Week 1**	**Week 2**	**Week 3**	**Week 4**
1a	DB bench press	5:1:1	7-8	3 × 8	3 × 8	4 × 8	4 × 8
1b	One-arm DB row	1:1:2	6-7	3 × 8 ea	3 × 8 ea	3 × 10 ea	3 × 10 ea
1c	Front plank	ISO		2 × 30 s	2 × 30 s	2 × 30 s	2 × 30 s
2a	Inverted row	1:1:3	7-8	3 × 10	3 × 10	3 × 12	3 × 12
2b	Half-kneeling KB overhead one-arm press	1:1:2	5-6	3 × 8 ea	3 × 8 ea	3 × 10 ea	3 × 10 ea
2c	Half-kneeling cable chop	Cont		2 × 8 ea	2 × 8 ea	2 × 8 ea	2 × 8 ea
3a	Pull-up ISO	ISO	5-6	2 × 25 s ea	2 × 30 s ea	3 × 25 s ea	3 × 30 s ea
3b	Band pull apart	Cont		2 × 12	2 × 12	2 × 15	2 × 15
3c	Landmine rainbow	1:1:2	6-7	2 × 12	2 × 12	3 × 12	3 × 12

Tuesday (day 2): lower body—strength

Order	Exercise	Tempo	RPE	Sets × reps or time	Sets × reps or time	Sets × reps or time	Sets × reps or time
			1-10	**Week 1**	**Week 2**	**Week 3**	**Week 4**
1a	DB goblet squat	5:1:1	7-8	3 × 8	3 × 8	4 × 6	4 × 6
1b	Cable pull-through	1:1:3	5-6	3 × 10 ea	3 × 10 ea	3 × 12 ea	3 × 12 ea
1c	Lateral band walk	Cont		2 × 10 ea	2 × 10 ea	3 × 10 ea	3 × 10 ea

Order	Exercise	Tempo	RPE 1-10	Sets × reps or time Week 1	Sets × reps or time Week 2	Sets × reps or time Week 3	Sets × reps or time Week 4
2a	DB SLDL	3:1:1	7-8	3 × 10	3 × 10	3 × 12	3 × 12
2b	KB goblet split squat	3:1:1	5-6	3 × 8 ea	3 × 10 ea	4 × 8 ea	4 × 10 ea
2c	Glute bridge	ISO		2 × 30 s	2 × 30 s	2 × 30 s	2 × 30 s
3a	DB lateral lunge	2:1:1	5-6	3 × 8 ea	3 × 8 ea	3 × 8 ea	3 × 8 ea
3b	Wall sit	ISO	5-6	2 × 30 s	2 × 45 s	3 × 30 s	3 × 45 s
3c	DB farmer's carry	ISO	6-7	2 × 25 m	2 × 25 m	3 × 25 m	3 × 25 m

Thursday (day 3): upper body—strength 2

Order	Exercise	Tempo	RPE 1-10	Sets × reps or time Week 1	Sets × reps or time Week 2	Sets × reps or time Week 3	Sets × reps or time Week 4
1a	Neutral grip pull-up	5:1:1	6-7	3 × 4	3 × 5	4 × 4	4 × 5
1b	One-arm DB incline press	3:1:1	6-7	3 × 8 ea	3 × 8 ea	4 × 8 ea	4 × 8 ea
1c	Single-leg glute bridge ISO	ISO		2 × 20 s ea	2 × 20 s ea	2 × 20 s ea	2 × 20 s ea
2a	One-arm DB row	1:1:2	6-7	3 × 10 ea	3 × 10 ea	3 × 12 ea	3 × 12 ea
2b	Tempo push-up ECC/ISO	3:3:1	7-8	3 × 8	3 × 10	3 × 12	3 × 15
2c	Pallof press	Cont		2 × 10 ea	2 × 10 ea	2 × 10 ea	2 × 10 ea
3a	Half-kneeling one-arm pulldown	1:1:3	5-6	3 × 10 ea	3 × 10 ea	3 × 12 ea	3 × 12 ea
3b	DB lateral raise	1:1:2	5-6	2 × 10	2 × 10	2 × 12	2 × 12
3c	Half-kneeling cable lift	Cont		2 × 10 ea	2 × 10 ea	2 × 12 ea	2 × 12 ea

Friday (day 4): lower body—strength 2

Order	Exercise	Tempo	RPE 1-10	Sets × reps or time Week 1	Sets × reps or time Week 2	Sets × reps or time Week 3	Sets × reps or time Week 4
1a	DB RFE split squat	3:1:1	6-7	3 × 8 ea	3 × 6 ea	4 × 8 ea	4 × 6 ea
1b	DB hip thrust	3:1:1	6-7	3 × 10	3 × 10	3 × 12	3 × 15
1c	Band hip flexion	ISO		2 × 20 s ea	2 × 20 s ea	2 × 20 s ea	2 × 20 s ea
2a	Front split squat	2:1:1	5-6	3 × 8 ea	3 × 8 ea	3 × 8 ea	3 × 8 ea
2b	DB SL RDL	2:1:1	5-6	3 × 6 ea	3 × 6 ea	3 × 8 ea	3 × 8 ea
2c	Single-leg calf raise	1:1:2		2 × 10 ea	2 × 10 ea	2 × 12 ea	2 × 12 ea
3a	Split squat ISO	ISO	5-6	2 × 25 s ea	2 × 30 s ea	3 × 25 s ea	3 × 30 s ea
3b	MB adductor squeeze	ISO	4-5	2 × 25 s	2 × 30 s	3 × 25 s	3 × 30 s
3c	Suitcase carry	Cont	5-6	2 × 25 m ea	2 × 25 m ea	2 × 25 m ea	2 × 25 m ea

Table 9.3   High School: Late Off-Season (Three Days)

Monday (day 1): total body—strength/power

Order	Exercise	Tempo	RPE	Sets × reps	Sets × reps	Sets × reps	Sets × reps
			1-10	**Week 1**	**Week 2**	**Week 3**	**Week 4**
1a	BB front squat	5:1:1	8-9	3 × 6	4 × 6	5 × 5	5 × 4
1b	Box jump	Exp		3 × 4	4 × 4	5 × 4	5 × 4
2a	Neutral grip pull-up	1:1:3	7-8	3 × 5	4 × 5	5 × 5	5 × 4
2b	Medicine ball slam	Exp		3 × 8	4 × 8	5 × 8	5 × 8
3a	DB reverse lunge	2:1:1	5-6	3 × 6 ea	3 × 6 ea	4 × 5 ea	4 × 5 ea
3b	DB chest-supported row	1:1:2	5-6	3 × 8	3 × 8	4 × 8	4 × 8
3c	Glute-ham raise	3:1:1	4-5	2 × 8	2 × 8	3 × 8	3 × 8

Wednesday (day 2): total body—strength/power

Order	Exercise	Tempo	RPE	Sets × reps or time	Sets × reps or time	Sets × reps or time	Sets × reps or time
			1-10	**Week 1**	**Week 2**	**Week 3**	**Week 4**
1a	BB hip thrust	1:1:3	7-8	3 × 8	3 × 8	4 × 8	4 × 8
1b	Broad jump	Exp		3 × 4	3 × 4	4 × 4	4 × 4
2a	BB bench press	5:1:1	7-8	3 × 6	3 × 6	4 × 6	4 × 6
2b	MB chest pass	Exp		3 × 8	3 × 8	4 × 8	4 × 8
3a	2 DB SLDL	2:1:1	5-6	3 × 6 ea	3 × 6 ea	4 × 6 ea	4 × 6 ea
3b	One-arm DB bench press	1:1:1	5-6	3 × 6 ea	3 × 6 ea	4 × 6 ea	4 × 6 ea
3c	Copenhagen plank	ISO		2 × 25 s ea	2 × 25 s ea	3 × 25 s ea	3 × 25 s ea

Friday (day 3): total body—strength/power

Order	Exercise	Tempo	RPE	Sets × reps	Sets × reps	Sets × reps	Sets × reps
			1-10	**Week 1**	**Week 2**	**Week 3**	**Week 4**
1a	Trap bar deadlift	1:1:3	7-8	3 × 6	4 × 6	5 × 5	5 × 4
1b	Hurdle hop	Exp		3 × 3	4 × 3	5 × 3	5 × 3
2a	Landmine push press	1:1:2	7-8	3 × 6	3 × 6	4 × 6	4 × 6
2b	MB scoop toss	Exp		3 × 3	3 × 3	4 × 3	4 × 3
3a	2 DB lateral lunge	2:1:1	5-6	3 × 8 ea	3 × 8 ea	3 × 8 ea	3 × 8 ea
3b	DB front raise	1:1:2	5-6	2 × 8	2 × 8	2 × 10	2 × 10
3c	Hamstring curl	1:1:2	5-6	2 × 8	2 × 8	2 × 10	2 × 10

Table 9.4 High School: Late Off-Season (Four Days)

Monday (day 1): upper body—strength/power

Order	Exercise	Tempo	RPE	Sets × reps	Sets × reps	Sets × reps	Sets × reps
			1-10	Week 1	Week 2	Week 3	Week 4
1a	BB bench press	5:1:1	7-8	3 × 6	3 × 6	4 × 6	4 × 6
1b	MB chest pass	Exp		3 × 8	3 × 8	4 × 8	4 × 8
2a	Neutral grip pull-up	1:1:3	7-8	3 × 5	4 × 5	5 × 5	5 × 4
2b	Medicine ball slam	Exp		3 × 8	4 × 8	5 × 8	5 × 8
3a	One-arm DB bench press	2:1:1	5-6	3 × 6 ea	3 × 6 ea	4 × 6 ea	4 × 6 ea
3b	DB chest-supported row	1:1:2	5-6	3 × 8	3 × 8	4 × 8	4 × 8
3c	DB front raise	1:1:2	5-6	2 × 8	2 × 8	2 × 10	2 × 10

Tuesday (day 2): lower body—strength/power

Order	Exercise	Tempo	RPE	Sets × reps or time	Sets × reps or time	Sets × reps or time	Sets × reps or time
			1-10	Week 1	Week 2	Week 3	Week 4
1a	BB front squat	5:1:1	8-9	3 × 6	4 × 6	5 × 5	5 × 4
1b	Box jump	Exp		3 × 4	4 × 4	5 × 4	5 × 4
2a	BB hip thrust	1:1:3	7-8	3 × 8	3 × 8	4 × 8	4 × 8
2b	Broad jump	Exp		3 × 4	3 × 4	4 × 4	4 × 4
3a	2 DB SLDL	2:1:1	5-6	3 × 6 ea	3 × 6 ea	4 × 6 ea	4 × 6 ea
3b	DB reverse lunge	2:1:1	5-6	3 × 6 ea	3 × 6 ea	4 × 5 ea	4 × 5 ea
3c	Glute-ham raise	3:1:1	4-5	2 × 30 s	2 × 30 s	3 × 30 s	3 × 30 s

Thursday (day 3): upper body—strength/power

Order	Exercise	Tempo	RPE	Sets × reps	Sets × reps	Sets × reps	Sets × reps
			1-10	Week 1	Week 2	Week 3	Week 4
1a	One-arm DB snatch	Exp	7-8	3 × 4 ea	4 × 4 ea	5 × 4 ea	5 × 3 ea
1b	MB side toss	Exp		3 × 3 ea	4 × 3 ea	5 × 3 ea	5 × 3 ea
2a	One-arm landmine push press	1:1:2	7-8	3 × 6 ea	3 × 6 ea	4 × 6 ea	4 × 6 ea
2b	MB scoop toss	Exp		3 × 3	3 × 3	4 × 3	4 × 3
3a	Inverted row	1:1:2	6-7	3 × 8	3 × 8	3 × 8	3 × 8
3b	Diamond push-up	2:1:x	6-7	2 × 8	2 × 10	3 × 8	3 × 10
3c	One-arm KB overhead carry	Cont	5-6	2 × 8-12	2 × 8-12	2 ×8-12	2 × 8-12

(continued)

Table 9.4 High School: Late Off-Season (Four Days) *(continued)*

Friday (day 4): lower body—strength/power

Order	Exercise	Tempo	RPE	Sets × reps or time	Sets × reps or time	Sets × reps or time	Sets × reps or time
			1-10	Week 1	Week 2	Week 3	Week 4
1a	Trap bar deadlift	1:1:3	7-8	3 × 6	4 × 6	5 × 5	5 × 4
1b	Hurdle hop	Exp		3 × 3	4 × 3	5 × 3	5 × 3
2a	KB swing	Exp	7-8	3 × 8	3 × 8	4 × 8	4 × 8
2b	DB step-up	1:1:2		3 × 6 ea	3 × 6 ea	4 × 6 ea	4 × 6 ea
3a	2 DB lateral lunge	2:1:1	5-6	3 × 8 ea	3 × 8 ea	3 × 8 ea	3 × 8 ea
3b	Hamstring curl	1:1:2	5-6	2 × 8	2 × 8	2 × 10	2 × 10
3c	Copenhagen plank	ISO		2 × 25 s ea	2 × 25 s ea	3 × 25 s ea	3 × 25 s ea

Table 9.5 College: Early Off-Season

Monday (day 1): total body—hypertrophy (LB push/UB pull emphasis)

Order	Exercise	Tempo	% of 1RM or RPE	Sets × reps or time	Sets × reps or time	Sets × reps or time
				Week 1	Week 2	Week 3
1a	Barbell front squat	2:1:1	65%-75%	3 × 10	3 × 10	3 × 10
1b	Half-kneeling landmine one-arm press	1:1:2	55%-65%	3 × 10 ea	3 × 10 ea	3 × 10 ea
1c	Banded-ankle dorsiflexion	1:1:4	RPE 6-7	3 × 4 ea	3 × 5 ea	3 × 6 ea
2a	Neutral grip pull-up (APRE 6)*	1:1:2	75%-85%	3 × 6	3 × 6	3 × 6
2b	Single-leg hamstring bridge	1:1:5	BW	3 × 3 ea	3 × 4 ea	3 × 5 ea
2c	Lying band hip flexion	1:2:1	RPE 6-7	3 × 8 ea	3 × 10 ea	3 × 12 ea
3a	KB goblet split squat	2:1:1	55%-65%	3 × 12 ea	3 × 14 ea	3 × 16 ea
3b	Single-leg glute bridge	ISO		3 × 30 s ea	30 × 35 s ea	3 × 40 s ea

*APRE sets use 1 submaximal set. Set 2 is an open-ended rep out. Set 3 is adjusted based on reps achieved within set 2.

Tuesday (day 2): total body—hypertrophy (LB pull/UB push emphasis)

Order	Exercise	Tempo	% of 1RM or RPE	Sets × reps	Sets × reps	Sets × reps
				Week 1	Week 2	Week 3
1a	Barbell SLDL (APRE 10)*	2:1:1	65%-75%	3 × 10	3 × 10	3 × 10
1b	Chest-supported row	1:3:1	55%-60%	3 × 10 ea	3 × 10 ea	3 × 10 ea
1c	Plank hold	1:4:1	BW	3 × 4 ea	3 × 5 ea	3 × 6 ea
2a	DB bench press (APRE 10)*	2:1:1	65%-75%	3 × 10	3 × 10	3 × 10

Order	Exercise	Tempo	% of 1RM or RPE	Sets × reps	Sets × reps	Sets × reps
				Week 1	Week 2	Week 3
2b	Single-leg skater squat	3:1:1	10%-15%	3 × 8 ea	3 × 10 ea	3 × 12 ea
2c	Cable external rotation	Cont	60%-70%	3 × 10 ea	3 × 10 ea	3 × 10 ea
3a	Half-kneeling Pallof press	1:2:4	RPE 6-7	3 × 5 ea	3 × 5 ea	3 × 5 ea
3b	Pilates ring adductor squeeze	1:5:1	RPE 6-7	2 × 3	2 × 4	2 × 5

*APRE sets use 1 submaximal set. Set 2 is an open-ended rep out. Set 3 is adjusted based on reps achieved within set 2.

Thursday (day 3): total body—hypertrophy (LB push/UB pull emphasis)

Order	Exercise	Tempo	% of 1RM	Sets × reps or time	Sets × reps or time	Sets × reps or time
				Week 1	Week 2	Week 3
1a	DB RFE split squat (APRE 10)*	2:1:1	65%-75%	3 × 10 ea	3 × 10 ea	3 × 10 ea
1b	Half-kneeling cable rotational press	1:1:3	50%-60%	3 × 6 ea	3 × 6 ea	3 × 6 ea
1c	Backward bear crawl	Slow	BW	3 × 8 ea	3 × 10 ea	3 × 12 ea
2a	One-arm DB row (APRE 10)*	1:1:2	65%-75%	3 × 6	3 × 6	3 × 6
2b	Slide leg curl	1:1:4	BW	3 × 8 ea	3 × 10 ea	3 × 12 ea
2c	Side plank	ISO	BW	3 × 30 s ea	3 × 30 s ea	3 × 30 s ea
3a	DB split squat	ISO	55%-65%	3 × 20 s ea	3 × 20 s ea	3 × 20 s ea
3b	Alt leg lower	1:1:3	BW	2 × 6 ea	2 × 7 ea	2 × 8 ea

*APRE sets use 1 submaximal set. Set 2 is an open-ended rep out. Set 3 is adjusted based on reps achieved within set 2.

Friday (day 4): total body—hypertrophy (LB pull/UB push emphasis)

Order	Exercise	Tempo	% of 1RM or RPE	Sets × reps or time	Sets × reps or time	Sets × reps or time
				Week 1	Week 2	Week 3
1a	Conventional deadlift (APRE 10)*	1:1:3	65%-75%	3 × 10	3 × 10	3 × 10
1b	Cable hip flexion	1:1:2	55%-65%	3 × 10 ea	3 × 10 ea	3 × 10 ea
2a	Barbell bench press (APRE 10)*	2:1:1	65%-75%	3 × 10	3 × 10	3 × 10
2b	DB goblet lateral lunge	1:3:1	55%-60%	3 × 5 ea	3 × 5 ea	3 × 5 ea
2c	Half-kneeling cable chop	Cont	RPE 6-7	3 × 8 ea	3 × 8 ea	3 × 8 ea
3a	Lat pulldown	1:3:1	55%-65%	3 × 8	3 × 8	3 × 8
3b	Glute-ham raise	3:0:1	BW	3 × 6	3 × 7	3 × 8
3c	Copenhagen plank	ISO	BW	2 × 15 s	2 × 20 s	2 × 25 s

*APRE sets use 1 submaximal set. Set 2 is an open-ended rep out. Set 3 is adjusted based on reps achieved within set 2.

Table 9.6   College: Mid Off-Season (Mesocycle 1)

Monday (day 1): total body—eccentric strength

Order	Exercise	Tempo	% of 1RM or RPE	Sets × reps Week 1	Sets × reps Week 2	Sets × reps Week 3
1a	Hands-asst safety bar rev lunge	6:1:1	80%-120%	4 × 2 ea	4 × 2 ea	3 × 2 ea
1b	Trap bar vertical jump	Exp	1.35-1.40 m/s	4 × 4	4 × 4	3 × 4
1c	One-arm DB row (cluster, 10 s rest)	1:1:6	85%-95%	3 × 1:1:1 ea	3 × 1:1:1 ea	3 × 1:1:1 ea
2a	Glute-ham raise	6:0:1	BW	3 × 1:1:1	3 × 2:1:1	3 × 2:2
2b	Standing one-arm landmine press	1:1:6	80%-90%	3 × 3 ea	3 × 3 ea	3 × 3 ea
2c	Side plank pos w/ hip abduction	1:1:3	BW	3 × 4 ea	3 × 5 ea	3 × 6 ea
3a	Suspension roll out	3:0:1	BW	2 × 6	2 × 7	2 × 8
3b	Band pull apart	1:1:3	RPE 7-8	2 × 8	2 × 9	2 × 10

Note: 1.35-1.40 m/s demonstrates the usage of programmed velocity ranges using LPT. 1:1:1 refers to cluster sets of 3 single repetitions with 20 to 30 s rest between each rep.

Tuesday (day 2): total body—dynamic effort

Order	Exercise	Tempo	% of 1RM	Sets × reps Week 1	Sets × reps Week 2	Sets × reps Week 3
1a	Trap bar deadlift	1:1:3	0.8-0.85 m/s	4 × 3	4 × 3	3 × 3
1b	Single-leg leap matrix	Exp	Max power	4 × 1 ea	4 × 1 ea	3 × 1 ea
1c	Rotational squat one-arm cable row	1:1:1	70%-75%	3 × 6 ea	3 × 6 ea	3 × 6 ea
2a	One-arm landmine push press	Exp	70%-75%	4 × 2 ea	4 × 2 ea	3 × 2 ea
2b	KB swing	Exp	55%-60%	3 × 10	3 × 10	3 × 10
2c	Suspension Y	1:1:4	BW	3 × 3	3 × 4	3 × 5
3a	Supine SL cable hip flexion	1:1:3	65%-70%	2 × 5 ea	2 × 5 ea	2 × 5 ea
3b	Alt side plank	1:5:1	BW	2 × 6 ea	2 × 7 ea	2 × 8 ea

Thursday (day 3): total body—concentric strength

Order	Exercise	% of 1RM	Sets × reps Week 1	Sets × reps Week 2	Sets × reps Week 3
1a	Barbell front squat	55%-60%	10 × 1	10 × 1	10 × 1
1b	Suspension inverted row	BW	10 × 1	10 × 1	10 × 1
1c	Half-kneeling cable lift	55%-60%	10 × 1	10 × 1	10 × 1
2a	DB SLDL	55%-60%	10 × 1	10 × 1	10 × 1
2b	Push-up	BW	10 × 1	10 × 1	10 × 1
2c	Stability ball roll out	BW	10 × 1	10 × 1	10 × 1
3a	KB goblet lateral squat	55%-60%	10 × 1	10 × 1	10 × 1
3b	DB OH press	55%-60%	10 × 1	10 × 1	10 × 1

Order	Exercise	% of 1RM	Sets × reps	Sets × reps	Sets × reps
			Week 1	Week 2	Week 3
3c	Side plank (hip dip)	BW	10 × 1	10 × 1	10 × 1
4a	Supine adductor ball squeeze	BW	2 × 3 (4 s ISO)	2 × 4 (4 s ISO)	2 × 5 (4 s ISO)
4b	Pallof press		2 × 6 ea (3 s ISO)	2 × 6 ea (3 s ISO)	2 × 6 ea (3 s ISO)

Friday (day 4): total body—work capacity circuits

Order	Exercise	Tempo	% of 1RM or RPE	Sets × reps	Sets × reps	Sets × reps
				Week 1	Week 2	Week 3
1a	Hands-asst safety bar rev lunge	1:6:1	80%-120%	3 × 2 ea	3 × 2 ea	2 × 2 ea
1b	Hurdle vertical jump	Exp	Max speed	3 × 5	3 × 5	2 × 5
1c	Trap bar vertical jump	Exp	1.35-1.40 m/s	3 × 4	3 × 4	2 × 4
1d	One-arm DB row (cluster, 10 s rest)	1:6:1	85%-95%	3 × 1:1:1 ea	3 × 1:1:1 ea	3 × 1:1:1 ea
2a	Suspension hamstring curl	1:6:1	BW	3 × 2	3 × 3	3 × 4
2b	Standing one-arm landmine press	1:6:1	80%-90%	3 × 3 ea	3 × 3 ea	3 × 3 ea
2c	Side plank with hip abduction	1:3:1	BW	3 × 4 ea	3 × 5 ea	3 × 6 ea
3a	Suspension roll out	1:3:1	BW	2 × 6	2 × 7	2 × 8
3b	Band pull apart	1:3:1	RPE 6-8	2 × 8	2 × 9	2 × 10

Note: Within each circuit, athletes complete 10 reps of each exercise, then the next set decreases by 1 rep. This descends until they finish at 1 rep of each exercise. 1:1:1 refers to cluster sets of 3 single repetitions with 20 to 30 s rest between each rep.

Table 9.7 College: Mid Off-Season (Mesocycle 2)

Monday (day 1): total body—isometric strength

Order	Exercise	Tempo	% of 1RM or RPE	Sets × reps	Sets × reps	Sets × reps
				Week 1	Week 2	Week 3
1a	Hands-asst safety bar rev lunge	1:6:1	80%-120%	3 × 2 ea	3 × 2 ea	2 × 2 ea
1b	Hurdle vertical jump	Exp	Max speed	3 × 5	3 × 5	2 × 5
1c	Trap bar vertical jump	Exp	1.35-1.40 m/s	3 × 4	3 × 4	2 × 4
1d	One-arm DB row (cluster, 10 s rest)	1:6:1	85%-95%	3 × 1:1:1 ea	3 × 1:1:1 ea	3 × 1:1:1 ea
2a	Suspension hamstring curl	1:6:1	BW	3 × 2	3 × 3	3 × 4
2b	Standing one-arm landmine press	1:6:1	80%-90%	3 × 3 ea	3 × 3 ea	3 × 3 ea
2c	Side plank with hip abduction	1:3:1	BW	3 × 4 ea	3 × 5 ea	3 × 6 ea
3a	Suspension roll out	1:3:1	BW	2 × 6	2 × 7	2 × 8
3b	Band pull apart	1:3:1	RPE 6-8	2 × 8	2 × 9	2 × 10

Note: 1:1:1 refers to cluster sets of 3 single repetitions with 20 to 30 s rest between each rep.

(continued)

Table 9.7   College: Mid Off-Season (Mesocycle 2)   *(continued)*

Tuesday (day 2): total body—dynamic effort

Order	Exercise	Tempo	% of 1RM or RPE	Sets × reps	Sets × reps	Sets × reps
				Week 1	**Week 2**	**Week 3**
1a	Trap bar deadlift	Exp	0.90-0.95 m/s	4 × 3	4 × 3	3 × 3
1b	Single-leg leap matrix	Exp	Max power	4 × 1 ea	4 × 1 ea	3 × 1 ea
1c	Rot split squat SA cable row	Exp	65%-70%	3 × 6 ea	3 × 6 ea	3 × 6 ea
2a	One-arm landmine push press	Exp	65%-70%	4 × 2 ea	4 × 2 ea	3 × 2 ea
2b	One-arm KB swing	Exp	65%-70%	3 × 6 ea	3 × 6 ea	3 × 6 ea
3a	Incline Y	1:2:1	RPE 5-7	3 × 8	3 × 10	3 × 12
3b	DB RFESS (dynamic reversal)	1:2:1	40%-55%	2 × 4 ea	2 × 4 ea	2 × 4 ea
3c	Alt side plank	1:5:1	BW	2 × 6 ea	2 × 7 ea	2 × 8 ea

Thursday (day 3): total body—concentric strength

Order	Exercise	Tempo	% of 1RM	Sets × reps	Sets × reps	Sets × reps
				Week 1	**Week 2**	**Week 3**
1a	Trap bar deadlift	1:1:2	90%-95%	4 × (1+1)	3 × (1+1)	2 × (1+1)
1b	Depth drop to broad jump	Exp	Max power	4 × 3	3 × 3	2 × 3
1c	Side lying ext rotation	Cont	70%-75%	3 × 8 ea	3 × 8 ea	3 × 8 ea
2a	Bench press	2:1:1	90%-95%	4 × (1+1)	3 × (1+1)	2 × (1+1)
2b	Lateral MB rot chest pass	Exp	Max power	4 × 3 ea	3 × 3 ea	2 × 3 ea
2c	Off-box DB single-leg squat	1:1:1	70%-75%	3 × 6 ea	3 × 6 ea	2 × 6 ea
3a	Split stance landmine rainbow	1:2:1	60%-70%	2 × 5 ea	2 × 5 ea	2 × 5 ea
3b	Stability ball single-leg curl	1:1:1	BW	2 × 8 ea	2 × 10 ea	2 × 12 ea

Friday (day 4): total body—work capacity circuits

Order	Exercise	Tempo	% of 1RM	Sets × reps	Sets × reps	Sets × reps
				Week 1	**Week 2**	**Week 3**
1a	Front squat	6 min	70%-75%	x 6	x 6	x 6
1b	KB one-arm row		65%-70%	x 8 ea	x 8 ea	x 8 ea
1c	Half-kneeling cable lift		55%-60%	x 10 ea	x 10 ea	x 10 ea
2a	Pull-up	6 min	BW	x 4	x 4	x 4
2b	DB lateral squat		65%-70%	x 6 ea	x 6 ea	x 6 ea
2c	Cable alt leg lower		55%-60%	x 8 ea	x 8 ea	x 8 ea
3a	Landmine single-leg SLDL	6 min	70%-75%	x 6 ea	x 6 ea	x 6 ea
3b	DB bench press		65%-70%	x 8	x 8	x 8
3c	Half-kneeling cable chop		55%-60%	x 10 ea	x 10 ea	x 10 ea
4a	Copenhagen plank	4 s ECC	BW	2 × 3 ea	2 × 4 ea	2 × 5 ea
4b	Inverted row		BW	2 × AMRAP	2 × AMRAP	2 × AMRAP

Note: Accumulate as many sets as possible within the given time frame; allow a 2:30 rest between blocks.

Table 9.8   College: Late Off-Season

Monday (day 1): total body—power

Order	Exercise	Tempo	% of 1RM or RPE	Sets × reps Week 1	Sets × reps Week 2	Sets × reps Week 3
1a	Trap bar jump	1:1:1	1.25-1.3 m/s	3 × 4	3 × 4	3 × 4
1b	MB rotational leap	Exp	Max speed	3 × 4 ea	3 × 4 ea	3 × 4 ea
1c	Staggered stance one-arm cable row	1:1:1	55%-60%	3 × 6 ea	3 × 6 ea	3 × 6 ea
2a	Landmine split jerk (with countermovement)	1:1:1	55%-60%	3 × 2 ea	3 × 2 ea	3 × 2 ea
2b	KB swing	Exp	55%-60%	3 × 10	3 × 10	3 × 8
2c	Bench reverse fly	1:5:1	RPE 6-8	3 × 5	3 × 5	3 × 5
3a	DB step-up	1:1:1	40%-55%	2 × 4 ea	2 × 4 ea	2 × 4 ea
3b	Standing cable hip flexion	1:1:1	RPE 4-6	2 × 6 ea	2 × 6 ea	2 × 6 ea

Wednesday (day 2): total body—speed

Order	Exercise	Tempo	% of 1RM or RPE	Sets × reps Week 1	Sets × reps Week 2	Sets × reps Week 3
1a	DB RFESS (dynamic reversal)	1:1:1	35%-40%	4 × 3	4 × 3	3 × 3
1b	45° Skater bound	Exp	Max power	4 × 1 ea	4 × 1 ea	3 × 1 ea
1c	Suspension one-arm rot inverted row	1:1:1	BW	3 × 4 ea	3 × 5 ea	3 × 6 ea
2a	Band-resisted barbell bench	1:1:1	35%-40%	4 × 4	4 × 4	3 × 4
2b	MB overhead scoop toss	Exp	RPE 7	3 × 5	3 × 5	3 × 5
2c	Stability ball roll out	1:3:1	BW	2 × 6	2 × 7	2 × 8
3a	Post-lateral banded slide lunge	1:1:1	25%-30%	2 × 8 ea	2 × 8 ea	2 × 8 ea
3b	Lateral mini band walk	Cont		2 × 8 yd (or m)	2 × 10 yd (or m)	2 × 12 yd (or m)

Friday (day 3): total body—strength

Order	Exercise	Tempo	% of 1RM	Sets × reps Week 1	Sets × reps Week 2	Sets × reps Week 3
1a	Front squat	2:1:1	80%-85%	3 × 4	3 × 4	3 × 4
1b	Alt DB bench press	3:1:1	80%-85%	3 × 4 ea	3 × 4 ea	3 × 4 ea
1c	Lateral kn abduction liftoff	1:5:1	BW	3 × 3 ea	3 × 4 ea	3 × 5 ea
2a	Parallel grip pull-up	1:2:1	80%-85%	3 × 4	3 × 4	3 × 4
2b	Two-arm SLDL	1:3:1	70%-75%	3 × 6 ea	3 × 6 ea	3 × 6 ea
2c	90° mini band step out	1:2:1		2 × 8 ea	2 × 10 ea	2 × 12 ea
3a	DB slide lat lunge + band	1:2:1	60%-65%	2 × 8 ea	2 × 8 ea	2 × 8 ea
3b	Sliding lateral lunge Pallof press	Slow	45%-55%	2 × 6 ea	2 × 6 ea	2 × 6 ea

Table 9.9 Professional: Early Off-Season

Monday (day 1): upper body

Order	Exercise	Tempo	Sets × reps	Sets × reps	Sets × reps
			Week 1	**Week 2**	**Week 3**
1a	Y, T, W ISO	1:4:1	3-4 × 4 ea	3-4 × 4 ea	3-4 × 4 ea
1b	Half-kneeling cable lift	Cont	3-4 × 6-8 ea	3-4 × 6-8 ea	3-4 × 6-8 ea
1c	Half-kneeling one-arm KB press	Cont	3 × 8-12 ea	3 × 8-12 ea	3 × 8-12 ea
2a	Parallel grip chin-up	Cont	3-4 × 4-6	3-4 × 4-6	3-4 × 4-6
2b	Half-kneeling landmine press	Cont	3-4 × 6-8 ea	3-4 × 6-8 ea	3-4 × 6-8 ea
3a	Half-kneeling Pallof press	1:6:1	2 × 6 ea	2 × 6 ea	2 × 6 ea
3b	Ab wheel roll out	Cont	2-3 × 8-12	2-3 × 8-12	2-3 × 8-12
4a	Side plank	6 s ISO	1 × 6 ea	1 × 6 ea	1 × 6 ea

Tuesday (day 2): lower body

Order	Exercise	Tempo	Sets × reps	Sets × reps	Sets × reps
			Week 1	**Week 2**	**Week 3**
1a	Barbell complex warm-up: clean/front squat/push press/RDL	Exp	3 × 5	3 × 5	3 × 5
1b	Front foot elevated split squat	5:1:1	3 × 6-8 ea	3 × 6-8 ea	3 × 6-8 ea
2a	Front squat	5:1:1	3-4 × 5-7	3-4 × 5-7	3-4 × 5-7
3a	Single-leg squat	3:0:1	2-3 × 10-15 ea	2-3 × 10-15 ea	2-3 × 10-15 ea
3b	Single-leg eccentric Valslide leg curl	6:0:1	2-3 × 4-6	2-3 × 4-6	2-3 × 4-6
4a	Copenhagen plank	1:6:1	1-2 × 4-6 ea	1-2 × 4-6 ea	1-2 × 4-6 ea

Thursday (day 3): upper body

Order	Exercise	Tempo	Sets × reps or time	Sets × reps or time	Sets × reps or time
			Week 1	**Week 2**	**Week 3**
1a	One-arm KB swing	Exp	3 × 6-8 ea	3 × 6-8 ea	3 × 6-8 ea
1b	Plank	ISO	2 × 30 s	2 × 40 s	2 × 50 s
2a	Single-leg MB anterior reach	1:4:1	2 × 4 ea	2 × 4 ea	2 × 4 ea
2b	Dead bug	4:1:1	2 × 6-8 ea	2 × 6-8 ea	2 × 6-8 ea
3a	Landmine deadlift	Cont	2 × 10-15	2 × 10-15	2 × 10-15
4a	Slide board lateral lunge	Cont	2 × 10-15	2 × 10-15	2 × 10-15
4b	Mini band lateral step out		2 × 15-20 ea	2 × 15-20 ea	2 × 15-20 ea
4c	Stability ball side plank		2 × 6 × 6 s	2 × 6 × 6 s	2 × 6 × 6 s

Friday (day 4): lower body

Order	Exercise	Tempo	Sets × reps	Sets × reps	Sets × reps
			Week 1	Week 2	Week 3
1a	Incline Y	1:4:1	3 × 6	3 × 6	3 × 6
1b	Half-kneeling cable chop	Cont	3 × 6-8 ea	3 × 6-8 ea	3 × 6-8 ea
1c	Single-arm DB bench press	4:1:1	3 × 7-10 ea	3 × 7-10 ea	3 × 7-10 ea
2a	One-arm DB incline bench press	4:0:1	3 × 7-10 ea	3 × 7-10 ea	3 × 7-10 ea
2b	One-arm DB row	4:1:1	3 × 7-10 ea	3 × 7-10 ea	3 × 7-10 ea
3a	Inverted row	1:2:1	2 × 6-8	2 × 6-8	2 × 6-8
3b	Rear delt lateral raise	3:1:1	2 × 8-12	2 × 8-12	2 × 8-12
4a	Half-kneeling Pallof press	1:6:1	2 × 6-8 ea	2 × 6-8 ea	2 × 6-8 ea

Table 9.10   Professional: Goalie Early Off-Season

Monday (day 1)

Order	Exercise	Tempo	Sets × reps or time	Sets × reps or time	Sets × reps or time
			Week 1	Week 2	Week 3
1a	Single-leg hip thrust on bench	3:1:1	3 × 7-10 ea	3 × 7-10 ea	3 × 7-10 ea
1b	Single-arm KB swing		3 × 10 ea	3 × 10 ea	3 × 10 ea
2a	Hands-free zombie front squat	6:1:1	3-4 × 4-6	3-4 × 4-6	3-4 × 4-6
3a	Single-leg box squat	3:0:0	2-3 × 10-15 ea	2-3 × 10-15 ea	2-3 × 10-15 ea
3b	One-arm KB row	3:1:1	2-3 × 8-12 ea	2-3 × 8-12 ea	2-3 × 8-12 ea
4a	Nordic eccentric curl	6:0:0	2 × 3-5	2 × 3-5	2 × 3-5
4b	Copenhagen plank	6 s ISO	2 × 4-6 × 6 s	2 × 4-6 × 6 s	2 × 4-6 × 6 s

Wednesday (day 2)

Order	Exercise	Tempo	Sets × reps	Sets × reps	Sets × reps
			Week 1	Week 2	Week 3
1a	Tall kneeling cable lift	Cont	3 × 6 ea	3 × 6 ea	3 × 6 ea
1b	One-arm KB swing	Exp	3 × 10 ea	3 × 10 ea	3 × 10 ea
2a	Suspension inverted row	4:1:1	3 × 5-7	3 × 5-7	3 × 5-7
2b	Nordic eccentric curl	6:0:0	3 × 3-5	3 × 3-5	3 × 3-5
2c	Ab wheel roll out	Cont	3 × 8-12	3 × 8-12	3 × 8-12
3a	Tripod one-arm DB row	3:1:1	3 × 7-10 ea	3 × 7-10 ea	3 × 7-10 ea
3b	Seated external rotation	Cont	3 × 7-10 ea	3 × 7-10 ea	3 × 7-10 ea
4a	Tall kneeling Pallof press	1:6:1	2 × 6 × 6 s ea	2 × 6 × 6 s ea	2 × 6 × 6 s ea
4b	Tall kneeling DB curl and press	Cont	2 × 7-10	2 × 7-10	2 × 7-10

(continued)

Table 9.10 Professional: Goalie Early Off-Season   *(continued)*

Friday (day 3)

Order	Exercise	Tempo	Sets × reps or time	Sets × reps or time	Sets × reps or time
			Week 1	**Week 2**	**Week 3**
1a	Plank	Hold	2 × 40 s	2 × 50 s	2 × 60 s
1b	Dead bug	Cont	2 × 6-8	2 × 6-8	2 × 6-8
2a	KB one-arm lateral squat	Cont	3 × 6-8 ea	3 × 6-8 ea	3 × 6-8 ea
2b	Alt DB row in push-up position	Cont	3 × 6-8 ea	3 × 6-8 ea	3 × 6-8 ea
3a	Glute-ham raise	4:0:1	3 × 4-6	3 × 4-6	3 × 4-6
3b	DB rear foot elevated split squat	4:1:1	3 × 5-7 ea	3 × 5-7 ea	3 × 5-7 ea
4a	Lateral lunge slide	Cont	2 × 7-10 ea	2 × 7-10 ea	2 × 7-10 ea
4b	Copenhagen plank	1:6:1	2 × 4-6 × 6 s	2 × 4-6 × 6 s	2 × 4-6 × 6 s

Table 9.11 Professional: Late Off-Season

Monday (day 1): upper body

Order	Exercise	Tempo	Sets × reps	Sets × reps	Sets × reps
			Week 1	**Week 2**	**Week 3**
1a	One-arm DB snatch	Exp	3 × 3 ea	3 × 3 ea	3 × 3 ea
1b	Half-kneeling cable lift	Cont	3 × 6-8 ea	3 × 6-8 ea	3 × 6-8 ea
2a	Medium grip pull-up	3:1:1	3 × 4-6	3 × 4-6	3 × 4-6
2b	Split stance landmine press	Cont	3 × 5-7 ea	3 × 5-7 ea	3 × 5-7 ea
3a	Landmine rainbow	Cont	2-3 × 4-6 ea	2-3 × 4-6 ea	2-3 × 4-6 ea
3b	Ab wheel roll out	Cont	2-3 × 8-12	2-3 × 8-12	2-3 × 8-12
4a	Side plank	1:6:1	1 × 6 × 6 s	1 × 6 × 6 s	1 × 6 × 6 s

Tuesday (day 2): lower body

Order	Exercise	Tempo	Sets × reps	Sets × reps	Sets × reps
			Week 1	**Week 2**	**Week 3**
1a	Barbell complex warm-up: clean/front squat/push press/RDL		3 × 3-5	3 × 3-5	3 × 3-5
2a	Hang clean*	Exp	3-4 × 3	3-4 × 3	3-4 × 3
2b	3-hurdle hop	Exp	3-4 × 3	3-4 × 3	3-4 × 3
3a	Front squat**		3 × 3-5	3 × 3-5	3 × 3-5
3b	Box jump	Exp	3 × 3	3 × 3	3 × 3
4a	Single-leg squat	3:1:1	2-3 × 5-7 ea	2-3 × 5-7 ea	2-3 × 5-7 ea
4b	Eccentric slider leg curl	5:1:1	2 × 5 × 5 s	2 × 5 × 5 s	2 × 5 × 5 s
5a	Copenhagen plank	1:6:1	1 × 4-6 × 6 s	1 × 4-6 × 6 s	1 × 4-6 × 6 s

*At >1.2 m/s. **At 0.5-0.6 m/s.

Thursday (day 3): upper body

Order	Exercise	Tempo	Sets × reps	Sets × reps	Sets × reps
			Week 1	**Week 2**	**Week 3**
1a	Half-kneeling cable chop	Cont	3 × 6 ea	3 × 6 ea	3 × 6 ea
1b	Bench press*	Cont	3 × 3-5	3 × 3-5	3 × 3-5
1c	Seated MB chest pass	Exp	3 × 5	3 × 5	3 × 5
2a	One-arm DB incline bench press	3:1:1	2-3 × 6-8 ea	2-3 × 6-8 ea	2-3 × 6-8 ea
2b	One-arm DB row	3:1:1	2-3 × 6-8 ea	2-3 × 6-8 ea	2-3 × 6-8 ea
3a	Inverted row	3:1:1	2-3 × 6-8	2-3 × 6-8	2-3 × 6-8
3b	Rear delt lateral raise	Cont	2-3 × 8-12	2-3 × 8-12	2-3 × 8-12
4a	Landmine rainbow	Cont	2 × 4-6 ea	2 × 4-6 ea	2 × 4-6 ea
4b	Ab wheel roll out	Cont	2 × 8-12	2 × 8-12	2 × 8-12

*At 0.45-0.6 m/s.

Friday (day 4): lower body

Order	Exercise	Tempo	Sets × reps	Sets × reps	Sets × reps
			Week 1	**Week 2**	**Week 3**
1a	Trap bar deadlift*	Cont	3-4 × 3	3-4 × 3	3-4 × 3
1b	Seated box jump	Exp	3-4 × 3	3-4 × 3	3-4 × 3
2a	KB swing	Exp	3 × 6	3 × 6	3 × 6
2b	Consecutive standing long jump	Exp	3 × 3	3 × 3	3 × 3
3a	Glute-ham raise	3:0:1	2-3 × 4-6	2-3 × 4-6	2-3 × 4-6
3b	One-arm single-leg SLDL	3:0:1	2-3 × 6-8 ea	2-3 × 6-8 ea	2-3 × 6-8 ea
3c	Lateral slide lunge	3:0:1	2-3 × 7-10	2-3 × 7-10	2-3 × 7-10
4a	Copenhagen plank	1:6:1	2 × 4-6 × 6 s	2 × 4-6 × 6 s	2 × 4-6 × 6 s

*At 0.45-0.6 m/s.

Table 9.12   Professional: Goalie Late Off-Season

Monday (day 1)

Order	Exercise	Tempo	Sets × reps	Sets × reps	Sets × reps
			Week 1	**Week 2**	**Week 3**
1a	Kneeling DB clean (knee pads recommended)	Exp	3-4 × 3	3-4 × 3	3-4 × 3
1b	Kneeling jump + lateral bound	Exp	3-4 × 3	3-4 × 3	3-4 × 3
2a	Front squat*	2:1:1	3-4 × 3-5	3-4 × 3-5	3-4 × 3-5
2b	Box jump	exp	3-4 × 1-3	3-4 × 1-3	3-4 × 1-3
3a	DB reverse lunge	Cont	2 × 4-6 ea	2 × 4-6 ea	2 × 4-6 ea
3b	One-arm DB row	3:1:1	3 × 8-12 ea	3 × 8-12 ea	3 × 8-12 ea
4a	Copenhagen plank	1:6:1	2 × 4-6 × 6 s	2 × 4-6 × 6 s	2 × 4-6 × 6 s
4b	Nordic eccentric hamstring curl	6:1:1	2 × 3-5	2 × 3-5	2 × 3-5

*At 0.45-0.6 m/s.

(continued)

Table 9.12 Professional: Goalie Late Off-Season *(continued)*

Wednesday (day 2)

Order	Exercise	Tempo	Sets × reps	Sets × reps	Sets × reps
			Week 1	Week 2	Week 3
1a	Trap bar deadlift*	Cont	3-4 × 3-5	3-4 × 3-5	3-4 × 3-5
1b	Seated box jump	Exp	3-4 × 3	3-4 × 3	3-4 × 3
2a	KB one-arm lateral squat	3:1:1	3-4 × 4-6 ea	3-4 × 4-6 ea	3-4 × 4-6 ea
2b	Half-kneeling slider lateral push	Cont	3-4 × 5 ea	3-4 × 5 ea	3-4 × 5 ea
3a	Glute-ham raise	3:0:1	2-3 × 4-6	2-3 × 4-6	2-3 × 4-6
3b	DB rear foot elevated split squat	3:1:1	2-3 × 5-7 ea	2-3 × 5-7 ea	2-3 × 5-7 ea
3c	Lateral slide lunge	3:1:1	2-3 × 7-10 ea	2-3 × 7-10 ea	2-3 × 7-10 ea
4a	Copenhagen plank	1:6:1	2 × 4-6 × 6 s ea	2 × 4-6 × 6 s ea	2 × 4-6 × 6 s ea

*At 0.45-0.6 m/s.

Friday (day 3)

Order	Exercise	Tempo	Sets × reps	Sets × reps	Sets × reps
			Week 1	Week 2	Week 3
1a	One-arm DB snatch	Exp	3-4 × 3 ea	3-4 × 3 ea	3-4 × 3 ea
1b	Tall kneeling cable lift	Cont	3-4 × 6	3-4 × 6	3-4 × 6
2a	Medium grip pull-up	4:1:1	3 × 4-6	3 × 4-6	3 × 4-6
2b	Nordic eccentric curl	6:0:0	3 × 3-5	3 × 3-5	3 × 3-5
2c	Ab wheel roll out	Cont	3 × 8-12	3 × 8-12	3 × 8-12
3a	Inverted row	3:1:1	2-3 × 7-10	2-3 × 7-10	2-3 × 7-10
3b	Seated external rotation	Cont	2-3 × 7-10 ea	2-3 × 7-10 ea	2-3 × 7-10 ea
4a	Tall kneeling landmine rainbow	Cont	2 × 5-7 ea	2 × 5-7 ea	2 × 5-7 ea
4b	Tall kneeling DB curl and press	Cont	2 × 8-12	2 × 8-12	2 × 8-12

10

PRESEASON PROGRAMMING

MARK FITZGERALD (HIGH SCHOOL), MATT SHAW (COLLEGE), MATT NICHOL (PROFESSIONAL)

The preseason period is a transitional period between off-season training and the start of the hockey in-season competition period. The main priority for the strength and conditioning professional is the physical preparation of the team for in-season practice and competition workloads. Included within this period is the onboarding of all athletes arriving back to their respective teams. Taking time to cover expectations, routines, proper communication, lifestyle management, and organizational resources helps the team members establish proper habits as they begin training as a full team for the first time. Strength and conditioning professionals should work directly with all newcomers to evaluate training age, training status, and an appropriate starting place for off-ice training as they join the team. It may be appropriate to create developmental groups within the team based upon training age, training status, and goal orientation to maximize athlete transition and prioritize the training of specific performance decrements ahead of the in-season period.

GOALS AND OBJECTIVES

In the preseason phase, it is recommended that the athletes focus primarily on their training on the ice. Resistance training in the weight room is still important, but off-ice work must now begin to complement the on-ice work and be planned around it. Whenever possible, speed and conditioning training should be performed in the most sport-specific fashion.

Off the ice, the focus of training should be to convert the gains in strength achieved in the previous phase of the off-season into sport-specific power. A high capacity to produce force is obviously important, but hockey athletes must be able to express this force rapidly and from a variety of positions under a variety of conditions.

During preseason training, strength and conditioning professionals must work directly with the hockey coaching staff to assist in managing and coordinating on- and off-ice training loads. In many instances, the on- and off-ice conditioning that the strength and conditioning professional has programmed is the singular objective starting place to serve as the foundation behind practice design. Likewise, it is advantageous for strength and conditioning professionals to have a strong understanding of late off-season voluntary on-ice training frequency, volume, and intensity across the team. This allows strength and conditioning professionals to work with the hockey coaching staff to find an appropriate starting place behind practice structure, identify any potential gaps in preparation, and progress on-ice loads toward in-season demand. Open and honest discussion with the athletes about the inclusion of voluntary on-ice practice without any hockey coaching staff present can assist the team in proper progression of on-ice volume. Proper communication with the hockey coaching staff and team can help the strength and conditioning professional prioritize the type of on-ice skating that would be most beneficial for the team or specific developmental groups.

The preseason period's off-ice training goal is to support physical development without competing against on-ice preparation for the season. With the transition of athletes back onto the ice practicing with coaches and the physical toll of battle or contact drills, physical stress is generally very high during the preseason period. Off-ice training should prioritize proper warm-up strategies, provide low-volume noncompeting stress on tissue, maintain varying exposure behind the force–velocity curve, and establish off-ice professionalism. With both physical and mental stress high during this transition, strength and conditioning professionals should be thoughtful in using the time to teach and prepare habits for in-season training. Teaching soft tissue warm-up routines, training intent, mobility work, and proper recovery can all be prioritized without adding physical stress. While the late off-season period is one of the most specific periods of off-ice training toward on-ice demand, the preseason period should shift away from on-ice specificity and transition back to more generalized training means.

LENGTH, STRUCTURE, AND ORGANIZATION

The design of preseason training programs depends upon the level of the athlete as well as the structure of the specific preseason. This section explains the differences and nuances of varying levels of the hockey athlete.

High School

Preseason training for the high school athlete is a reflection of the work that was done in the off-season. If the off-season work was done well, the preseason phase should be a smooth transition where the sport takes priority and training volume and intensity are adjusted. Planning the training sessions becomes more important, and the athlete wants to ensure the highest levels of performance for the sport. This could mean training before or after the sport as well as doing some at-home work to fill in the gaps.

The preseason program can be anywhere from two to four weeks in length, depending on the sport participation and length of training camp. Although hockey is not typically a "peaking" sport, the preseason phase aims to place the athlete into the beginning of the season in the most ideal position to be successful. The structure of the preseason phase can be adjusted to the schedule of the athlete and the sport while still aiming to emphasize the qualities built in the off-season. During this phase there is flexibility for the athlete to adjust to the demands of the sport. There is a range of training days, from three to four, based on the intensity of the ice sessions. Similar to the off-season, there is a daily focus on multijoint movements followed by supplementary work as well as anatomical core exercises. This allows the athlete to continue to progress and gain strength and power while leading up to the beginning of competition. As the four-week program progresses, the volume decreases and intensity increases to ensure that the athlete is maximizing the work done off-ice while conserving resources for on-ice practice.

College

The preseason incorporates a single three-week concurrent training mesocycle. During this time strength and conditioning professionals may find it appropriate to individualize training based on newcomer onboarding, returners, or other specific developmental groups. This allows for the strength and conditioning professional to scale the technical demands of training and manage intensity based upon training age and training status as the team arrives back to campus. The preseason example (see table 10.3) uses a three-day total body split with a different emphasis each day: day 1, power; day 2, speed; day 3, strength. Much like late off-season, high-volume repetition methods are dropped so they do not impede upon on-ice training. If specific developmental groups need higher volume training, placing the highest volume training day toward the end of the week and before an off day should not interfere with practice.

Each individual session is generally 60 minutes in length. Athletes should begin the training session with self-myofascial release and an organized team-based warm-up. Warm-up should prepare the athlete not only for the tissue ranges of motion and motor patterns that are performed within the training session but also the on-ice demands if training takes place before practice. Warm-up should transition the athlete from ground-based isolated mobilizations into increasingly more complex multiplanar and higher-velocity movements to increase both mental and physical readiness of the athletes for the individual training session. The selection of power, speed, and strength-based exercises should be organized based upon the athletes' previous exposure, technical competence, and appropriateness to elicit the specific adaptation goal within each training session. As the team is going through high-stress practice and transitioning to greater on-ice training volumes, previous exposure to exercise variations decreases the likelihood of an acute change in tissue stress and high levels of soreness. Assistance, anatomical core, prehabilitation, and mobility-based exercises should round out daily programming considerations.

Professional

Resistance training is planned for three days per week. The first session of the week has a high neurological demand but otherwise creates very little muscular soreness. This session is best performed while fresh and well rested and enhances the performance on the ice, so it is performed before the first on-ice practice of the week. The remaining sessions are performed after the on-ice training on that scheduled day so they do not detract from the quality of the on-ice practice, which is of greater importance.

RECOMMENDED EXERCISES

Exercise selection during the preseason period should be organized to maintain physical performance and support daily readiness for on-ice practice. Major exercise selection should continue previously trained movement patterns from the late off-season period yet continue the progression of velocity and intensity relative to individual session training goals. During on-ice practice with coaches and additional voluntary skill sessions, athletes receive high volumes of stress on the adductors and hip flexors. Lower body exercise selection should shift stress to more knee-dominant and concentric-only exercise selections (such as the front squat or deadlift, respectively) to limit additional stress upon the adductors and hip musculature. Hip-dominant exercises can still be used; however, the intensity and volume should be significantly decreased and then linearly transitioned back in as athletes adjust to the intensity and volume of skating stress. The use of both overcoming and yielding isometrics can also be an effective method of training the lower body without increasing tissue stress around the hip musculature. Likewise, the frequency of contact drills can elicit a higher volume of shoulder soreness as athletes progress back into on-ice battle drills. Upper body exercise selection may need to be adjusted individually based on the stress response from practice. In general, upper body training should continue to prioritize posterior strength and stability of the scapula and shoulder joint over anterior pressing exercises.

Assistance, prehabilitation, and anatomical core exercises should support performance through more isolated weak point training and corrective strategies. Although the overarching main training stress within each day may target power, speed, or strength, assistance exercises can use higher volume or tempo methods to develop isolated strength, stability, and end-range control and should focus on developing the strength or work capacity of nonconflicting more-isolated movements such as foot and ankle exercises, knee flexion, or isolated shoulder movements. Prehabilitation exercises should focus on the improvement of mechanics through low-intensity, higher-repetition means for scapular control, rotator cuff, and isolated hip work. Single exposure of one to two sets of hip flexion, extension, abduction, and adduction weekly in training can assist in the maintenance of isolated hip strength and active range of motion. Training for the anatomical core should continue the development of multiplanar trunk and pelvic stability. Exercise selection can be regressed within the preseason to more isolated, less-intense variations than late off-season, accounting for the stress experienced on-ice.

Athletes should use the preseason to establish in-season professional habits for warm-up and recovery. Strength and conditioning professionals should educate and assist in the establishment of proper warm-up strategies on non-resistance-training practice days. Athletes should get in the habit of individually assessing and managing their daily muscle tension, soreness, and range of motion during self-myofascial release and warm-up. Structuring time for the athletes to individually warm up and establish routines assists in creating self-efficacy and ownership of their bodies away from team-based training sessions.

As the team is transitioning to normalized workloads during the in-season phase, modifications should be made to goalie training. The total volume of hip stress on goalies is different than among skating positions. Goalies, who may number only two to three on most rosters, have some of the highest chronic loads on hip musculature across the entire roster. As noted within the off-season chapter, goalies should be put in more knee-dominant unilateral or bilateral exercises and reduced range of motion in hip-dominant exercises as on-ice volume increases. Their total volume within off-ice training may need to be decreased based upon their on-ice training volumes leading into preseason to assist in managing recovery. Goalie routines should include additional mobility work and self-myofascial release to maintain tissue quality.

INTENSITY

Training intensity during preseason can continue under conservative total volumes of stress and appropriate to the athlete's individual training status. For returning athletes that have progressed through the entirety of the off-season training period, training intensity can continue to progress without much disruption unless on-ice volumes exceed what they have been physically prepared to handle. The autoregulation of load using linear position transducer (LPT) can be especially useful because athlete output can fluctuate acutely based on fatigue during preseason training. Training velocity ranges may therefore be a more appropriate use of regulating intensity than percentages of estimated 1RMs. Power training during preseason can range from 1.3 m/s (35%

of an athlete's estimated 1RM) using loaded jumping methods to 0.95 m/s (60% of the 1RM) if athletes are using exercises such as band-resisted trap bar deadlifts (see table 10.1, day 1). For newcomers or younger training age athletes, less technical and higher force power exercises should be prioritized over higher velocity options because the base of force production should be a higher priority, developmentally. In the previous example, loaded jump variations may not be advised for newcomers because the landing force may exceed their ability to stabilize. Speed training should incorporate ballistic and explosive methods that are below 20% of an athlete's estimated 1RM. The use of jumping, medicine ball throwing, and traditional exercises should be performed with the athlete trying to achieve maximal velocity under very light loads. Resistance training intensity during the preseason period can range from 75% to 85% of an athlete's estimated 1RM or 0.65 to 0.5 m/s if programming is based on velocity ranges (1). The intensity and volume of resistance training during preseason should decrease to allow the athlete to maximize general force and velocity transfer of off-season training to the skill of on-ice skating without interference. Newcomers and younger training age athletes should start with more conservative resistance training intensities, establishing technique, and progress training linearly as they are onboarded to handle daily and weekly stress.

VOLUME

Volume of off-ice training is the most important factor to control during the preseason period. The overprescription of volume can have detrimental outcomes on individual performance, increasing the likelihood of soft tissue injury, delayed onset muscle soreness, and decreases in performance. Volume should be based upon prior exposure to training stress during previous weeks, volume of prescribed on-ice training loads, and external factors such as academic stress and lifestyle. The ability of the athlete to recover and sustain progression of on-ice technical and tactical skills should take priority. In specific circumstances where athletes are committed late, returning athletes report out of shape, or an athlete is returning from injury, supplementary training and conditioning may need to occur. In these instances, the volume of off-ice training should be closely managed and still prioritize on-ice training up to the athlete's threshold. The supplementation of general methods of training and conditioning off-ice can be used to support the athlete's progression of specific physical limitations.

Interpreting the Sample Program Tables

+ = *Do the two exercises back-to-back*

AA = Anatomical adaptation

Alt = Alternated

AMRAP = As many as possible (but quality repetitions)

APRE = Autoregulatory progressive resistance exercise

Asst = Assisted

BB = Barbell

BW = Body weight

Cont = Continuous

DB = Dumbbell

(continued)

Interpreting the Sample Program Tables *(continued)*

Ea = Each side (arm or leg), direction, or exercise

ECC = Eccentric

Exp = Explosive

Ext = External

FFE = Front foot elevated

Fwd = Forward

Goblet = Holding DB or KB with both hands below the chin and elbows pointed out to the side in the midline of the body

GPP = General preparation phase

ISO = Isometric

KB = Kettlebell

Kn = Kneeling

Lat = Lateral

LB = Lower body

LPT = Linear position transducer

MB = Medicine ball

m/s = meters per second

OH = Overhead

Order = Performing one set of each exercise (1a, 1b, 1c) in the group one after the other. After the first set is completed, go back to the first exercise in the group and do the second set of each exercise. If certain exercises call for fewer sets than others in the group, perform those sets on the back end of the grouping. For example, if exercise 1a calls for 4 sets and exercise 1b calls for 3 sets, perform exercise 1b during sets 2 through 4 of exercises 1a.

Plyo = plyometric

Pos = Position

RDL = Romanian deadlift

Rev = Reverse

RFE = Rear foot elevated

RFESS = Rear foot elevated split squat

RM = Repetition maximum

Rot = Rotation

RPE = Rating of perceived exertion (intensity based on level of perceived difficulty)

SA = Single arm

SB = Stability ball

SL = Single leg

SLDL = Single-leg deadlift

Tempo = The time, in seconds, for each phase or portion of the exercise, written as "eccentric phase: top (or bottom) position: concentric phase" (King, I., How to write strength training programs. In *Speed of Movement*, p. 123, 1998). For example, a tempo of "1:5:1" for the back squat means 1 second to lower, 5 seconds held at the bottom position, and 1 second to stand back up. *Note:* "Exp" means that the athlete should explode during the movement. A tempo of "Exp" is associated with power exercises because there is not a prescriptive time allotted to each portion of the movement. *Note:* All tempos are written with the first number referring to the movement that is performed first (either eccentric or concentric).

Tib = Tibialis

UB = Upper body

CONCLUSION

The preseason training period should prioritize the use of general physical developmental exercises to maintain and continue the progression of physical skills while avoiding any interference with on-ice training loads. A successful preseason physically prepares all athletes to perform daily within their potential and prepare for the training and competition loads of the in-season workload. Athlete availability in practice may be the most important preseason key performance indicator for the success of off-season development, along with the progression of individual athlete developmental markers. The preseason should serve as the transitional link between generalized off-season training and the specific refinement of the team's on-ice technical and tactical performance in-season.

Table 10.1 High School: Preseason (Three Days)

Monday (day 1): total body—power

Order	Exercise	Tempo	RPE	Sets × reps	Sets × reps	Sets × reps	Sets × reps
			1-10	Week 1	Week 2	Week 3	Week 4
1a	SA DB snatch	Exp	6-7	5 × 3 ea	5 × 3 ea	6 × 3 ea	6 × 3 ea
1b	BB front squat	2:1:1	8-9	5 × 3	5 × 3	6 × 3	6 × 3
1c	BB squat jump	Exp	5-6	5 × 5	5 × 5	5 × 5	5 × 5
1d	DB bent-over row	1:1:2	5-6	4 × 6 ea	4 × 6 ea	4 × 6 ea	4 × 6 ea
2a	Neutral grip pull-up	1:1:2	7-8	4 × 3	4 × 3	4 × 3	4 × 3
2b	MB slam	Exp	6-7	4 × 10	4 × 10	4 × 10	4 × 10

Wednesday (day 2): total body—power

Order	Exercise	Tempo	RPE	Sets × reps	Sets × reps	Sets × reps	Sets × reps
			1-10	Week 1	Week 2	Week 3	Week 4
1a	Trap bar deadlift	1:1:2	8-9	5 × 5	5 × 4	5 × 3	5 × 3
1b	Trap bar jump	Exp		5 × 3	5 × 3	5 × 3	5 × 3
1c	One-arm DB bench press	2:1:1	6-7	4 × 5 ea	4 × 5 ea	4 × 5 ea	4 × 5 ea
1d	Cable lift	Cont		3 × 8 ea	3 × 8 ea	3 × 8 ea	3 × 8 ea
2a	BB bench press	2:1:1	7-8	5 × 5	5 × 4	5 × 3	5 × 3
2b	One-arm MB throw	Exp		5 × 3 ea	5 × 3 ea	5 × 3 ea	5 × 3 ea
2c	Inverted row	1:1:2	6-7	4 × 6	4 × 6	4 × 6	4 × 6

(continued)

Table 10.1 High School: Preseason (Three Days) *(continued)*

Friday (day 3): total body—power

Order	Exercise	Tempo	RPE	Sets × reps	Sets × reps	Sets × reps	Sets × reps
			1-10	Week 1	Week 2	Week 3	Week 4
1a	BB squat jump	Exp	7-8	4 × 4	4 × 4	4 × 4	4 × 4
1b	One-arm rotational cable row	1:1:2	7-8	4 × 8 ea	4 × 8 ea	4 × 8 ea	4 × 8 ea
1c	Landmine deadlift	2:1:1	6-7	4 × 6	4 × 6	4 × 6	4 × 6
1d	Rotary cable chop	Cont		3 × 8 ea	3 × 8 ea	3 × 8 ea	3 × 8 ea
2a	One-arm landmine push press	1:1:2	6-7	4 × 4 ea	4 × 4 ea	4 × 4 ea	4 × 4 ea
2b	DB lateral lunge	2:1:1	6-7	4 × 6 ea	4 × 6 ea	4 × 6 ea	4 × 6 ea
2c	Lateral MB shotput toss	Exp		4 × 3 ea	4 × 3 ea	4 × 3 ea	4 × 3 ea

Table 10.2 High School: Preseason (Four Days)

Monday (day 1): upper body—power

Order	Exercise	Tempo	RPE	Sets × reps	Sets × reps	Sets × reps	Sets × reps
			1-10	Week 1	Week 2	Week 3	Week 4
1a	One-arm DB snatch	Exp	6-7	5 × 3 ea	5 × 3 ea	6 × 3 ea	6 × 3 ea
1b	Lateral MB shotput toss	Exp	Plyo	4 × 3 ea	4 × 3 ea	4 × 3 ea	4 × 3 ea
1c	One-arm landmine push press	1:1:2	6-7	4 × 4 ea	4 × 4 ea	4 × 4 ea	4 × 4 ea
1d	DB bent-over row	1:1:2	5-6	4 × 6 ea	4 × 6 ea	4 × 6 ea	4 × 6 ea
2a	Neutral grip pull-up	2:1:1	7-8	4 × 3	4 × 3	4 × 3	4 × 3
2b	MB slam	Exp		4 × 10	4 × 10	4 × 10	4 × 10
2c	2 DB push press	1:1:2	6-7	3 × 6	3 × 6	3 × 6	3 × 6
2d	Cable lift	Cont		3 × 8 ea	3 × 8 ea	3 × 8 ea	3 × 8 ea

Tuesday (day 2): lower body—power

Order	Exercise	Tempo	RPE	Sets × reps or distance	Sets × reps or distance	Sets × reps or distance	Sets × reps or distance
			1-10	Week 1	Week 2	Week 3	Week 4
1a	Trap bar deadlift	1:1:2	8-9	5 × 5	5 × 4	5 × 3	5 × 3
1b	Trap bar jump	Exp		5 × 3	5 × 3	5 × 3	5 × 3
1c	SL box squat	2:1:1	6-7	4 × 5 ea	4 × 5 ea	4 × 5 ea	4 × 5 ea
1d	Lateral band walk	Cont		3 × 8 ea	3 × 8 ea	3 × 8 ea	3 × 8 ea
2a	BB split squat	2:1:1	7-8	4 × 4 ea	4 × 4 ea	4 × 4 ea	4 × 4 ea
2b	Single-leg DB SLDL	2:1:1		4 × 6 ea	4 × 6 ea	4 × 6 ea	4 × 6 ea
2c	Single-leg box jump	Exp	6-7	4 × 3 ea	4 × 3 ea	4 × 3 ea	4 × 3 ea
2d	Farmer's carry	Cont		3 × 25 m ea	3 × 25 m ea	3 × 25 m ea	3 × 25 m ea

Thursday (day 3): upper body—power

Order	Exercise	Tempo	RPE	Sets × reps or distance	Sets × reps or distance	Sets × reps or distance	Sets × reps or distance
			1-10	Week 1	Week 2	Week 3	Week 4
1a	BB bench press	2:1:1	7-8	5 × 5	5 × 4	5 × 3	5 × 3
1b	One-arm MB chest pass	Exp		5 × 3 ea	5 × 3 ea	5 × 3 ea	5 × 3 ea
1c	Inverted row	1:1:2	6-7	4 × 6	4 × 6	4 × 6	4 × 6
1d	One-arm waiter carry	Cont		3 × 25 m ea	3 × 25 m ea	3 × 25 m ea	3 × 25 m ea
2a	One-arm cable rotational row	1:1:2	7-8	4 × 8 ea	4 × 8 ea	4 × 8 ea	4 × 8 ea
2b	One-arm DB bench press	2:1:1	6-7	4 × 5 ea	4 × 5 ea	4 × 5 ea	4 × 5 ea
2c	Lateral MB shotput toss	Exp	Plyo	4 × 3 ea	4 × 3 ea	4 × 3 ea	4 × 3 ea
2d	Side plank row	1:1:1		3 × 10 ea	3 × 10 ea	3 × 10 ea	3 × 10 ea

Friday (day 4): lower body—power

Order	Exercise	Tempo	RPE	Sets × reps	Sets × reps	Sets × reps	Sets × reps
			1-10	Week 1	Week 2	Week 3	Week 4
1a	BB squat jump	Exp	7-8	4 × 4	4 × 4	4 × 4	4 × 4
1b	DB RFE split squat	2:1:1	7-8	4 × 6 ea	4 × 6 ea	4 × 6 ea	4 × 6 ea
1c	Landmine deadlift	2:1:1	6-7	4 × 6	4 × 6	4 × 6	4 × 6
1d	Rotary cable chop	Cont		3 × 8 ea	3 × 8 ea	3 × 8 ea	3 × 8 ea
2a	KB swing	Exp		4 × 10	4 × 10	4 × 10	4 × 10
2b	DB lateral lunge	2:1:1	6-7	4 × 6 ea	4 × 6 ea	4 × 6 ea	4 × 6 ea
2c	Alt lateral bound	Exp		4 × 6 ea	4 × 6 ea	4 × 6 ea	4 × 6 ea
2d	Single-leg stability ball hamstring curl	1:1:2	BW	3 × 8 ea	3 × 8 ea	3 × 8 ea	3 × 8 ea

Table 10.3   College: Preseason

Monday (day 1): total body—power

Order	Exercise	Tempo	% of 1RM or RPE	Sets × reps or time	Sets × reps or time	Sets × reps or time
				Week 1	Week 2	Week 3
1a	Band-resisted trap bar deadlift	Exp	0.90-0.95 m/s	3 × 3	4 × 3	4 × 3
1b	Barbell vertical jump	Exp	Bar only	3 × 4	3 × 4	3 × 4
1c	Supine cable hip flexion	1:1:3	50%-60%	2 × 5 ea	2 × 5 ea	2 × 5 ea
2a	Barbell bench press	1:1:1	70%-75%	3 × 4	4 × 4	4 × 4
2b	DB goblet lateral lunge	1:3:1	50%-55%	3 × 5 ea	3 × 5 ea	3 × 5 ea
2c	Cable dead bug	3:0:1	RPE 7	2 × 4 ea	2 × 5 ea	2 × 6 ea
1a	Stability ball leg curl	1:5:1	BW	2 × 3	2 × 4	2 × 5
1b	Bottom leg support side plank	ISO	RPE 4-6	2 × 15 s ea	2 × 20 s ea	2 × 25 s ea

(continued)

Table 10.3 College: Preseason *(continued)*

Wednesday (day 2): total body—speed

Order	Exercise	Tempo	% of 1RM or RPE	Sets × reps Week 1	Sets × reps Week 2	Sets × reps Week 3
1a	Barbell step-up	1:1:1	50%-55%	3 × 3 ea	4 × 3 ea	4 × 3 ea
1b	Off box alt split vertical jump	Exp	Max Power	3 × 3 ea	3 × 3 ea	3 × 3 ea
1c	Split squat pos one-arm cable row	1:1:1	50%-55%	3 × 6 ea	3 × 6 ea	3 × 6 ea
2a	One-arm KB SLDL	1:1:1	50%-55%	3 × 5 ea	3 × 5 ea	3 × 5 ea
2b	DB incline bench press	1:1:1	50%-55%	3 × 5	3 × 5	3 × 5
2c	Half-kn cable chop	1:3:1	RPE 6-8	2 × 6 ea	2 × 6 ea	2 × 6 ea
3a	Side-lying reverse fly	1:1:3	RPE 6-8	2 × 8 ea	2 × 8 ea	2 × 8 ea
3b	One-arm KB slide cross-behind lunge	3:1:1	RPE 6-8	2 × 8 ea	2 × 8 ea	2 × 8 ea

Friday (day 3): total body—strength

Order	Exercise	Tempo	% of 1RM	Sets × reps Week 1	Sets × reps Week 2	Sets × reps Week 3
1a	Front squat	2:1:1	75%-80%	2 × 4	3 × 4	3 × 4
1b	DB bench press	2:1:1	75%-80%	2 × 6	3 × 6	3 × 6
1c	Standing cable external rotation	Cont	60%-65%	2 × 10 ea	3 × 10 ea	3 × 10 ea
2a	Athletic stance one-arm row	1:1:1	65%-70%	2 × 8 ea	3 × 8 ea	3 × 8 ea
2b	Glute-ham raise	2:0:1	BW	2 × 8	3 × 8	3 × 10
2c	Side plank top leg support	1:6:1	BW	2 × 2 ea	2 × 3 ea	2 × 4 ea
3a	Off-bench DB single-leg squat	2:1:1	60%-65%	2 × 5 ea	2 × 5 ea	2 × 5 ea
3b	Stability ball knee tuck	1:2:1	BW	2 × 8	2 × 10	2 × 12

Table 10.4 Professional: Preseason

Monday (day 1): upper body

Order	Exercise	Tempo	Load	Sets × reps Week 1	Sets × reps Week 2	Sets × reps Week 3
1a	Dynamic cable lift	Cont		3-4 × 6 ea	3-4 × 6 ea	3-4 × 6 ea
1b	Parallel grip chin-up	2:1:1	BW	3-4 × 4-6	3-4 × 4-6	3-4 × 4-6
1c	Split stance landmine throw	Exp		3-4 × 4-6 ea	3-4 × 4-6 ea	3-4 × 4-6 ea
2a	Bent-over rear delt lateral raise	3:1:1		2 × 10-15	2 × 10-15	2 × 10-15
2b	Standing lateral raise	3:1:1		2 × 10-15	2 × 10-15	2 × 10-15

Tuesday (day 2): lower body

Order	Exercise	Tempo	Load or velocity	Sets × reps or time	Sets × reps or time	Sets × reps or time
				Week 1	Week 2	Week 3
1a	Hang clean	Exp	>1.3 m/s	3-4 × 2-3	3-4 × 2-3	3-4 × 2-3
1b	3 consecutive broad jump	Exp	BW	3-4 × 3	3-4 × 3	3-4 × 3
2a	Front squat	Cont	0.75-0.95 m/s	2-3 × 3	2-3 × 3	2-3 × 3
2b	3 consecutive hurdle hop	Exp	BW	2-3 × 3	2-3 × 3	2-3 × 3
3a	Copenhagen plank	1:6:1	BW	1 × 4-6 × 6 s ea	1 × 4-6 × 6 s ea	1 × 4-6 × 6 s ea

Wednesday (day 3): upper body

Order	Exercise	Tempo	Velocity	Sets × reps or time	Sets × reps or time	Sets × reps or time
				Week 1	Week 2	Week 3
1a	Dynamic cable chop	Cont		3-4 × 6 ea	3-4 × 6 ea	3-4 × 6 ea
1b	Bench press	Cont	0.75-0.95 m/s	3-4 × 3-5	3-4 × 3-5	3-4 × 3-5
1c	Seated med ball chest pass	Exp		3-4 × 5	3-4 × 5	3-4 × 5
2a	Inverted row	3:1:1		2-3 × 4-6	2-3 × 4-6	2-3 × 4-6
2b	External rotation	Cont		2-3 × 7-10 ea	2-3 × 7-10 ea	2-3 × 7-10 ea
3a	Alt side bridge	6 s ISO		1-2 × 2 × 6 s	1-2 × 2 × 6 s	1-2x 2 × 6 s

Friday (day 4): lower body

Order	Exercise	Tempo	Load or velocity	Sets × reps or time	Sets × reps or time	Sets × reps or time
				Week 1	Week 2	Week 3
1a	Trap bar deadlift	Cont	0.55-0.7 m/s	3-4 × 3	3-4 × 3	3-4 × 3
1b	Seated box jump	Exp	BW	3-4 × 1	3-4 × 1	3-4 × 1
2a	KB swing	Exp		3 × 6	3 × 6	3 × 6
2b	Consecutive standing broad jump	Exp	BW	3 × 3	3 × 3	3 × 3
3a	One-leg DB reverse lunge + knee drive	Cont		3 × 5 ea	3 × 5 ea	3 × 5 ea
4a	Copenhagen plank	1:6:1	BW	1 × 4-6 × 6 s ea	1 × 4-6 × 6 s ea	1 × 4-6 × 6 s ea

Table 10.5   Professional: Goalie Preseason

Monday (day 1)

Order	Exercise	Tempo	Load or velocity	Sets × reps	Sets × reps	Sets × reps
				Week 1	Week 2	Week 3
1b	Kneeling clean (pads recommended)	Exp		3-4 × 3	3-4 × 3	3-4 × 3
1b	Lateral bound	Exp	BW	3-4 × 6	3-4 × 6	3-4 × 6
2a	Front squat	Cont	0.7-0.9 m/s	3-4 × 3-5	3-4 × 3-5	3-4 × 3-5
2b	Box jump	Exp	BW	3-4 × 1-3	3-4 × 1-3	3-4 × 1-3
3a	DB rear foot elevated split squat	2:1:1		3 × 4-6 ea	3 × 4-6 ea	3 × 4-6 ea
3b	One-arm DB row	3:1:1		3 × 7-10 ea	3 × 7-10 ea	3 × 7-10 ea

Wednesday (day 2)

Order	Exercise	Tempo	Load	Sets × reps	Sets × reps	Sets × reps
				Week 1	Week 2	Week 3
1a	One-arm DB snatch	Exp		3-4 × 3 ea	3-4 × 3 ea	3-4 × 3 ea
1b	Tall kneeling cable lift	Cont		3-4 × 6-8 ea	3-4 × 6-8 ea	3-4 × 6-8 ea
2a	One-arm cable rotational row	Cont		3 × 5 ea	3 × 5 ea	3 × 5 ea
2b	Glute-ham raise	3:0:1	BW	3 × 4-6	3 × 4-6	3 × 4-6
3a	Inverted row	3:1:1		3 × 5-7	3 × 5-7	3 × 5-7
3b	External rotation	Cont		3 × 7-10 ea	3 × 7-10 ea	3 × 7-10 ea
3c	Tall kneeling DB curl and press	Cont		2 × 10	2 × 10	2 × 10

Friday (day 3)

Order	Exercise	Tempo	Load or velocity	Sets × reps or time	Sets × reps or time	Sets × reps or time
				Week 1	Week 2	Week 3
1a	Trap bar deadlift	Cont	0.55-0.7 m/s	3-4 × 3-5	3-4 × 3-5	3-4 × 3-5
1b	Seated box jump	Exp	BW	3-4 × 3	3-4 × 3	3-4 × 3
2a	One-arm dumbbell lateral squat	Cont		3-4 × 4-6 ea	3-4 × 4-6 ea	3-4 × 4-6 ea
2b	Half-kneeling slider lateral push	Cont		2-3 × 6-8 ea	2-3 × 6-8 ea	2-3 × 6-8 ea
3a	Front split squat	Cont		2-3 × 6-8 ea	2-3 × 6-8 ea	2-3 × 6-8 ea
3b	Nordic hamstring curl	3:0:1	BW	2-3 × 3-5	2-3 × 3-5	2-3 × 3-5
3c	Tall kneeling cable chop	Cont		2-3 × 6-8 ea	2-3 × 6-8 ea	2-3 × 6-8 ea
4a	Copenhagen plank	1:6:1	BW	2 × 4-6 × 6 s ea	2 × 4-6 × 6 s ea	2 × 4-6 × 6 s ea

11

IN-SEASON PROGRAMMING

**MARK FITZGERALD (HIGH SCHOOL), MATT SHAW (COLLEGE),
MATT NICHOL (PROFESSIONAL)**

During the in-season period, the fundamental goal of every team is putting forth an optimal active roster of healthy high-performing athletes to create the highest likelihood of success against their competition, dependent on the opposition's strengths and weaknesses. Within each week of the in-season period, athlete performance and health status dictates lineup decisions. Unlike off-season or preseason training, where every athlete may be participating in somewhat similar volumes of total stress within the week, in-season competition playing time can create large discrepancies in physical and mental stress among athletes. Playing time can range from none at all to 100% of a competition. With most teams competing multiple times per week throughout the in-season period, playing time can create significant individual differences in stress both weekly and chronically across the season. The in-season period requires a holistic approach to individualize performance development, manage stress, and support athlete recovery.

GOALS AND OBJECTIVES

In-season performance development is uniquely based upon the goal orientation of each individual athlete and the prescription of both on-ice and off-ice stress to support long-term hockey development and wellness. The main goal of the weekly preparation period (WPP) is the physical, technical, and tactical preparation of the team going into competition. The WPP varies depending on the level of the athletes. Most youth and collegiate hockey conferences have two competitions per week, on Friday and Saturday. The WPP in this case would occur from Sunday through Thursday. However, competition schedules can vary to include midweek contests, which would shorten the WPP to three to four days. During the WPP, all athletes are generally receiving the same prescription of on-ice and off-ice training volumes. Off-ice training goals include the maintenance or development of specific physical outputs and tissue resiliency while supporting recovery through both physical and educational means.

Professional hockey athletes can have competitions multiple times per week with very little time to develop a WPP. Off-ice programming must be fluid and based on individual athletes' needs to best prepare them for competition.

LENGTH, STRUCTURE, AND ORGANIZATION

The design of the in-season training programs depends upon the level of the athlete as well as the game schedule. Each level lends itself to different goals and influences the structure and organization of training during the season.

High School

In-season training for the high school hockey athlete incorporates several different objectives. The sport, the reason the athlete participates, always takes priority; training is in place to support that. The in-season should be focused on including as many different qualities as possible (mobility, strength, flexibility, hypertrophy) and managing those qualities across the season. Building routines around the different aspects of the season aids in organizing resistance training (table 11.1).

Table 11.1   Organizing In-Season Resistance Training

Event	Timing	Focus of training	Qualities
Game day	Postgame	Total body	Hypertrophy/endurance
Practice day	Pre- or postpractice	Strength, power development	Max effort and power
Rest and recovery	Athlete choice	Movement	Mobility
Travel day	Before or after	Total body	Hypertrophy/endurance

The in-season portion covers the entire competition phase, which can be anywhere between three and six months. With the variability in the game schedules, having flexibility in the training program is key to keeping the athlete engaged in training. One of the most detrimental things a young hockey athlete can do is to discontinue training during the in-season. If the athlete chooses not to participate in resistance training during the season, it can negatively affect athletic development and potentially affect on-ice performance. Ensuring the athlete is addressing the major physical qualities of strength, hypertrophy, power, and endurance is helpful when entering the following off-season.

The in-season phase is determined by the competition schedule and must have some flexibility within it. Table 11.2 is an example of what a weekly schedule could look like based on a team traveling to play two away games over a weekend.

Table 11.2   Weekly In-Season Schedule

Sunday	Monday	Tuesday	Wednesday	Thursday	Friday	Saturday
Travel home Rest and recovery	*Morning* Total body resistance training session	*Morning* Mobility session	*Morning* Total body resistance training session	*Morning* Movement session	*Game day* Morning skate	*Game day* Morning skate
No training	*Afternoon* Practice	*Afternoon* Practice	*Afternoon* Practice	Travel	Game	Game

For the high school athlete, the positional requirements are determined by the role the athlete has on the team. An athlete with heavy playing time must manage resistance training volume to avoid doing too much and negatively affecting performance on the ice. Conversely, the athlete who is not playing as much or may be in and out of gameplay must keep up enough exposure to training to maintain the qualities built in the off-season and preseason. This becomes a more challenging endeavor for the high school athlete, and ideally, athletes have support from both a sport coach and a strength and conditioning professional.

College

The complexity of the in-season period requires organization, communication, flexibility, and thoughtful integration to maximize individual and team performance. The college environment combines academic, social, lifestyle, and physical stress upon athletes; they are required to maintain a minimum of 12 credit hours, yet many enroll in up to 16 credit hours per term. For each credit hour taken, outside study and homework may constitute an additional 1 to 4 hours weekly. Thus, the minimum time spent engaging in academic-related hours can range from 24 to 64 hours per week. During the in-season competition period, student-athletes may engage in up to 20 hours of mandatory athletic-related activity (practice, workouts, meetings, competition). Therefore, just between the academic and athletic requirements, most student-athletes are working the equivalent of one or two full-time (40-hour) jobs. The addition of environmental and lifestyle stressors, such as social situations, alcohol consumption, poor sleep habits, limited nutritional resources, and organizational time constraints are ever-present.

During team off-ice training, prescribed loads are largely determined based upon logistical factors such as team travel considerations the prior weekend, the strength of the opponent, number of days out from competition, and which week it is within the in-season period. The largest deviations in individual stress occur during the weekly competition period (WCP) and should therefore be one of the most individually managed aspects of in-season training volume. While athletes engaging in competitions should be focused on maximizing performance, healthy scratches (uninjured players who are not in the game lineup) and athletes with low playing times may need supplemental work to avoid detraining due to chronically low WCP stress. Supplementing on-ice specific skill development, which is overseen by the hockey coaching staff, and off-ice developmental training can assist in managing weekly workloads and progressing physical development. The orientation of supplemental off-ice training is dependent on factors such as competition playing time, training age, and training goals identified through physical testing.

One of the most important aspects of the in-season period is quantifying training and competition stress. This provides the practitioner an objective way to evaluate the discrepancies of training intensity and volume among everyone on the team across on-ice and off-ice environments. Resources to accomplish this may look different for every institution, but methods such as calculating duration of stress exposure, RPE, drill, or exercise repetition counts can all provide valuable insight. Team monitoring of accelerometry and heart rate can provide improved accuracy in measuring individual differences in physical output and stress response but requires financial investment. This information should be used to improve the decision-making behind stress prescription on-ice and off-ice while considering team and individual goals across the length of the in-season period.

The management of athlete recovery plays a significant role in the success of teams across such a long in-season period. During the first half of the in-season, the hockey coaching staff spends the majority of practice time teaching technical and tactical habits within team systems and preparing the team to play as a cohesive group. Many teams experience higher on-ice skating loads in practice and competition due to tactical and positional inefficiencies, contributed to by the limitations in practice hours before the in-season period. Strength and conditioning professionals should start conservatively with off-ice training volume early and then build training volume up during the first half of the in-season period. Establishing recovery routines and education early within the season creates a foundation behind proper lifestyle skills to leverage recovery. Sleep, nutritional habits, compression, and the use of hot or cold therapies are the lowest hanging fruit for collegiate recovery. Education of athletes should center around the value of managing these areas and establishing consistent habits.

As athletes transition into the second half of the season, practice stress should be optimized to reduce volume and increase the quality and intensity of drills. Just as on-ice volumes are decreased as athletes become more proficient in technical and tactical abilities, off-ice training should parallel this in the second half of the season. The schedule for decreasing off-ice training stress in the second half of the season occurs based upon the amount of time remaining until the last guaranteed competition. For some teams this may be the end of the regular season, heading into the conference tournament, or the start of the NCAA tournament. Reducing the total amount of stress within the WPP while maximizing recovery from all controllable areas allows athletes the best possible opportunity to peak for success.

The college hockey regular season starts the first weekend in October and runs through the beginning of March, making it one of the longest collegiate sport seasons. Conference tournaments and the NCAA tournament can extend the in-season period to the second week in April. The first half of the regular college in-season is generally dense with nonconference competitions and the beginning of conference competitions. The first half expands from the start of the in-season period until most teams depart for the holiday break, around mid-December. Many teams get a two-week break from competitions, and athletes can head home to spend time with family. The second half of the regular season spans from late December until the beginning of conference tournaments in March. The second half of competition is almost entirely focused on conference competition, with maybe a few exceptions for nonconference games, depending on team scheduling. The length for the in-season period allows most strength and conditioning professionals to program 23 guaranteed weeks of in-season training, divided into approximately eight three-week mesocycles.

Within most conferences the weekly preparation period allows for consistent training structure across the in-season period. Within a typical competition week, with games on Friday and Saturday, full-team training sessions should occur Monday and Wednesday. Additional warm-ups, supplementary training, and in-season testing can occur on nontraining days such as Tuesdays and Thursdays. The first training session of the week (four days prior to competition) should focus on higher-force training (60%-90% of an estimated 1RM) to expand or maintain the athlete's strength and strength–speed development. The second training day, two days out from competition, should consistently focus on speed–strength or speed because that does not create high levels of tissue soreness. At the conclusion of each WPP leading up to competition, lineup selections for competition are made. At that point, stress prescription for those out of the active lineup for Friday's competition shifts toward the development of on-ice technical skills and off-ice generalized physical development to support on-ice performance. This can include healthy scratches or injured athletes that are not medically cleared to compete. When adding supplemental training for those not competing, it is advised to properly organize training stress to account for possible lineup changes between Friday and Saturday competitions. A higher-intensity low-volume dynamic-effort-focused training session Friday can still allow athletes to perform at a high level if they transition into the lineup for Saturday's competition. Athletes that are scratched for Saturday can then receive a higher volume off-ice training session focused on strength deficiencies, because they will have a rest day on Sunday. The tiering of stress in this manner allows for those competing in games to receive two total body training sessions of moderate- to low-volume off-ice training, while developmental athletes not actively competing train four sessions per week.

Managing training loads and specific qualities across the length of the in-season period should be organized by a few underlying principles. Early in-season stress can be very demanding because teams are quickly trying to progress on-ice habits and tactics to generate success. As the hours shift from an 8-hour week in preseason to a 20-hour week in-season, off-ice training load should be moderate to low to account for the high volume of total stress. As training progresses across the first half of the regular season, off-ice training volume can linearly increase as athletes adjust to in-season training loads. Progressing training volume and intensity gives athletes a larger foundation from which to taper toward late in-season competitions. By the second half of the in-season, day 1 training can shift from strength emphasis to moderate- or high-intensity power training. The second day can then shift toward absolute speed work, giving the athletes a linear transition toward peaking. Difficult travel across time zones, game lengths extending into overtime, and sustained competition weeks without a bye week should all be considered when managing load. An acute decrease in training volume following these circumstances can dramatically assist in recovery from chronic stress across the season. It is also important to consider the impact of high-stress academic periods such as midterms and finals on sleep and recovery. A reduction in stress from both on-ice and off-ice training can help reduce total stress acting on athletes while sleep is reduced and academic stress may be abnormally high.

Physical adaptations to training can be rotated across the in-season period to assist in maintaining residual training effects. The use of different training tempos during the first training session of the week maintains the specific muscle action force potential, whether it be eccentric, concentric, or isometric. Likewise, varying the use of exercises completed with a stretch-shortening cycle, compared to those trained concentric only, differentiates mechanical stress across the in-season period. Differentiation of stress by training age can continue to be used in-season. Higher training age athletes can be trained with less overall frequency of resistance training and a higher proportion of training focused on power or speed development. Younger training age athletes may be able to sustain positive adaptations to resistance training in-season compared to their older training age counterparts who train at higher relative intensity without technical limitations. Although these deviations in programming can be coordinated in-season, strength and conditioning professionals should still be flexible with prescribed volume to account for differences in playing time.

Professional

There are more than a dozen recognized professional men's hockey leagues around the world. The National Hockey League is widely regarded as the best league in the world. While the official start and end dates and game schedules of the various other leagues (in particular the European-based leagues) are different than in the NHL, they are similar enough in general pattern that the strategies listed here can be extrapolated and applied with little difficulty. Therefore, these principles would apply to those leagues as well.

Professional women's hockey has several different professional leagues around the world, but the scheduling of those games (both volume and frequency) is highly variable and vastly different from the men's leagues. The professional women's hockey schedule is more similar to the college hockey season, with two weekend competitions.

Strength and conditioning training for elite athletes at all levels is always a blend of art and science, but in-season training for professional hockey athletes, specifically, is often more art than science. Recommendations on programming for this population that are offered by anyone who has not spent time doing the job should always be taken with a grain of salt. Many intangibles simply cannot be factored in appropriately when planned in a spreadsheet. Some of the confounding factors that can compromise a planned in-season training schedule include the following:

- Travel to and from away games comes with complications, such as crossing international borders and time zones, staying in unfamiliar hotels and eating in unfamiliar restaurants, and dealing with all sorts of schedule interruptions and delays.
- Athletes can be traded or sent down at various times of the season and, subsequently, new athletes with whom the coach has no training history can join the team unexpectedly.
- Individual athletes (and occasionally the team as a whole) can have appearance obligations for corporate partners or community outreach initiatives that can conflict with training times.
- Personal family issues such as births, deaths, illnesses may limit an athlete's availability.
- The mental aspect of the game leaves coaches dealing with athletes who may not want to participate when struggling on the ice.

Note that because the National Hockey League is the highest level of the sport, it attracts the most elite and highly talented athletes. As is true in any skill-based team sport, there are athletes who are physical outliers. These athletes may not respond to training in the same manner as the majority of athletes. Some are extremely responsive and adaptive to training and therefore require far less volume to achieve similar results. These athletes are more prone to overtraining, and caution must be exercised when using cookie-cutter programs without constant monitoring for readiness. Perhaps a more challenging problem is that many of these athletes have been able to achieve great levels of success in their sport without the same level of commitment to training. Even though biological age and sport level would suggest an advanced program, many of these athletes have a much lower training age and require a more rudimentary approach. Athletes such as this need coaches who can educate them and help them understand why they need to make a commitment to their training and how best to go about doing so in a manner specific to their unique needs and abilities.

The NHL hockey season can encompass anywhere from seven to ten months of the calendar year. Preseason exhibition games typically commence in late September, and the regular season typically ends in early April. The NHL playoff season can be as long as two months for teams that make it to the Stanley Cup finals. For example, in the 2022 NHL season, preseason training camps opened on September 14. Teams played four to six preseason exhibition games between September 14 and October 10. Regular season league play started on October 12, and all teams completed 82 games by April 30. Teams that are fortunate enough to qualify for the Stanley Cup playoffs could have the potential to play as many as 28 additional games over the course of the next two months. All told, the NHL season, including exhibition and playoff games, could last anywhere from 210 to 258 days and encompass from 86 to 116 games. This results in an average of one game every 2.5 days. However, when factoring in the extended breaks for December holidays and the NHL All-Star week, then this becomes much closer to one game every two days. This volume of competition and density of game schedule is not conducive to high in-season training loads.

Furthermore, ice hockey is a high-speed collision sport, and athletes are constantly dealing with injuries. Even when these injuries are not significant enough to keep the athletes out of the lineup, they are often significant enough to affect their ability to participate freely in resistance training. Numerous accommodations must be made to find ways to maintain strength and power during this long season in a way that is tolerable by these bodies that are often bruised and battered. The experienced strength and conditioning professional understands that regardless of what workout was planned for any given day, a system should be in place to assess each athlete's physical readiness to perform resistance training exercises because some dysfunctions not yet diagnosed by the medical staff but significant enough to prevent safely participating in training can occur.

Due to the volume and frequency that the athletes are on the ice performing sport-specific movements, the training off the ice shifts to generalized goals of strength and power. For some younger athletes at a lower training age, and for those who have a lower workload of minutes played per game, there may also be some hypertrophy-specific work to maintain or even gain lean body mass during the long and arduous season.

There are a variety of tools available to sport scientists and strength and conditioning professionals to help to assess and monitor the readiness of the athletes to train. These range from low-tech and basic (subjective questionnaires, resting heart rate, and basal temperature) to the more advanced and higher-tech (wearable monitoring devices to measure sleep and heart rate variability, force plates, and accelerometers). Even with all this monitoring it can still be extremely challenging for strength and conditioning professionals to know exactly how and when to apply external loading in the weight room and when rest may be the more appropriate choice.

Apart from goaltenders, no accommodation is made on a position-specific basis. In the case of goaltenders, it is also important to differentiate between starting goaltenders, back-up goaltenders, or goaltending tandems who share the workload.

The planning of the resistance training program for goaltenders in-season is highly challenging on some teams because there can be highly variable workloads in any given week or month. The average length of a shift for a forward in the NHL is 46 seconds, with an average recovery time between shifts of 3 to 5 minutes and an average total ice time of approximately 16 minutes (2). The average length of a shift for an NHL defense athlete is 55 seconds, with an average recovery time between shifts of 2 to 4 minutes and an average total ice time of approximately 20 minutes (2). A starting goaltender, on the other hand, is expected to play the entire game and is not able to come to the bench to be relieved for shifts like the other athletes can. When the starting goaltender is playing well, the backup goaltender does not play at all during the game and thus requires an increased workload outside of the stimulus of the game to maintain sport-specific power and conditioning. However, should the coach determine that the starting goaltender is not playing well, a backup can be substituted in at any time, and therefore the backup goalie must always be prepared (and sufficiently recovered from training) to be called into action midgame. As a result, it is always wise for the backup goaltender to do a significant portion of training either immediately after any games with no playing time or the following morning, if the weekly game schedule allows it.

RECOMMENDED EXERCISES

In-season training should mirror the off-season's developmental strategies, with a few unique considerations. A large portion of off-season development is spent on unilateral training because it has the highest transferability within the three-dimensional force application of the stride. In-season training should continue to use single-leg exercises such as the rear foot elevated split squat, lunge variations, single-leg squat and single-leg deadlift (SLDL) to progress or maintain force production. The volume of three-dimensional variations, however, should decrease because hockey skating volume largely fills this need. During periods of acute increased skating volume, such as early in-season and after the holiday break, it may be beneficial to transition to bilateral exercises to reduce stress on the adductors and hip stabilizers from unilateral training. Bilateral variations such as the trap bar deadlift and front squat are more valuable options because the limiting factor behind loading is postural stability and not absolute loading on lower body musculature. Furthermore, both exercises can help improve lumbo-pelvic stability and postural orientation of the pelvis with the rib cage in-season. Lower and upper body posterior chain exercises should continue to be prioritized as essential exercises in offsetting the anterior dominance of stress in-season. Although the hamstring is not a dominant contributor to stride force production, it is a large stabilizer of the knee and the pelvis (1). Both hip- and knee-dominant hamstring variations should be included weekly. Upper body training should be posteriorly dominant but still include landmine, dumbbell, barbell, and push-up variations for anterior strength and teaching proper scapular movement. Upper body posterior training should include overhead, horizontal, and arm abduction variations because these contribute to maintaining the strength and function of the glenohumeral and scapulothoracic joints.

Accessory work and prehabilitation exercises should continue to develop the strength, endurance, and stability of isolated single-joint or multijoint agonists that may be limiting performance. Movements for the hip, anatomical core, rotator cuff, and scapular stabilizers should make up the majority of these types of exercises. Programming should prioritize the three-dimensional stability, strength, and endurance of these structures to maintain athlete tissue health and help decrease the likelihood of common compensations across the in-season period.

Because both time and energy are at a premium, it is imperative that the strength and conditioning professional be maximally efficient with the athletes' available training time. It is best to choose a relatively small number of exercises that have a relatively large return on investment.

INTENSITY

In-season training intensity is largely based upon the interdependent relationship between the volume of stress acting upon the athletes and the ability to recover from sessions. When the total volume of prescribed on-ice practice, off-ice training, and external stressors are in balance with athlete recovery, intensity can be maintained or increased to elicit an adaptation. However, when these stressors exceed the athletes' ability to maintain proper recovery through sleep, nutritional, and lifestyle habits, intensity needs to be decreased. Throughout the in-season period, training intensity and recovery go through fluctuations. Early identification of difficult team travel, creating sleep disruptions, and sustained high weekly loads can help strength and conditioning professionals properly plan decreases in intensity or volume. In most situations, in-season training intensity can be kept consistent by taking a moderate to very low volume approach to training. However, if there is an acute training volume increase, it may be advantageous to adjust intensity.

High School

The sport and sport practice account for most of the load throughout the in-season. Understanding when the athlete can insert and apply more load and higher intensities through training is a learning process. Resistance training becomes a secondary but necessary tool for the athlete and must be managed appropriately. Most high school athletes can continue to make progress from moderate training intensities because they are still learning how to coordinate multiple joints and muscle activation patterns to accomplish movements.

College

Within the weekly training structure, contrasting intensities are used to balance adaptations between high force and high velocity. When specific mesocycles use heavier loads (i.e., above 80% of an estimated 1RM) during the first day of training, the second day of training shifts the intensity to below 35% of the 1RM (see table 11.4). This polarization of training intensities creates balance in exposure between high force and high velocity. Likewise, when mesocycles call for strength–speed power training between 57.5% and 80% of the 1RM, training on the second day shifts speed–strength to between 35% and 57.5% of the 1RM (see table 11.5). During the first half of the regular season, training intensities should be incrementally increased, with a higher percentage of mesocycles focusing on high-force foundational strength and power. In the second half of the regular season, mesocycles should begin to decrease training intensity and start biasing the lower range of prescribed intensities to elicit higher velocities toward peaking for conference or NCAA tournament play. The ability to maintain training intensity across the long in-season requires careful planning of proper exercise selection and accounting for fluctuations in training volume to offset stress. The culmination of in-season training intensity should provide the athlete with a robust and highly developed force–velocity curve to leverage on-ice performance.

Training age, exercise selection, and technical ability of the athlete largely determine individually based intensity prescription. Younger training age athletes need lower relative intensities of training with higher volume-based approaches. Strategies such as this allow athletes appropriate intensity ranges to maintain technique within specific exercise prescriptions. As athletes progress across different exercise variations, each unique movement has a specific maximum load that can be achieved. Creating a progression of exercise variations that naturally increase absolute loading potential or challenges the stability of posture and position against external loads push athletic development further. Older trained athletes that have developed postural stability and nervous system efficiency are able to train at much higher relative intensity without technique or postural failure limiting their loading ability. Coaches should consider a higher intensity and lower volume approach with older training age athletes, who can more efficiently train up to their force potential.

Professional

Low-volume and high-intensity training is preferable, due to the decreased likelihood of postexercise soreness and fatigue. For this same reason, be very judicious about the use of eccentric overload training, which can cause unnecessary soreness.

For the primary multijoint exercises, athletes should perform 2 to 3 working sets (not including warm-up sets) using repetition ranges of 1 to 4 and intensities of between 80% and 90% of the 1RM. For any isolation movements, athletes should use 1 to 3 working sets of 6 to 10 repetitions at intensities of 70% to 80% of the 1RM.

VOLUME

Total off-ice training volume in-season should usually be kept within moderate to low ranges. The largest goal in-season is to develop and maintain the force–velocity curve without interfering with on-ice performance and negatively affecting recovery. As discussed, total off-ice training volume should be deprioritized during the largest increases in on-ice training volume. Any large deviation in on-ice volume should create an equal and opposite decrease in total off-ice volume of training. Across in-season programming, small fluctuations in training volume are key for proper adaptation. Large changes in training volume can create tissue soreness and overreaching or can lead to detraining if the stimulus is chronically smaller than normal. This applies to total on-ice stress and off-ice training volumes. The progression of on-ice and off-ice volumes usually reaches a peak as the technical, tactical, and physical performance of athletes reach diminishing returns in outcomes. During most seasons, the progression of volume should occur within the first half of the in-season period, allowing for the optimization of higher intensity performance within practice and competition during the second half of the in-season period. Higher-volume training should be used cautiously and with planned objectives in mind. For younger training age athletes or for developmental athletes not competing, volume can be a useful tool to maintain or develop specific physical adaptations. Training up to fatigue and not to failure should be used in-season in most situations. The use of training to failure should be based upon the need of the athlete and can be used to promote muscular hypertrophy, which is a rare in-season training goal.

Interpreting the Sample Program Tables

+ = Do the two exercises back-to-back

AA = Anatomical adaptation

Alt = Alternated

AMRAP = As many as possible (but quality repetitions)

APRE = Autoregulatory progressive resistance exercise

Asst = Assisted

BB = Barbell

BW = Body weight

Cont = Continuous

DB = Dumbbell

Ea = Each side (arm or leg), direction, or exercise

ECC = Eccentric

Exp = Explosive

Ext = External

FFE = Front foot elevated

Fwd = Forward

Goblet = Holding DB or KB with both hands below the chin and elbows pointed out to the side in the midline of the body

GPP = General preparation phase

ISO = Isometric

KB = Kettlebell

Kn = Kneeling

Lat = Lateral

LB = Lower body

LPT = Linear position transducer

MB = Medicine ball

m/s = meters per second

OH = Overhead

Order = Performing one set of each exercise (1a, 1b, 1c) in the group one after the other. After the first set is completed, go back to the first exercise in the group and do the second set of each exercise. If certain exercises call for fewer sets than others in the group, perform those sets on the back end of the grouping. For example, if exercise 1a calls for 4 sets and exercise 1b calls for 3 sets, perform exercise 1b during sets 2 through 4 of exercises 1a.

Plyo = plyometric

Pos = Position

RDL = Romanian deadlift

Rev = Reverse

RFE = Rear foot elevated

RFESS = Rear foot elevated split squat

RM = Repetition maximum

Rot = Rotation

RPE = Rating of perceived exertion (intensity based on level of perceived difficulty)

SA = Single arm

SB = Stability ball

SL = Single leg

SLDL = Single-leg deadlift

Tempo = The time, in seconds, for each phase or portion of the exercise, written as "eccentric phase: top (or bottom) position: concentric phase" (King, I., How to write strength training programs. In *Speed of Movement*, p. 123, 1998). For example, a tempo of "1:5:1" for the back squat means 1 second to lower, 5 seconds held at the bottom position, and 1 second to stand back up. *Note:* "Exp" means that the athlete should explode during the movement. A tempo of "Exp" is associated with power exercises because there is not a prescriptive time allotted to each portion of the movement. *Note:* All tempos are written with the first number referring to the movement that is performed first (either eccentric or concentric).

Tib = Tibialis

UB = Upper body

CONCLUSION

In-season training should be carefully planned to properly stimulate adaptation or maintain physical qualities developed in the off-season, depending on the individual stress and goal orientation of the athlete. Working with the hockey coaching staff, strength and conditioning professionals are in a unique position to provide valuable information related to the monitoring of athlete performance and stress, allowing them to assist in the planning and execution of stress prescriptions over the course of the in-season period. The establishment of periodized volume, intensity, and recovery in-season should take into account both the physical prescribed stress and the environmental stressors with respect to the competitive level of the athlete to improve performance outcomes. The old adages are true: Quality trumps quantity, and less is more. Strength and conditioning professionals have to learn to accept that the conditions and schedules they are faced with are radically different than they might have learned in a textbook or in a course. They need to be adaptable and never lose sight of the main objective: keeping the athletes healthy and available for the game and making sure their team is prepared to handle the rigors of a season that extends over several months.

Table 11.3 High School: In-Season

Monday (day 1): total body—hypertrophy/endurance

Order	Exercise	Tempo	RPE	Sets × reps, time, or distance	Sets × reps, time, or distance	Sets × reps, time, or distance	Sets × reps, time, or distance
			1-10	Week 1	Week 2	Week 3	Week 4
1a	DB FFE split squat	3:1:1	6-7	2 × 6 ea	2 × 6 ea	3 × 6 ea	3 × 6 ea
1b	One-arm DB incline press	3:1:1	6-7	2 × 6 ea	2 × 6 ea	3 × 6 ea	3 × 6 ea
1c	Inverted row	1:1:3	6-7	2 × 8	2 × 8	3 × 8	3 × 8
2a	DB single-leg SLDL	2:1:1	5-6	2 × 6 ea	2 × 6 ea	3 × 8 ea	3 × 8 ea
2b	One-arm DB row	2:1:1	6-7	2 × 8 ea	2 × 8 ea	3 × 8 ea	3 × 8 ea
2c	Tempo push-up ECC/ISO	3:3:1	6-7	2 × 6	2 × 6	3 × 8	3 × 8
3a	Split squat ISO	ISO	5-6	2 × 20 s ea	2 × 20 s ea	2 × 20 s ea	2 × 20 s ea
3b	Suitcase carry	Cont	5-6	2 × 25 m ea	2 × 25 m ea	2 × 25 m ea	2 × 10 m ea

Wednesday (day 2): total body—strength/power

Order	Exercise	Tempo	RPE	Sets × reps	Sets × reps	Sets × reps	Sets × reps
			1-10	Week 1	Week 2	Week 3	Week 4
1a	One-arm DB snatch	Exp	7-8	3 × 3 ea	3 × 3 ea	3 × 3 ea	3 × 3 ea
1b	MB side toss	Exp		3 × 3 ea	3 × 3 ea	3 × 3 ea	3 × 3 ea
2a	Trap bar deadlift	1:1:2	7-8	3 × 3	3 × 3	3 × 3	3 × 3
2b	Medicine ball slam	Exp		3 × 5	3 × 5	3 × 5	3 × 5
3a	One-arm landmine push press	1:1:2	7-8	3 × 3 ea	3 × 3 ea	3 × 3 ea	3 × 3 ea
3b	Rotary chop	Cont		2 × 6 ea	2 × 6 ea	2 × 6 ea	2 × 6 ea
4a	DB lateral lunge	1:1:1	5-6	2 × 5 ea	2 × 5 ea	2 × 5 ea	2 × 5 ea
4b	One-arm cable rotational row	1:2:1	5-6	2 × 5 ea	3 × 5 ea	2 × 5 ea	2 × 5 ea

Table 11.4 College: In-Season (First Half of Season)

Monday (day 1): total body—strength

Order	Exercise	Tempo	% of 1RM or RPE	Sets × reps	Sets × reps	Sets × reps
				Week 1	Week 2	Week 3
1a	Safety bar reverse lunge	1:1:1	80%-85%	3 × 5 ea	3 × 4 ea	3 × 3 ea
1b	Sitting broad jump	Exp	BW	3 × 3	3 × 3	3 × 3
1c	Supine cable hip flexion	1:2:1	RPE 5-7	2 × 6 ea	2 × 6 ea	2 × 6 ea
2a	Bench press	2:1:1	75%-85%	3 × 8	3 × 6	3 × 4
2b	DB SLDL	4:1:1	75%-80%	3 × 4 ea	3 × 4 ea	3 × 4 ea
2c	Copenhagen plank	1:4:1	BW	2 × 2 ea	2 × 3 ea	2 × 4 ea
3a	Neutral pull-up	1:2:2	BW	2 × AMRAP	2 × AMRAP	2 × AMRAP
3b	SB roll out (elbows)	1:2:1	BW	2 × 8	2 × 10	2 × 12

Wednesday (day 2): total body—speed

Order	Exercise	Tempo	% of 1RM or RPE	Sets × reps	Sets × reps	Sets × reps
				Week 1	Week 2	Week 3
1a	Trap bar vertical jump	Exp	1.5-1.55 m/s	3 × 4	3 × 4	3 × 4
1b	Staggered stance cable row	1:2:1	60%-65%	3 × 8 ea	3 × 8 ea	3 × 8 ea
1c	Side plank pos bottom leg support	1:5:1	BW	2 × 2 ea	2 × 3 ea	2 × 4 ea
2a	Landmine split jerk	1:1:1	35%-40%	3 × 2 ea	3 × 2 ea	3 × 2 ea
2b	Rot split squat MB shot put	Exp		3 × 3 ea	3 × 3 ea	3 × 3 ea
2c	Stability ball hamstring curl	1:5:1	BW	2 × 3	2 × 4	2 × 5
3a	Tall kn landmine rainbow	3:0:1	RPE 6-8	2 × 5 ea	2 × 5 ea	2 × 5 ea
3b	Band external rotation	Cont	Band	2 × 8	2 × 10	2 × 12

Table 11.5   College: In-Season (Second Half of the Season)

Monday (day 1): total body—strength–speed

Order	Exercise	Tempo	% of 1RM or RPE	Sets × reps	Sets × reps	Sets × reps
				Week 1	Week 2	Week 3
1a	Safety bar reverse lunge	1:1:1	65%-70%	3 × 3 ea	3 × 3 ea	3 × 3 ea
1b	Repeat broad jump	Exp	BW	3 × 3	3 × 3	3 × 3
1c	Standing cable hip flexion	1:1:4	RPE 6-8	2 × 4 ea	2 × 4 ea	2 × 4 ea
2a	Bench press with chains	2:1:1	65%-70%	3 × 4	3 × 4	3 × 4
2b	DB SLDL (dynamic reversal)	1:2:1	55%-60%	3 × 5 ea	3 × 5 ea	3 × 5 ea
2c	Copenhagen plank	1:4:1	BW	2 × 2 ea	2 × 3 ea	2 × 4 ea
3a	Half-kn rot cable pulldown	1:2:2	65%-70%	2 × 6 ea	2 × 6 ea	2 × 6 ea
3b	SB roll out (hands)	3:1:1	BW	2 × 6	2 × 7	2 × 8

Wednesday (day 2): total body—speed–strength

Order	Exercise	Tempo	% of 1RM or RPE	Sets × reps	Sets × reps	Sets × reps
				Week 1	Week 2	Week 3
1a	Trap bar vertical jump	Exp	1.15-1.2 m/s	3 × 4	3 × 4	3 × 4
1b	Rot split stance cable row	1:2:1	45%-50%	3 × 5 ea	3 × 5 ea	3 × 5 ea
1c	Side plank pos bottom leg support	1:3:1	BW	3 × 3 ea	3 × 4 ea	3 × 5 ea
2a	One-arm landmine split jerk	1:1:1	45%-50%	3 × 2 ea	3 × 2 ea	3 × 2 ea
2b	Lateral MB chest pass	Exp		3 × 3 ea	3 × 3 ea	3 × 3 ea
2c	Stability ball single-leg hamstring curl	1:1:3	BW	2 × 3 ea	2 × 4 ea	2 × 5 ea
3a	Standing landmine rainbow	Cont	RPE 7-9	2 × 5 ea	2 × 5 ea	2 × 5 ea
3b	DB seated external rotation	Cont	RPE 6-8	2 × 8 ea	2 × 8 ea	2 × 8 ea

Table 11.6   Professional: In-Season

Day 1: skaters

Order	Exercise	Tempo	Sets × reps	Sets × reps	Sets × reps
			Week 1	Week 2	Week 3
1a	Hang clean*	Exp	2-3 × 2-3	2-3 × 2-3	2-3 × 2-3
1b	Vertical jump	Exp	2-3 × 3	2-3 × 3	2-3 × 3
2a	Trap bar deadlift**	Cont	2-3 × 3	2-3 × 3	2-3 × 3
2b	Floor press	4:2:x	2-3 × 3-5	2-3 × 3-5	2-3 × 3-5
2c	Inverted row	3:1:1	3 × 6-8	3 × 6-8	3 × 6-8

*At >1.3 m/s. **At 0.55-0.7 m/s.

Day 1: goalies

Order	Exercise	Tempo	Sets × reps	Sets × reps	Sets × reps
			Week 1	Week 2	Week 3
1a	Trap bar deadlift (high handle)*	Cont	3 × 3-5	3 × 3-5	3 × 3-5
1b	Inverted row	3:1:1	3 × 7-10	3 × 7-10	3 × 7-10
1c	Rear delt reverse fly	Cont	3 × 10-15	3 × 10-15	3 × 10-15
2a	Glute bridge	6 s ISO	1-2 × 3-4	1-2 × 3-4	1-2 × 3-4
2b	Side plank	6 s ISO	1-2 × 6 ea	1-2 × 6 ea	1-2 × 6 ea

*At >0.5 m/s.

Day 2: skaters

Order	Exercise	Tempo	Sets × reps	Sets × reps	Sets × reps
			Week 1	Week 2	Week 3
1a	Incline Y	Cont	2-3 × 7-10	2-3 × 7-10	2-3 × 7-10
1b	Half-kn cable chop	Cont	2-3 × 7-10	2-3 × 7-10	2-3 × 7-10
1c	Inverted row	3:1:1	2-3 × 7-10	2-3 × 7-10	2-3 × 7-10
2a	Half-kn one-arm cable row	3:1:1	2-3 × 7-10	2-3 × 7-10	2-3 × 7-10
2b	Rear delt reverse fly	Cont	2-3 × 10-15	2-3 × 10-15	2-3 × 10-15
3a	Side plank	6 s ISO	1-2 × 4-6	I-2 × 4-6	I-2 × 4-6
3b	Single-leg slider eccentric hamstring curl	6:0:0	1-2 × 4-6	1-2 × 4-6	1-2 × 4-6

Day 2: goalies

Order	Exercise	Tempo	Sets × reps	Sets × reps	Sets × reps
			Week 1	Week 2	Week 3
1a	Incline Y	Cont	2-3 × 7-10	2-3 × 7-10	2-3 × 7-10
1b	Half-kn cable chop	Cont	2-3 × 7-10	2-3 × 7-10	2-3 × 7-10
1c	Inverted row	3:1:1	2-3 × 7-10	2-3 × 7-10	2-3 × 7-10
2a	Half-kn one-arm cable row	3:1:1	2-3 × 7-10	2-3 × 7-10	2-3 × 7-10
2b	Rear delt reverse fly	Cont	2-3 × 10-15	2-3 × 10-15	2-3 × 10-15
3a	Dead bug	4:1:1	1-2 × 5-7	1-2 × 5-7	1-2 × 5-7
3b	Single-leg slider eccentric hamstring curl	6:0:0	1-2 × 4-6	1-2 × 4-6	1-2 × 4-6

POSTSEASON PROGRAMMING

**MARK FITZGERALD (HIGH SCHOOL), MATT SHAW (COLLEGE),
MATT NICHOL (PROFESSIONAL)**

In the immediate postseason phase, the focus shifts from performance to health. Directly after the competition season is concluded, it is crucial to do a thorough biomechanical assessment of the athletes so that any injuries can be properly evaluated and a baseline level of function can be determined. Once this assessment is completed and the data is assessed, a rehabilitation plan should be designed with input from all members of the health and performance team.

GOALS AND OBJECTIVES

One important aspect of postseason training that is often overlooked is the need to reset athletes' mental health, which is even more important than their physical health. Athletes should take some time away to have a complete break from hockey and training. This should not be viewed as a lack of discipline or commitment but rather an important component of regeneration and recovery. The strength and conditioning professional and team nutritionist can serve as resources to help these athletes find a happy medium where they are able to relax and enjoy themselves without straying too far from the nutrition and lifestyle habits that are important for their health and well-being. Some athletes could also use this as an opportunity to seek the counsel of a sport psychologist if there is any lingering resentment over their personal or team's performance. Athletes are often eager to get away and forget all the stressors of the season, and after a brief hiatus they immediately jump back into regular strength and conditioning routines. It is often more effective to take some time to reflect and process any negative feelings about the season that just passed while concurrently setting goals and objectives for the following season.

As a result of the high volume and frequency of competitions as well as the fact that hockey is a high-speed collision sport, it is almost inevitable that athletes conclude the season with some degree of injury. For some athletes these are simply cases of overuse and repetitive strain, while others may require extensive surgeries.

The primary goal of the postseason training period is to reestablish range of motion, foundational motor patterns, and work capacity, providing a functional base to prepare athletes for off-season training. At the beginning of the postseason training period, fundamental habits of training should be rediscussed. Concepts such as training to full range of motion, executing exercises with intent, and establishing technical consistency should be reinforced. In-season competition predominantly exposes athletes to volumes and intensities within sport-specific motor patterns and tissue lengths. While in-season training assists in maintaining tissue range of motion, the postseason mesocycle should reprioritize tissue length and end-range control. The use of fundamental motor patterns should shift athletes away from the specificity of hockey stress toward establishing general basic coordination, technique, and endurance. Daily training sessions should rise and fall in volume, tempo, and rest to improve work capacity in a manner that progresses all athletes toward the demands of off-season training.

LENGTH, STRUCTURE, AND ORGANIZATION

The length of the postseason varies from level to level but also depends on how long the playoff run has taken. The postseason training phase is a crucial time to create the foundation for future intensive off-season training and should not be an afterthought.

High School

Postseason training for the high school athlete should be focused on rest and rejuvenation. Ideally the athlete has had some dedicated time away from the sport of hockey and has been allowed to take a mental and physical break. The time away should serve as a time to get excited for the next phase of training and look forward to the next challenge. The main goal of the postseason phase is to address any physical ailments that inhibit the athlete from getting into a new training program. Once the athlete is ready to commence the postseason phase, the initial goal is to begin building a base of overall strength and fitness (i.e., general physical preparedness, or GPP). The GPP phase encompasses many different qualities that support the athlete upon entering the more rigorous off-season phase.

The postseason phase can differ depending on the individual, but having two to four weeks is ideal. Working with a four-week plan, the athlete completes three total body resistance training sessions a week, with the other days left for other sports, activities, and rest. This time is also ideal to address any injuries and other ailments with a sports medicine practitioner. The three total body exercise days should have a least one day of rest in between them. Each day includes some foundational movements (knee-dominant, hip-dominant, and push/pull) for the athlete to build some tolerance for when the off-season program begins. This is also time for some type of work capacity training within the exercises that prepare the athlete for more strenuous training. Again, the high school athlete benefits greatly from time spent practicing and learning the basics of resistance training.

The GPP approach benefits any athlete, regardless of position on the ice. Hockey athletes are athletes first, and this training is useful in slowly building up volume and tolerance ahead of a more intense training period. Assuming this time is spent away from any type of hockey, it can also be important for the athlete to address areas of need. Athletes looking to put on lean body mass or improve overall strength can use this time to fill in those gaps.

College

By the time the postseason period begins, most college hockey teams have played the maximum allowable competition limit of 34 games as part of the regular season—or more if teams qualify for conference and NCAA tournament competition. This can take the total games played past 42 competitions within the in-season period if teams make it to the NCAA national championship game. The college postseason is a period of recovery and physical restoration following the in-season period. At the conclusion of the collegiate season, it is important to reflect upon the prior year and evaluate areas for improvement. Key performance indicators such as wearable data from games and practices, sprint or jump data, anthropometric trends from the year, team injury data, and subjective feedback from athletes and coaches should all be collected. Reviewing objective and subjective information can assist in individual and team goal setting. This process can create clarity in planning out the goals of postseason recovery and properly planning foundational training prior to the off-season training period.

Immediately following the conclusion of the in-season competition period, athletes go through a discretionary period of mental and physiological recovery away from training, practice, and competition stress. One to three weeks may be taken off for individual and team recovery from the in-season competition period before reacclimating athletes to training. During this time athletes need an appropriate amount of complete rest to physiologically allow recovery from the in-season period. The use of cross-training activities can be beneficial to bridge between complete rest and the start of a general preparation mesocycle. Athletes can complete two or three sessions of nonspecific activity before reengaging in off-ice training. Prior to transitioning athletes back to formal training, strength and conditioning professionals should be aware of any lingering injuries, asymmetries, or individual contraindications to training. Athlete posture can reflect the positions of skating and stick handedness. Notably, many athletes have short hip flexors, high upper trap tension, weak posterior chain strength, and asymmetries that reflect their flexed skating posture, stride, and shooting patterns from the season.

The general preparation phase is a two- to three-week mesocycle focused on the restoration of training frequency, tissue range of motion, foundational movement patterns, and general work capacity. Working backward from the training frequency prescribed within the early off-season can assist strength and conditioning professionals in developing a linear increase in training stress. Training frequency can begin with two to three sessions per week and then linearly increase to four sessions per week, improving the athletes' tolerance to parallel the organization of stress in later off-season mesocycles. Training within the general preparatory phase should progress to expose athletes to four 1-hour total body training sessions. Training during this period should include a mix of strategies that target tissue remodeling at end range of motion and the reintroduction of low- to moderate-intensity foundational exercises. Special consideration should be made for the hockey athlete's progression back into jump, plyometric, and throw training. The fixed foot position within skating during the in-season period can detrain the resilience of the Achilles tendon. Progressive volume of remedial ankling, jumps, hops, and leaps should reestablish tendon health and preparation for off-season training. This is not the focus of the program examples in this chapter but is still important to note because jump training requires a proper base before off-season training.

Each day of training within the general preparatory phase includes unique methods, volumes, and intensities while consistently incorporating underlying metabolic stress. Day 1 uses a variation of 1 set of 20 repetitions (see table 12.2), focusing on a single set for muscular endurance through the combination of complex foundational exercises and isolated single-joint assistance exercises. Day 2 (see table 12.3) focuses on yielding isometrics performed as a circuit to improve end-range tissue tolerance and decrease strength deficits in flexion. Day 3 (see table 12.4) uses a three-round, 15-repetition circuit with loading constraints based upon completion time. Athletes are given a 30-second work period to complete 15 repetitions and a 30-second rest period. Load is progressed each round based upon the amount of time remaining after the athlete hits the 15-repetition benchmark within the work period. Day 4 (see table 12.5) uses a very low intensity three-dimensional contralateral circuit to develop unilateral pelvic stability and tissue endurance. It is not the isolated method of any single day that creates results but the accumulated stress of the general preparatory phase that sets the stage for high tolerance to stress and work capacity.

Specialized supplementary training exercises outside of the main training emphasis should be used to progress specific training objectives. Foundational plyometric, jump, throw, and anatomical core endurance training are added prior to or at the conclusion of the main training blocks. Jump, plyometric, and throwing exercises should be added before the normal lifting stress after warm-up, while the athletes are not fatigued. Anatomical core training or additional areas of specialized focus in the early off-season can be added at the conclusion of sessions, because they should not interfere with the athletes' ability to execute the primary stress each day. Early tendon preparation for off-season training, underlying anatomical core or postural stability, and other limiting factors behind off-season training progression can be incorporated.

Professional

Just as a hockey team requires different types of athletes in different positions who possess different skill sets, optimizing the health and performance of an NHL hockey athlete requires an equally capable team. It is important for a strength and conditioning professional to develop a good working relationship with the medical professionals that deal with the athletes (athletic therapists, physiotherapists, chiropractors, osteopaths, medical doctors, and others) because communication around training restrictions and time lines during this phase is critical to a successful off-season program.

National Hockey League athletes sometimes use private coaches during the off-season period. Many athletes choose to enlist the services of these private coaches, especially when they live during the off-season somewhere other than in the city in which they play. The team strength and conditioning professional must establish and maintain a good working relationship with these professionals. Since the collective bargaining agreement between the NHL and the National Hockey League Players' Association (NHLPA) significantly restricts the ability of the team to monitor or intervene in the off-season activities of its athletes, the team strength and conditioning professional must rely upon the private coach to be able to properly prepare the athlete. Likewise, it is beneficial for the private coach to maintain good relationships with the team personnel to ensure the long-term success for the athlete client and to help increase the likelihood of receiving future referrals or recommendations from those same team personnel.

The strength and conditioning objectives in this phase need to be secondary to the health and wellness objectives. Providing a boilerplate program for this phase that is applicable to all (or even to most) athletes is extremely difficult. For athletes who played fewer overall minutes and finished the season with no injury issues whatsoever, this phase could be as short as two to three weeks.

For other athletes, this phase might be anywhere from one to several months long. Some surgeries may require as many as ten months of intensive rehabilitation. Even in those cases there remains a crucial role for the strength and conditioning professional to ensure that the athlete can adjust and adapt the normal resistance training program to stay as close as possible to the goals while not negatively affecting the healing process. Resistance training not only affects the prime mover muscles of a particular exercise but also stimulates the nervous system and the hormonal system. It is possible to do maximum resistance training with the upper or the lower body while simultaneously following a rehabilitation or corrective exercise protocol with the opposite half of the body. Also, due to what is known as "cross education," strength gains in one limb alone result in a transfer of strength improvement in the contralateral limb (1). Thus, not only is it possible to do resistance or power training with one limb while the other is undergoing rehabilitation but it may also enhance the recovery rate of the affected limb.

RECOMMENDED EXERCISES

Proper exercise selection can be one of the main tools to address physical development and the restoration of posture and function following a hockey season. Early off-season training should find balance restoring the athlete's posture, tissue range of motion within each plane of motion, and work capacity. It is common to find athletes' posture reflecting the positions of the game. Many hockey athletes have tight hip flexors, anterior pelvic tilt, tight spinal erectors, dominant upper trapezius, and protracted head position. Having a high percentage of posterior chain exercises during postseason training and reinforcing proper joint position can aid in offsetting these postures. The inclusion of fundamental patterns of movement is important because it resets technical habits and tissue length under light-loading, higher repetition work. Lower body training should be based around exposing the athlete to both bilateral and unilateral variations of pushing and pulling. Athletes should be able to squat, lunge, hinge at the hip, and flex and extend at the knee. Upper body training should expose athletes to overhead, horizontal, and rotational push and pull exercises. Scapular movement and stability should be reinforced through upper body exercises. However, programming rotator cuff and isolated scapular exercise variations can correct specific issues. Organizationally, it is important to create weekly exposure of these movement categories across each plane of motion. Getting athletes to reengage in general multiplanar movement can improve range of motion at the ankle, hip, thoracic spine, and scapulothoracic joints. The use of total body three-dimensional movement patterns can teach strategic movement variations that combine lower and upper body fundamental patterns.

Isolated single-joint or isometric exercises targeting the stabilizers of the ankle, hip, anatomical core, and glenohumeral joints can assist in reestablishing localized muscular endurance and can decrease asymmetries developed across the in-season period. With hockey being a very asymmetrical sport because of stick handedness and high-volume rotational patterning dominant to one side, it is important to redevelop unilateral limb work capacity. This can be accomplished with unilateral exercise selections or independent limb loading through equipment such as dumbbells. Both mobility and isolated single-joint exercises should target sagittal, frontal, and transverse function of each joint listed in this paragraph. The use of yielding isometrics at end ranges, low-intensity high-repetition sets, and moderate-intensity loading to fatigue can assist in progressing foundational strength and muscular endurance within these areas. These methods are used exclusively throughout the week in each training session.

Training the anatomical core within the general preparatory phase is done twice a week at the conclusion of training focused on reestablishing multiplanar stability and foundational muscular endurance. The anatomical core endurance circuit (see tables 12.3 and 12.5) allows athletes to navigate through a repeated plank series with progressively harder variations within anti-extension, anti-lateral flexion, and anti-rotary training. Athletes are progressed until they can no longer maintain technique or until they can complete the 4-and-a-half-minute circuit with technical proficiency.

INTENSITY

The general physical preparation training can range from bodyweight training to 60% of an athlete's estimated 1RM. Very low to moderate-intensity training should serve to establish technique within each foundational exercise in the postseason, prior to intensification during off-season training. Athletes that cannot maintain technique or have large asymmetries during this phase should not be progressed until they demonstrate proficiency in required foundational exercises. Total time under tension (TUT) is a more prominent goal of the programming than external load or repetitions. For most of the key exercises, the goal is a time under tension of 45 to 75 seconds per set, which can be achieved through high repetition sets of 15 to 25 repetitions, sets employing very slow eccentric tempos (6:1:1 or 5:2:2), or even isometric exercises. Rest intervals between sets are kept lower to allow for an aerobic training effect, which enables the athletes to achieve a training effect similar to a zone 2 steady-state workout while accomplishing more work in a more sport-specific fashion. The weekly structure of training intensities undulates to allow athletes to maintain high frequencies of training without creating conflicting fatigue. The highest training intensities, yet lower total session volumes are placed after rest days to maximize athlete recovery going into the sessions (days 1 and 3). Day 2 uses yielding isometrics for 30-second durations to improve end-range work capacity and strength. At the end of the week, the three-dimensional contralateral circuit provides the lowest overall training intensity but the highest accumulated volume across all muscle tissue. Each of these independent training methodologies increases either intensity or volume to linearly progress athlete training readiness toward off-season training demands.

VOLUME

Training volume is one of the most important considerations during the postseason acclimation to training stress. During the late in-season period when teams are making their final push to qualify for playoffs, off-ice training can significantly decrease. During that time, peaking for on-ice performance and recovery between competitions becomes the largest priority, and off-ice training is deprioritized. As individuals recover from the chronic physical and mental stress accumulated across the length of the in-season period, off-ice training tolerance begins to detrain. Individual training status shifts because those with the largest playing time may go through higher detraining than those that are scratched for competitions and still training through the end of the season. Strength and conditioning professionals should consider individual training status to determine an appropriate starting place for volume and training frequency. Both the individual volume prescribed within a single training session and the total volume accumulated across the week should be managed. For this reason, it can be beneficial to have not only a cross-training period of activity but also a transitional week that reintroduces individuals to generalized bodyweight training or lightly loaded general workouts done at low volume. This can help individuals linearly increase general activity, training volume, and training frequency until they reach the normal programming structure that will be used within the general preparation phase. Weekly progression of the total workload allows the athlete to achieve higher volumes of training and time under tension, which raises the specific work capacity to handle greater volumes of training in the off-season.

Interpreting the Sample Program Tables
+ = *Do the two exercises back-to-back*
AA = Anatomical adaptation
Alt = Alternated
AMRAP = As many as possible (but quality repetitions)
APRE = Autoregulatory progressive resistance exercise

Asst = Assisted

BB = Barbell

BW = Body weight

Cont = Continuous

DB = Dumbbell

Ea = Each side (arm or leg), direction, or exercise

ECC = Eccentric

Exp = Explosive

Ext = External

FFE = Front foot elevated

Fwd = Forward

Goblet = Holding DB or KB with both hands below the chin and elbows pointed out to the side in the midline of the body

GPP = General preparation phase

ISO = Isometric

KB = Kettlebell

Kn = Kneeling

Lat = Lateral

LB = Lower body

LPT = Linear position transducer

MB = Medicine ball

m/s = meters per second

OH = Overhead

Order = Performing one set of each exercise (1a, 1b, 1c) in the group one after the other. After the first set is completed, go back to the first exercise in the group and do the second set of each exercise. If certain exercises call for fewer sets than others in the group, perform those sets on the back end of the grouping. For example, if exercise 1a calls for 4 sets and exercise 1b calls for 3 sets, perform exercise 1b during sets 2 through 4 of exercises 1a.

Plyo = plyometric

Pos = Position

RDL = Romanian deadlift

Rev = Reverse

RFE = Rear foot elevated

RFESS = Rear foot elevated split squat

RM = Repetition maximum

Rot = Rotation

RPE = Rating of perceived exertion (intensity based on level of perceived difficulty)

SA = Single arm

SB = Stability ball

(continued)

Interpreting the Sample Program Tables *(continued)*

SL = Single leg

SLDL = Single-leg deadlift

Tempo = The time, in seconds, for each phase or portion of the exercise, written as "eccentric phase: top (or bottom) position: concentric phase" (King, I., How to write strength training programs. In *Speed of Movement*, p. 123, 1998). For example, a tempo of "1:5:1" for the back squat means 1 second to lower, 5 seconds held at the bottom position, and 1 second to stand back up. *Note*: "Exp" means that the athlete should explode during the movement. A tempo of "Exp" is associated with power exercises because there is not a prescriptive time allotted to each portion of the movement. *Note*: All tempos are written with the first number referring to the movement that is performed first (either eccentric or concentric).

Tib = Tibialis

UB = Upper body

CONCLUSION

Success in the postseason phase requires an integrated approach, with all the members of the medical and performance teams having vital input. Strength and conditioning professionals must be careful to restrain themselves and not to rush through the steps and time lines of this phase. The long-term health and success of the athlete depend on this. Athletes should be linearly progressed from their starting training status to safely handle the requirements of early off-season training intensity and volume. Within the postseason, athlete recovery and reestablishing training habits should occur. Special consideration should be made to establish proper technique within all foundational motor patterns and to assist the athlete in reacquiring tissue range of motion and work capacity.

Table 12.1   High School: Postseason

Monday (day 1): total body—AA/GPP

Order	Exercise	Tempo	RPE	Sets × reps, time, or distance	Sets × reps, time, or distance	Sets × reps, time, or distance	Sets × reps, time, or distance
			1-10	Week 1	Week 2	Week 3	Week 4
1a	Single-leg step-down	3:1:1	5-6	2 × 10	2 × 10	3 × 10	3 × 10
1b	Push-up	2:2:1	5-6	2 × 8	2 × 8	3 × 8	3 × 8
1c	Lateral band walk	Cont		2 × 12	2 × 12	2 × 12	2 × 12
2a	Band pull-through	1:2:2	5-6	2 × 12	2 × 12	3 × 12	3 × 12
2b	Seated cable row	1:2:2	5-6	2 × 10	2 × 10	3 × 10	3 × 10
2c	Front plank	Cont		2 × 30 s	2 × 30 s	2 × 30 s	2 × 30 s
3a	Walking lunge	1:1:1	6-7	2 × 20	2 × 20	3 × 20	3 × 20
3b	Farmer's carry	Cont	5-6	2 × 25 m	2 × 25 m	2 × 25 m	2 × 25 m
3c	Single-leg glute bridge	ISO		2 × 25 s ea	2 × 25 s ea	2 × 25 s ea	2 × 25 s ea

Wednesday (day 2): total body—AA/GPP

Order	Exercise	Tempo	RPE	Sets × reps or time	Sets × reps or time	Sets × reps or time	Sets × reps or time
			1-10	Week 1	Week 2	Week 3	Week 4
1a	One-leg step-up	1:1:3	5-6	2 × 10 ea	2 × 10 ea	3 × 10 ea	3 × 10 ea
1b	Suspension row	1:1:2	5-6	2 × 10	2 × 10	3 × 10	3 × 10
1c	Bird dog	1:5:1		2 × 3 ea	2 × 3 ea	2 × 3 ea	2 × 3 ea
2a	KB deadlift	3:1:1	5-6	2 × 10	2 × 10	3 × 10	3 × 10
2b	Shoulder tap	Cont	5-6	2 × 10 ea	2 × 10 ea	3 × 10 ea	3 × 10 ea
2c	Alt leg lower	Cont		2 × 10 ea	2 × 10 ea	2 × 10 ea	2 × 10 ea
3a	Hamstring curl	1:1:2	5-6	2 × 12	2 × 12	3 × 12	3 × 12
3b	Split squat	ISO	5-6	2 × 20 s ea	2 × 20 s ea	2 × 20 s ea	2 × 20 s ea
3c	Dead bug	Cont		2 × 10 ea	2 × 10 ea	2 × 10 ea	2 × 10 ea

Friday (day 3): total body—AA/GPP

Order	Exercise	Tempo	RPE	Sets × reps, time, or distance	Sets × reps, time, or distance	Sets × reps, time, or distance	Sets × reps, time, or distance
			1-10	Week 1	Week 2	Week 3	Week 4
1a	Skater squat	2:1:1	5-6	2 × 8 ea	2 × 8 ea	3 × 8 ea	3 × 8 ea
1b	Band face pull	1:1:1	5-6	2 × 15	2 × 15	3 × 15	3 × 15
1c	Side plank	ISO		2 × 30 s ea	2 × 30 s ea	2 × 30 s ea	2 × 30 s ea
2a	Glute bridge march	1:2:1	5-6	2 × 10 ea	2 × 10 ea	3 × 10 ea	3 × 10 ea
2b	Push-up	2:1:1	5-6	2 × 8	2 × 8	3 × 8	3 × 8
2c	Calf raise	1:1:2		2 × 15	2 × 15	2 × 15	2 × 15
3a	Forward lunge	2:1:1	5-6	2 × 8 ea	2 × 8 ea	3 × 8 ea	3 × 8 ea
3b	Band hip flexion	Cont		2 × 10 ea	2 × 10 ea	2 × 10 ea	2 × 10 ea
3c	Bear crawl	Cont		2 × 25 m	2 × 25 m	2 × 25 m	2 × 25 m

Table 12.2 College: Postseason GPP (Weeks 1-3)

Monday (day 1): 1 × 20 circuit

Order	Exercise	% of 1RM or RPE	Sets × reps Week 1	Sets × reps Week 2	Sets × reps Week 3
1	Landmine squat	40%-50%	1 × 10	1 × 20	1 × 20
2	Banded anterior tib	RPE 6-8	1 × 10 ea	1 × 20 ea	1 × 20 ea
3	Suspension inverted row	RPE 6-8	1 × 10	1 × 20	1 × 20
4	Glute bridge	RPE 6-8	1 × 10 ea	1 × 20 ea	1 × 20 ea
5	Banded hip abduction	RPE 6-8	1 × 10 ea	1 × 20 ea	1 × 20 ea
6	Trap bar deadlift	40%-50%	1 × 10	1 × 20	1 × 20
7	Weighted push-up	RPE 6-8	1 × 10	1 × 20	1 × 20
8	Bench T	RPE 6-8	1 × 10	1 × 20	1 × 20
9	DB step-up to hip flexion	40%-50%	1 × 10 ea	1 × 20 ea	1 × 20 ea
10	Standing banded adduction	RPE 6-8	1 × 10 ea	1 × 20 ea	1 × 20 ea
11	Half-kn landmine press	40%-50%	1 × 10 ea	1 × 20 ea	1 × 20 ea
12	Band-resisted dead bug (alt)	RPE 6-8	1 × 14	1 × 20	1 × 20
13	Landmine deadlift	40%-50%	1 × 10	1 × 20	1 × 20
14	DB biceps curl	40%-50%	1 × 10	1 × 20	1 × 20
15	Banded external rotation	RPE 6-8	1 × 10	1 × 20	1 × 20
16	Half-kn cable pulldown	40%-50%	1 × 10 ea	1 × 20 ea	1 × 20 ea
17	Tall kneeling Pallof press	40%-50%	1 × 10 ea	1 × 20 ea	1 × 20 ea
18	DB lateral raise	40%-50%	1 × 10	1 × 20	1 × 20
19	DB lying triceps extension	40%-50%	1 × 10	1 × 20	1 × 20
20	DB shoulder elevated SL glute bridge	RPE 6-8	1 × 10 ea	1 × 20 ea	1 × 20 ea

Note: Extensive plyometrics and throws should be completed prior to this session.

Table 12.3 College: Postseason GPP (Weeks 1-3)

Tuesday (day 2): yielding isometric circuit

Order	Exercise	Tempo	Order	Exercise	Tempo
1	DB split squat (right)	30 s ISO	9	One-arm DB row (left)	30 s ISO
2	One-arm DB bench press (left)	30 s ISO	10	DB goblet split squat (right)	30 s ISO
3	DB split squat (left)	30 s ISO	11	Tall DB overhead press (90°)	30 s ISO
4	One-arm DB bench press (right)	30 s ISO	12	DB goblet split squat (left)	30 s ISO
5	SB roll out	30 s ISO	13	Copenhagen plank at knee (right)	30 s ISO
6	SB single-leg hamstring curl (left)	30 s ISO	14	90-90 pull-up	30 s ISO
7	One-arm DB row (right)	30 s ISO	15	Copenhagen plank at knee (left)	30 s ISO
8	SB single-leg hamstring curl (right)	30 s ISO			

Week 1	Week 2	Week 3
Sets	**Sets**	**Sets**
2 rounds	3 rounds	4 rounds
Rest/round	**Rest/round**	**Rest/round**
2:30	2:30	2:30
% of 1RM	**% of 1RM**	**% of 1RM**
30%-40%	35%-45%	40%-50%

Note: Extensive plyometrics and throws should be completed prior to this session.

Anatomical core endurance (post-workout)	
Work time is 30 s per exercise variation.	
1	Front plank
2	Side plank L
3	Side plank R
4	Front plank alt leg lift (alt every 5 s)
5	Side plank hip dip L (dip every 5 s)
6	Side plank hip dip R (dip every 5 s)
7	Push-up alt lateral reach (alt every 5 s)
8	Side plank top leg lift L (2 s up, 3 s down)
9	Side plank top leg lift R (2 s up, 3 s down)

Note: Extensive plyometrics and throws should be completed prior to this session.

Table 12.4   College: Postseason GPP (Weeks 1-3)

Thursday (day 3): 3 × 15 time-constraint circuit

Order	Exercise	% of 1RM	Reps	Order	Exercise	% of 1RM	Reps
1	DB goblet squat	45%-60%	15	7	SB hamstring curl	45%-60%	8 ea
2	SA DB row	45%-60%	8 ea	8	DB squat to overhead press	45%-60%	15
3	Landmine deadlift	45%-60%	15	9	Plank position body saw	45%-60%	15
4	DB bench press	45%-60%	15	10	Trap bar deadlift	45%-60%	15
5	DB reverse lunge	45%-60%	8 ea				
6	Two-arm cable row	45%-60%	15				

Week 1	Week 2	Week 3
Sets	**Sets**	**Sets**
2 rounds	3 rounds	3 rounds
Rest/round	**Rest/round**	**Rest/round**
3:00	3:00	3:00

Notes: Extensive jumping should be completed prior to this session. Athletes have a 30-second work period to accomplish 15 repetitions (or 8 each for one-arm or single-leg exercises) and a 30-second rest period. If athletes complete the repetitions within the given work time, loading increases. If 5 seconds remain within the work period, loading increases 5 lb (2.3 kg). If 10 seconds remain within the work period, loading increases 10 lb (4.5 kg). Body-weight movements are progressed by increasing range of motion (flexion or extension) without momentum acting within the movements.

Table 12.5   College: Postseason GPP (Weeks 1-3)

Friday (day 4): 3D contralateral circuit

Order	Exercise	Order	Exercise	Order	Exercise
1	L split squat to R band row	15	L fwd lunge w/ viper rot press	28	R split squat to L DB overhead press
2	R split squat to L band row	16	R fwd lunge w/ viper rot press	29	L reverse lunge to R DB upright row
3	L lateral lunge to R DB overhead press	17	L lateral lunge to R band row	30	R reverse lunge to L DB upright row
4	R lateral lunge to L DB overhead press	18	R lateral lunge to L band row	31	L skater squat to viper press
5	RDL to L band rotational row	19	RDL to viper OH rotational press	32	R skater squat to viper press
6	RDL to R band rotational row	20	RDL to viper press	33	L SL RDL ISO viper row
7	L rotational lunge to R band press	21	L skater squat to R band row	34	R SL RDL ISO viper row
8	R rotational lunge to L band press	22	R skater squat to L band row	35	L step-up to R DB OH press
9	R cross behind lunge to R band row	23	L cross-under lunge to R OH press	36	R step-up to L DB OH press
10	L cross behind lunge to L band row	24	R cross-under lunge to L OH press	37	R cross-under to band pull apart
11	L SL RDL to overhead viper press	25	RDL to banded two-hand row	38	L cross-under to band ext rotation
12	R SL RDL to overhead viper press	26	RDL to band face pull	39	R staggered RDL to R band press
13	L step-up to R band row	27	L split squat to R DB overhead press	40	L staggered RDL to L band press
14	R step-up to L band row				

Anatomical core endurance (post-workout)	
Work time is 30 s per exercise variation.	
1	Front plank
2	Side plank L
3	Side plank R
4	Front plank alt leg lift (alt every 5 s)
5	Side plank hip dip L (dip every 5 s)
6	Side plank hip dip R (dip every 5 s)
7	Push-up alt lateral reach (alt/5 s)
8	Side plank top leg lift L (2 s up, 3 s down)
9	Side plank top leg lift R (2 s up, 3 s down)

Week 1	Week 2	Week 3
Work/rest	Work/rest	Work/rest
20 s / 10 s	30 s / 15 s	35 s / 15 s

Half-inch to one-inch bands (1-3 cm), 10-15 lb (4.5-6.8 kg) DB, 6-8 kg (13-17 lb) viper

Table 12.6 Professional: Postseason

Day 1

Order	Exercise	Tempo	Sets × reps or time	Sets × reps or time	Sets × reps or time	Sets × reps or time
			Week 1	Week 2	Week 3	Week 4
1a	Bird dog	1:5:1	2 × 3-5 × 5 s ea	2 × 3-5 × 5 s ea	2 × 3-5 × 5 s ea	2 × 3-5 × 5 s ea
1b	Dead bug	Cont	2 × 45-60 s	2 × 45-60 s	2 × 45-60 s	2 × 45-60 s
1c	Side plank	1:6:1	4-6 × 6-8 s ea	4-6 × 6-8 s ea	4-6 × 6-8 s ea	4-6 × 6-8 s ea
1d	Kneel isometric end-range hip abduction	1:6:1	4-6 × 6 s ea	4-6 × 6 s ea	4-6 × 6 s ea	4-6 × 6 s ea
2a	Half-kneeling sequential cable chop	Cont	2-3 × 7-10 ea	2-3 × 7-10 ea	2-3 × 7-10 ea	2-3 × 7-10 ea
2b	Front foot elevated split squat	2:2:1	2-3 × 6-8 ea	2-3 × 6-8 ea	2-3 × 6-8 ea	2-3 × 6-8 ea
2c	Half-kneeling one-arm cable row	1:2:2	2-3 × 8-12 ea	2-3 × 8-12 ea	2-3 × 8-12 ea	2-3 × 8-12 ea
3a	Lateral step-down (one-leg squat off box)	2:1:1	2-3 × 6-8 ea	2-3 × 6-8 ea	2-3 × 6-8 ea	2-3 × 6-8 ea
3b	One-arm single-leg SLDL	2:1:1	2-3 × 7-10 ea	2-3 × 7-10 ea	2-3 × 7-10 ea	2-3 × 7-10 ea
3c	Half-kneeling one-arm cable push	1:1:2	2-3 × 8-12 ea	2-3 × 8-12 ea	2-3 × 8-12 ea	2-3 × 8-12 ea
4a	Isometric split squat	ISO	1 × 45-60 s ea	1 × 45-60 s ea	1 × 45-60 s ea	1 × 45-60 s ea
4b	Copenhagen plank	1:6:1	1 × 3-5 × 6 s hold ea	1 × 3-5 × 6 s hold ea	1 × 3-5 × 6 s hold ea	1 × 3-5 × 6 s hold ea

Day 2

Order	Exercise	Tempo	Sets × reps or time	Sets × reps or time	Sets × reps or time	Sets × reps or time
			Week 1	Week 2	Week 3	Week 4
1a	Bird dog	1:5:1	2 × 3-5 × 5 s ea	2 × 3-5 × 5 s ea	2 × 3-5 × 5 s ea	2 × 3-5 × 5 s ea
1b	Dead bug	Cont	2 × 40-60 s	2 × 40-60 s	2 × 40-60 s	2 × 40-60 s
1c	Side plank	1:6:1	2 × 4-6 × 6-8 s ea	2 × 4-6 × 6-8 s ea	2 × 4-6 × 6-8 s ea	2 × 4-6 × 6-8 s ea
1d	Kneel isometric hip adduction	1:6:1	2 × 4-6 × 6 s ea	2 × 4-6 × 6 s ea	2 × 4-6 × 6 s ea	2 × 4-6 × 6 s ea
2a	Half-kneeling sequential cable lift	Cont	2-3 × 7-10 ea	2-3 × 7-10 ea	2-3 × 7-10 ea	2-3 × 7-10 ea
2b	One-leg skater squat	2:1:1	2-3 × 7-10 ea	2-3 × 7-10 ea	2-3 × 7-10 ea	2-3 × 7-10 ea
2c	Half-kneeling bottom up one-arm KB press	1:1:2	2-3 × 8-12 ea	2-3 × 8-12 ea	2-3 × 8-12 ea	2-3 × 8-12 ea

(continued)

Table 12.6 Professional: Postseason *(continued)*

Day 2 *(continued)*

Order	Exercise	Tempo	Sets × reps or time	Sets × reps or time	Sets × reps or time	Sets × reps or time
			Week 1	Week 2	Week 3	Week 4
3a	Eccentric Nordic curl (for hamstrings)	6:0:1	2-3 × 3-5	2-3 × 3-5	2-3 × 3-5	2-3 × 3-5
3b	Half-kneeling one-arm cable pulldown	1:2:1	2-3 × 8-12 ea	2-3 × 8-12 ea	2-3 × 8-12 ea	2-3 × 8-12 ea
3c	Incline Y	1:2:1	2-3 × 8-12	2-3 × 8-12	2-3 × 8-12	2-3 × 8-12
4a	ISO supported split squat + soleus raise	ISO	1 × 45-60 s ea	1 × 45-60 s ea	1 × 45-60 s ea	1 × 45-60 s ea
4b	Copenhagen plank	1:6:1	1 × 3-5 × 6 s hold	1 × 3-5 × 6 s hold	1 × 3-5 × 6 s hold	1 × 3-5 × 6 s hold

Note: Alternate the day 1 and day 2 schedules as follows:

Week 1: Monday, day 1; Wednesday, day 2; Friday, day 1

Week 2: Monday, day 2; Wednesday, day 1; Friday, day 2

Week 3: Monday, day 1; Wednesday, day 2; Friday, day 1

Week 4: Monday, day 2; Wednesday, day 1; Friday, day 2

Table 12.7 Professional: Goalie Postseason

Day 1

Order	Exercise	Tempo	Sets × reps or time	Sets × reps or time	Sets × reps or time	Sets × reps or time
			Week 1	Week 2	Week 3	Week 4
1a	Bird dog	1:5:1	2 × 3-5 × 5 s ea	2 × 3-5 × 5 s ea	2 × 3-5 × 5 s ea	2 × 3-5 × 5 s ea
1b	Dead bug	Cont	2 × 40-60 s	2 × 40-60 s	2 × 40-60 s	2 × 40-60 s
1c	Side plank	1:6:1	2 × 4-6 × 6-8 s ea	2 × 4-6 × 6-8 s ea	2 × 4-6 × 6-8 s ea	2 × 4-6 × 6-8 s ea
1d	Swiss ball isometric squat	ISO	2 × 40-60 s	2 × 40-60 s	2 × 40-60 s	2 × 40-60 s
2a	Tall kneeling sequential cable chop	Cont	2-3 × 7-10 ea	2-3 × 7-10 ea	2-3 × 7-10 ea	2-3 × 7-10 ea
2b	Tall kneeling one-arm cable row	3:1:1	2-3 × 8-12 ea	2-3 × 8-12 ea	2-3 × 8-12 ea	2-3 × 8-12 ea
2c	Eccentric reverse Nordic curl (for quads)	6:0:0	2-3 × 3-5	2-3 × 3-5	2-3 × 3-5	2-3 × 3-5
3a	Hands-free zombie front squat	5:1:1	2-3 × 4-6	2-3 × 4-6	2-3 × 4-6	2-3 × 4-6
3b	One-arm single-leg SLDL	Cont	2-3 × 7-10 ea	2-3 × 7-10 ea	2-3 × 7-10 ea	2-3 × 7-10 ea
3c	Suspension inverted row	1:1:2	2-3 × 7-10	2-3 × 7-10	2-3 × 7-10	2-3 × 7-10
3d	Cable external rotation	Cont	2-3 × 8-12	2-3 × 8-12	2-3 × 8-12	2-3 × 8-12
4a	Copenhagen plank	1:6:1	1 × 3-5 × 6 s hold ea	1 × 3-5 × 6 s hold ea	1 × 3-5 × 6 s hold ea	1 × 3-5 × 6 s hold ea

Day 2

Order	Exercise	Tempo	Sets × reps or time	Sets × reps or time	Sets × reps or time	Sets × reps or time
			Week 1	Week 2	Week 3	Week 4
1a	Bird dog	1:5:1	2 × 3-5 × 5 s ea	2 × 3-5 × 5 s ea	2 × 3-5 × 5 s ea	2 × 3-5 × 5 s ea
1b	Dead bug	Cont	2 × 40-60 s	2 × 40-60 s	2 × 40-60 s	2 × 40-60 s
1c	Side plank	1:6:1	2 × 4-6 × 6-8 s ea	2 × 4-6 × 6-8 s ea	2 × 4-6 × 6-8 s ea	2 × 4-6 × 6-8 s ea
1d	Swiss ball isometric	ISO	2 × 40-60 s	2 × 40-60 s	2 × 40-60 s	2 × 40-60 s
2a	Tall kneeling sequential cable lift	Cont	2-3 × 6-8 ea	2-3 × 6-8 ea	2-3 × 6-8 ea	2-3 × 6-8 ea
2b	One-leg skater squat	2:1:1	2-3 × 6-8 ea	2-3 × 6-8 ea	2-3 × 6-8 ea	2-3 × 6-8 ea
2c	Tall kneeling DB curl and press	Cont	2-3 × 8-12	2-3 × 8-12	2-3 × 8-12	2-3 × 8-12
3a	Eccentric Nordic curl (for hamstrings)	6:0:0	2-3 × 3-5	2-3 × 3-5	2-3 × 3-5	2-3 × 3-5
3b	Half-kneeling one-arm cable pulldown	3:1:1	2-3 × 8-12 ea	2-3 × 8-12 ea	2-3 × 8-12 ea	2-3 × 8-12 ea
3c	Incline Y	1:2:1	2-3 × 8-12	2-3 × 8-12	2-3 × 8-12	2-3 × 8-12
4a	Single-leg eccentric hamstring Valslide	6:0:1	1 × 4-6 × 6 s	1 × 4-6 × 6 s	1 × 4-6 × 6 s	1 × 4-6 × 6 s
4b	Copenhagen plank	1:6:1	1 × 3-5 × 6 s hold	1 × 3-5 × 6 s hold	1 × 3-5 × 6 s hold	1 × 3-5 × 6 s hold

Note: Alternate the day 1 and day 2 schedules as follows:

Week 1: Monday, day 1; Wednesday, day 2; Friday, day 1

Week 2: Monday, day 2; Wednesday, day 1; Friday, day 2

Week 3: Monday, day 1; Wednesday, day 2; Friday, day 1

Week 4: Monday, day 2; Wednesday, day 1; Friday, day 2

REFERENCES

Chapter 1

1. Agel, J, Dompier T, Dick, R, and Marshall, S. Descriptive epidemiology of collegiate men's ice hockey injuries: National Collegiate Athletic Association injury surveillance system, 1988-89 through 2003-04. *J Athl Train* 42:241-248, 2007.

2. Agre, J, Casal, D, Leon, AS, McNally, C, Baxter, TL, and Serfass, R. Professional ice hockey players: Physiologic, anthropometric, and musculoskeletal characteristics. *Arch Phys Med Rehabil* 69:188-192, 1988.

3. Bae, JH, Kim, DK, Seo, KM, Kang, SH, and Hwang, J. Asymmetry of the isokinetic trunk rotation strength of Korean male professional golf players. *Annals of Rehabilitation Medicine* 36(6):821-827, 2012.

4. Beam, William, Adams, C, and Gene, M. *Exercise Physiology Laboratory Manual, 7th edition*. New York, NY: McGraw-Hill, 95-109, 2014.

5. Botton, CE, Radaelli, R, Wilhelm, EN, Silva, BGC, Brown, LE, and Pinto, RS. Bilateral deficit between concentric and isometric muscle actions. *Isokinet Exerc Sci* 21:161-165, 2013.

6. Bracko, MR, and Fellingham, GW. Prediction of ice skating performance with off-ice testing in youth hockey players. *Med Sci Sports Exerc* 29:S172, 1997.

7. Burr, JF, Jamnik, RK, Baker, J, Macpherson, A, Gledhill, N, and McGuire, EJ. Relationship of physical fitness test results and hockey playing potential in elite-level ice hockey players. *J Strength Cond Res* 22(5):1535-1543, 2008.

8. Burr, JF, Jamnik, RK, Dogra, S, and Gledhill, N. Evaluation of jump protocols to assess leg power and predict hockey playing potential. *J Strength Cond Res* 21(4):1139-1145, 2007.

9. Cormie, P, McCaulley, GO, Triplett, NT, and McBride, JM. Optimal loading for maximal power output during lower-body resistance exercises. *Med Sci Sport Exerc* 39(2):340-349, 2007.

10. Delisle-Houde, P, Reid, RE, Insogna, JA, Prokop, NW, Buchan, TA, Fontaine, SL, and Andersen, RE. Comparing DXA and air displacement-plethysmography to assess body composition of male collegiate hockey players. *J Strength Cond Res* 33(2):474-478, 2019.

11. Farlinger, CM, Kruisselbrink, LD, and Fowles, JR. Relationships to skating performance in competitive hockey players. *J Strength Cond Res* 21(3):915-922,2007.

12. Felser, S, Behrens, M, Fischer, S, Heise, S, Baumler, M, Salomon, R, and Bruhn, S. Relationship between strength qualities and short track speed skating performance in young athletes. *Scand J Med Sci Sports* 26:165-171, 2016.

13. Geithner, CA, Lee, AM, and Bracko, MR. Physical and performance differences among forwards, defensemen, and goalies in elite women's ice hockey. *J Strength Cond Res* 20(3):500-505, 2006.

14. Green, MR, Pivarnik, JM, Carrier, DP, and Womack, CJ. Relationship between physiological profiles and on-ice performance of a National Collegiate Athletic Association Division I hockey team. *J Strength Cond Res* 20(1):43-46, 2006.

15. Häkkinen, K, Komi, P, and Alen, M. Effect of explosive type strength training on isometric force- and relaxation-time, electromyographic and muscle fibre characteristics of leg extensor muscles. *Acta Physiol Scand* 125:587-600, 1985.

16. Hoff, J, Kemi, OJ, and Helgerud, J. Strength and endurance differences between elite and junior elite ice hockey players: The importance of allometric scaling. *Int J Sports Med* 26(7):537-541, 2005.

17. Howard, JD, and Enoka, RM. Maximum bilateral contractions are modified by neurally mediated interlimb effects. *J Appl Physiol* 70:306-316, 1991.

18. Kuruganti, U, and Seaman, K. The bilateral leg strength deficit is present in old, young and adolescent females during isokinetic knee extension and flexion. *Eur J Appl Physiol* 97:322-326, 2006.

19. Lauersen, JB, Bertelsen, DM, and Andersen, LB. The effectiveness of exercise interventions to prevent sports injuries: A systematic review and meta-analysis of randomized controlled trials. *Br J Sports Med* 48(11):871-877, 2014.

20. Mascaro, T, Seaver, BL, and Swanson, L. Prediction of skating speed with off-ice testing in professional hockey players. *J Orthop Sport Phys* 15(2):92-98, 1992.

21. Ohtsuki, T. Decrease in human voluntary isometric arm strength induced by simultaneous bilateral exertion. *Behav Brain Res* 7:165-178, 1983.

22. Peyer, KL, Pivarnik, JM, Eisenmann, JC, and Vorkapich, M. Physiological characteristics of National Collegiate Athletic Association Division I ice hockey players and their relation to game performance. *J Strength Cond Res* 25(5):1183-1192, 2011.

23. Potteiger J, Smith, DL, and Maier, ML. Relationship between body composition, leg strength, anaerobic power, and on-ice skating performance in Division 1 men's hockey athletes. *J Strength Cond Res* 24(7):1755-1762, 2010.

24. Quinney, HA, Dewart, R, Game, A, Snydmiller, G, Warburton, D, and Bell, G. A 26 year physiological description of a National Hockey League team. *Appl Physiol Nutr Metab* 33:753-760, 2008.

25. Ransdell, LB, and Murray, T. A physical profile of elite female ice hockey players from the USA. *J Strength Cond Res* 25(9):2358-2363, 2011.

26. Suchomel, TJ, Nimphius, S, Bellon, CR, and Stone, MH. The importance of muscular strength: Training considerations. *Sports Med* 48:765-785, 2018.

27. Taniguchi, Y. Lateral specificity in resistance training: The effect of bilateral and unilateral training. *Eur J Appl Physiol Occup Physiol* 75:144-150, 1997.

28. Twist, P, and Rhodes, T. A physiological analysis of ice hockey positions. *National Strength and Conditioning Journal* 15:44-46, 1993.

29. Tyler T, Nicholas S, Campbell R, and McHugh M. The association of hip strength and flexibility with the incidence of adductor muscle strains in professional ice hockey players. *Am J Sports Med* 29(2):124-128, 2001.

30. Vandervoort, AA, Sale, DG, and Moroz, J. Comparison of motor unit activation during unilateral and bilateral leg extension. *J Appl Physiol Respir Environ Exerc Physiol* 56:46-51, 1984.

31. Wilson, K, Snydmiller, G, Game, A, Quinney, A, and Bell, G. The development and reliability of a repeated anaerobic cycling test in female ice hockey players. *J Strength Cond Res* 24(2):580-584, 2010.

Chapter 2

1. Behm, DG, Wahl, MJ, Button, DC, Power, KE, and Anderson, KG. Relationship between hockey skating speed and selected performance measures. *J Strength Cond Res* 19:326-331, 2005.

2. Bompa, TO, and Chambers, D. *Total Hockey Conditioning: From Pee-Wee to Pro.* Firefly Books, 2003.

3. Budarick, AR, Shell, JR, Robbins, SM, Wu, T, Renaud, PJ, and Pearsall, DJ. Ice hockey skating sprints: Run to glide mechanics of high calibre male and female athletes. *Sports Biomech* 1-17, 2018.

4. Canadian Hockey Association. *Intermediate Level Manual.* Ottawa, ON: Canadian Hockey Association, 1989.

5. Cox, MH, Miles, DS, Verde, TJ, and Rhodes, EC. Applied physiology of ice hockey. *Sports Med* 19:184-201, 1995.

6. De Koning, J, and van Ingen Schenau, G. Performance-determining factors in speed skating. In *Biomechanics in Sport: Performance Enhancement and Injury Prevention*, Zatsiorsky, VM, ed. Wiley Online Library, 232-246, 2000.

7. De Koning, J, De Groot, G, and van Ingen Schenau, G. Ice friction during speed skating. *J Biomech* 25:565-571, 1992.

8. Donskov, A. *Physical Preparation for Ice Hockey II: The Gain, Go, Grow Manual.* AuthorHouse, 2020.

9. Donskov, A. *Physical Preparation for Ice Hockey: Biological Principles and Practical Solutions.* AuthorHouse, 2016.

10. Douglas, A, Rotondi, MA, Baker, J, Jamnik, VK, and Macpherson, AK. On-ice physical demands of world-class women's ice hockey: From training to competition. *Int J Sports Physiol Perform* 14:1227-1232, 2019.

11. Douglas, AS, and Kennedy, CR. Tracking in-match movement demands using local positioning system in world-class men's ice hockey. *J Strength Cond Res* 34:639-646, 2020.

12. Farlinger, CM, Kruisselbrink, LD, and Fowles, JR. Relationships to skating performance in competitive hockey players. *J Strength Cond Res* 21:915-922, 2007.

13. Gaitanos, GC, Williams, C, Boobis, LH, and Brooks, S. Human muscle metabolism during intermittent maximal exercise. *J Appl Physiol* 75:712-719, 1993.

14. Green, MR, Pivarnik, JM, Carrier, DP, and Womack, CJ. Relationship between physiological profiles and on-ice performance of a National Collegiate Athletic Association Division I hockey team. *J Strength Cond Res* 20:43-46, 2006.

15. Haché, A. *The Physics of Hockey.* JHU Press, 2002.

16. Hargreaves, M, and Spriet, LL. Overview of exercise metabolism. In *Exercise Metabolism*, Hargreaves, M, and Spriet, LL, eds. Champaign, IL: Human Kinetics, 1, 2006.

17. Holloszy, J, and Coyle, EF. Adaptations of skeletal muscle to endurance exercise and their metabolic consequences. *J Appl Physiol* 56:831-838, 1984.

18. Janot, JM, Beltz, NM, and Dalleck, LD. Multiple off-ice performance variables predict on-ice skating performance in male and female Division III ice hockey players. *J Sports Sci Med* 14:522, 2015.

19. Jovanović, M, and Flanagan, EP. Researched applications of velocity-based strength training. *J Aust Strength Cond* 22:58-69, 2014.

20. Lafontaine, D. Three-dimensional kinematics of the knee and ankle joints for three consecutive push-offs during ice hockey skating starts. *Sports Biomech* 6:391-406, 2007.

21. Lieber, RL, and Fridén, J. Functional and clinical significance of skeletal muscle architecture. *Muscle & Nerve* 23:1647-1666, 2000.

22. Lignell, E, Fransson, D, Krustrup P, and Mohr, M. Analysis of high-intensity skating in top-class ice hockey match-play in relation to training status and muscle damage. *J Strength Cond Res* 32:1303-1310, 2018.

23. MacDougall, J, Sale, D, Moroz, J, Elder, G, Sutton, J, and Howald, H. Mitochondrial volume density in human skeletal muscle following heavy resistance training. *Med Sci Sports* 11:164-166, 1979.

24. MacLean, E. A theoretical review of the physiological demands of ice-hockey and a full year periodized sport specific conditioning program for the Canadian junior hockey player. www.functionalhockey.com/files/Physiological_Demands_of_Ice-Hockey_and_Full_Yr_Periodized_Cond_Program.pdf. Accessed on September 12, 2023.

25. Marino, GW. Biomechanics of power skating: Past research, future trends. Presented at ISBS-Conference Proceedings Archive, 1995.

26. Marino, GW. Kinematics of ice skating at different velocities. *Res Q* 48:93-97, 1977.

27. McPherson, MN, Wrigley, A, and Montelpare, WJ. The biomechanical characteristics of development-age hockey players: Determining the effects of body size on the assessment of skating technique. In *Safety in Ice Hockey: Fourth Volume*. ASTM International, 2004.

28. Montgomery, DL. Physiological profile of professional hockey players—A longitudinal comparison. *Appl Physiol Nutr* 31:181-185, 2006.

29. Neeld, K, Peterson, B, Dietz, C, Cappaert, T, and Alvar, B. Differences in external workload demand between session types and positions in collegiate men's ice hockey. *International Journal of Kinesiology and Sports Science* 9:36-44, 2021.

30. Pearsall, DJ, Paquette, YM, Baig, Z, Albrecht, J, and Turcotte, RA. Ice hockey skate boot mechanics: Direct torque and contact pressure measures. *Procedia Engineering* 34:295-300, 2012.

31. Pearsall, DJ, Turcotte, RA, and Murphy, SD. Biomechanics of ice hockey. In *Exercise and Sport Science*, Garrett, WE, and Kirkendall, DT, eds. Philadelphia: Lippincott, Williams & Wilkins, 675-694, 2000.

31a. Peterson, BJ, Fitzgerald, JS, Dietz, CC, Ziegler, KS, Ingraham, SJ, Baker, SE, and Snyder, EM. Aerobic capacity is associated with improved repeated sprint performance in hockey. *J Strength Cond Res* 29:1465-1472, 2015.

32. Pierce, CM, LaPrade, RF, Wahoff, M, O'Brien, L, and Philippon, MJ. Ice hockey goaltender rehabilitation, including on-ice progression, after arthroscopic hip surgery for femoroacetabular impingement. *J Orthop Sports Phys Ther* 43:129-141, 2013.

33. Shell, JR, Robbins, SM, Dixon, PC, Renaud, PJ, Turcotte, RA, Wu, T, and Pearsall, DJ. Skating start propulsion: Three-dimensional kinematic analysis of elite male and female ice hockey players. *Sports Biomech* 16:313-324, 2017.

34. Stidwill, T, Pearsall, D, and Turcotte, R. Comparison of skating kinetics and kinematics on ice and on a synthetic surface. *Sports Biomech* 9:57-64, 2010.

35. Tanaka, H. Effects of cross-training: transfer of training effects on VO2max between cycling, running and swimming. *Sports Medicine* 18:330-339, Nov 1994.

36. Thompson, KM, Safadie, A, Ford, J, and Burr, JF. Off-ice resisted sprints best predict all-out skating performance in varsity hockey players. *J Strength Cond Res* 36(9):2597-2601, 2020.

37. Turcotte, R, Pearsall, D, Montgomery, D, Lefebvre, R, Nicolaou, M, and Loh, J. Plantar force measures during forward skating in ice hockey. Presented at ISBS-Conference Proceedings Archive, 2001.

38. Turner, AN, and Stewart, PF. Repeat sprint ability. *Strength & Conditioning Journal* 35:37-41, 2013.

39. Twist, P, and Rhodes, T. Exercise physiology: A physiological analysis of ice hockey positions. *Strength & Conditioning Journal* 15:44-46, 1993.

40. Upjohn, T, Turcotte, R, Pearsall, DJ, and Loh, J. Three-dimensional kinematics of the lower limbs during forward ice hockey skating. *Sports Biomech* 7:206-221, 2008.

41. Vescovi, JD, Murray, TM, and VanHeest, JL. Positional performance profiling of elite ice hockey players. *Int J Sports Physiol Perform* 1:84-94, 2006.

42. Wijdicks, CA, Philippon, MJ, Civitarese, DM, and LaPrade, RF. A mandated change in goalie pad width has no effect on ice hockey goaltender hip kinematics. *Clin J Sport Med* 24:403-408, 2014.

43. Wu, T, Pearsall, DJ, Russell, PJ, and Imanaka, Y. Kinematic comparisons between forward and backward skating in ice hockey. Presented at ISBS-Conference Proceedings Archive, 2016.

Chapter 3

1. Baker, DG, and Newton, RU. An analysis of the ratio and relationship between upper body pressing and pulling strength. *J Strength Cond Res* 18(3):594-598, 2004.

2. Bendus, V. Unpublished raw data. Brock University. 2023.

3. Bond, CW, Bennett, TW, and Noonan, BC. Evaluation of skating top speed, acceleration, and multiple repeated sprint speed ice hockey performance tests. *J Strength Cond Res* 32(8), 2273-2283, 2018.

4. Brady, CJ, Harrison, AJ, and Comyns, TM. A review of the reliability of biomechanical variables produced during the isometric mid-thigh pull and isometric squat and the reporting of normative data. *Sports Biomechanics* 19(1):1-25, 2020.

5. Burr, JF, Jamnik, VK, Dogra, S, and Gledhill, N. Evaluation of jump protocols to assess leg power and predict hockey playing potential. *J Strength Cond Res* 21(4):1139-1145, 2007.

6. Chiarlitti, NA, Delisle-Houde, P, Reid, RER, Kennedy, C, and Andersen, RE. Importance of body composition in the National Hockey League Combine physiological assessments. *J Strength Cond Res* 32(11):3135-3142, 2018.

7. Farlinger, CM, Kruisselbrink, LD, and Fowles, JR. Relationships to skating performance in competitive hockey players. *J Strength Cond Res* 21(3):915-922, 2007.

8. Layer, J, Grenz, C, Hinshaw, T, Smith, D, Barrett, S, and Dai, B. Kinetic analysis of isometric back squats and isometric belt squats. *J Strength Cond Res* 32(12):3301-3309, 2018.

9. Lignell, E, Fransson, D, Krustrup, P, and Mohr, M. Analysis of high-intensity skating in top-class ice hockey match-play in relation to training status and muscle damage. *J Strength Cond Res* 32(5), 1303-1310, 2018.

10. McConnell, D. [Unpublished raw data]. University of Massachusetts Lowell, 2018.

11. McConnell, D. [Unpublished raw data]. Arizona Coyotes, 2022.

12. Neeld, K. [Unpublished raw data]. USA Hockey, 2016a.

13. Neeld, K. [Unpublished raw data]. Endeavor Sports Performance, 2016b.

14. Nuzzo J, McBridge, J, Cormie, P, and McCaulley, G. Relationship between countermovement jump performance and multijoint isometric and dynamic tests of strength. *J Strength Cond Res* 22:699-707, 2008.

15. Patel, B. [Unpublished raw data]. Quinnipiac University, 2022.

16. Potenza, M. [Unpublished raw data]. San Jose Sharks, 2016.

17. Potenza, M. [Unpublished raw data]. San Jose Sharks, 2017.

18. Potenza, M. [Unpublished raw data]. San Jose Sharks, 2018.

19. Runner, AR, Lehnhard, RA, Butterfield, SA, Tu, S, and O'Neill, T. Predictors of speed using off-ice measures of college hockey players. *J Strength Cond Res* 30(6):1626-1632, 2016.

20. Schmitt, KU, Muser, MH, Thueler, H, and Bruegger, O. Crash-test dummy and pendulum impact tests of ice hockey boards: Greater displacement does not reduce impact. *Brit J Sport Med* 52(1):41-46, 2017.

Chapter 4

1. Aagaard, P. Training-induced changes in neural function. *Exerc Sport Sci Rev* 31:61-67, 2003.

2. Aagaard, P, Simonsen, EB, Andersen, JL, Magnusson, P, and Dyhre-Poulsen, P. Increased rate of force development and neural drive of human skeletal muscle following resistance training. *J Appl Physiol* 93:1318-1326, 2002.

3. Aboodarda, SJ, Byrne, JM, Samson, M, Wilson, BD, Mokhtar, AH, and Behm, DG. Does performing drop jumps with additional eccentric loading improve jump performance? *J Strength Cond Res* 28:2314-2323, 2014.

4. Andersen, LL, and Aagaard P. Influence of maximal muscle strength and intrinsic muscle contractile properties on contractile rate of force development. *Eur J Appl Physiol* 96:46-52, 2006.

5. Andersen, LL, Andersen, JL, Zebis, MK, and Aagaard, P. Early and late rate of force development: Differential adaptive responses to resistance training? *Scand J Med Sci Sports* 20:e162-e169, 2010.

6. Baar, K. Stress relaxation and targeted nutrition to treat patellar tendinopathy. *Int J Sport Nutr Exerc Metab* 29:453-457, 2019.

7. Baar, K. Isometric exercises. *Sportsmith*, 2022.

8. Behm, DG, and Anderson, KG. The role of instability with resistance training. *J Strength Cond Res* 20:716-722, 2006.

9. Behm, DG, and Sale, DG. Intended rather than actual movement velocity determines velocity-specific training response. *J Appl Physiol* 74:359-368, 1993.

10. Bell, DR, Sanfilippo, JL, Binkley, N, and Heiderscheit, BC. Lean mass asymmetry influences force and power asymmetry during jumping in collegiate athletes. *J Strength Cond Res* 28:884, 2014.

11. Blimkie, CJ, and Bar-Or, O. Trainability of muscle strength, power and endurance during childhood. *The Child and Adolescent Athlete* 6:113-129, 1996.

12. Bompa, T, and Haff, G. *Periodization: Theory and Methodology of Training*, 5th ed. Champaign, IL: Human Kinetics, 2009.

13. Campos, GE, Luecke, TJ, Wendeln, HK, Toma, K, Hagerman, FC, Murray, TF, Ragg, KE, Ratamess, NA, Kraemer, WJ, and Staron, RS. Muscular adaptations in response to three different resistance-training regimens: Specificity of repetition maximum training zones. *Eur J Appl Physiol* 88:50-60, 2002.

14. Carey Smith, R, and Rutherford, O. The role of metabolites in strength training: I. A comparison of eccentric and concentric contractions. *Eur J Appl Physiol Occup Physiol* 71:332-336, 1995.

15. Cholewicki, J, McGill, SM, and Norman, RW. Lumbar spine loads during the lifting of extremely heavy weights. *Med Sci Sports Exerc* 23:1179-1186, 1991.

16. Cintineo, HP, Freidenreich, DJ, Blaine, CM, Cardaci, TD, Pellegrino, JK, and Arent, SM. Acute physiological responses to an intensity and time-under-tension equated single-vs. multiple-set resistance training bout in trained men. *J Strength Cond Res* 32:3310-3318, 2018.

17. Comfort, P, Dos' Santos, T, Thomas, C, McMahon, JJ, and Suchomel, TJ. An investigation into the effects of excluding the catch phase of the power clean on force-time characteristics during isometric and dynamic tasks: An intervention study. *J Strength Cond Res* 32:2116-2129, 2018.

18. Coratella, G, and Schena, F. Eccentric resistance training increases and retains maximal strength, muscle endurance, and hypertrophy in trained men. *Appl Physiol Nutr Me* 41:1184-1189, 2016.

19. Cormie P, McCaulley, GO, Triplett, NT, and McBride, JM. Optimal loading for maximal power output during lower-body resistance exercises. *Med Sci Sports Exerc* 340-349, 2007.

20. Cormie, P, McGuigan, MR, and Newton, RU. Developing maximal neuromuscular power. Part 1: Biological basis of maximal power production. *Sports Med* 41:17-38, 2011.

21. Cormier, P, Freitas, TT, Loturco, I, Turner, A, Virgile, A, Haff, GG, Blazevich, AJ, Agar-Newman, D, Henneberry, M, and Baker, DG. Within-session exercise sequencing during programming for complex training: Historical perspectives, terminology, and training considerations. *Sports Med* 52:2371-2389, 2022.

22. Cronin, JB, McNair, PJ, and Marshall, RN. Force-velocity analysis of strength-training techniques and load: Implications for training strategy and research. *J Strength Cond Res* 17:148-155, 2003.

23. Cuenca-Fernández, F, Smith, IC, Jordan, MJ, MacIntosh, BR, López-Contreras, G, Arellano, R, and Herzog, W. Nonlocalized postactivation performance enhancement (PAPE) effects in trained athletes: A pilot study. *Appl Physiol Nutr Me* 42:1122-1125, 2017.

24. Cuthbert, M, Haff, GG, Arent, SM, Ripley, N, McMahon, JJ, Evans, M, and Comfort, P. Effects of variations in resistance training frequency on strength development in well-trained populations and implications for in-season athlete training: A systematic review and meta-analysis. *Sports Med* 51:1967-1982, 2021.

25. Emery, C, and Meeuwisse, W. The effectiveness of a neuromuscular prevention strategy to reduce injuries in youth soccer: A cluster-randomised controlled trial. *Brit J Sports Med* 44:555-562, 2010.

26. Erskine, RM, Fletcher, G, and Folland, JP. The contribution of muscle hypertrophy to strength changes following resistance training. *Eur J Appl Physiol* 114:1239-1249, 2014.

27. Franchi, MV, Atherton, PJ, Reeves, ND, Flück, M, Williams, J, Mitchell, WK, Selby, A, Beltran Valls, R, and Narici, MV. Architectural, functional and molecular responses to concentric and eccentric loading in human skeletal muscle. *Acta Physiologica* 210:642-654, 2014.

28. Francis, C. *Structure of Training for Speed.* Charliefrancis.com, 2008.

29. Friedmann-Bette, B, Bauer, T, Kinscherf, R, Vorwald, S, Klute, K, Bischoff, D, Müller, H, Weber, M-A, Metz, J, and Kauczor, H-U. Effects of strength training with eccentric overload on muscle adaptation in male athletes. *Eur J Appl Physiol* 108:821-836, 2010.

30. Fry, AC, and Kraemer, WJ. Resistance exercise overtraining and overreaching: Neuroendocrine responses. *Sports Med* 23:106-129, 1997.

31. Grgic, J, Schoenfeld, BJ, Skrepnik, M, Davies, TB, and Mikulic, P. Effects of rest interval duration in resistance training on measures of muscular strength: A systematic review. *Sports Med* 48:137-151, 2018.

32. Häkkinen, K, Pakarinen, A, Alen, M, Kauhanen, H, and Komi, P. Relationships between training volume, physical performance capacity, and serum hormone concentrations during prolonged training in elite weightlifters. *Int J Sports Med* 8:S61-S65, 1987.

33. Handford, MJ, Bright, TE, Mundy, P, Lake, J, Theis, N, and Hughes, JD. The need for eccentric speed: A narrative review of the effects of accelerated eccentric actions during resistance-based training. *Sports Med* 52:2061-2083, 2022.

34. Hornberger, TA, and Chien, S. Mechanical stimuli and nutrients regulate rapamycin-sensitive signaling through distinct mechanisms in skeletal muscle. *J Cell Biochem* 97:1207-1216, 2006.

35. Hyldahl, RD, Nelson, B, Xin, L, Welling, T, Groscost, L, Hubal, MJ, Chipkin, S, Clarkson, PM, and Parcell, AC. Extracellular matrix remodeling and its contribution to protective adaptation following lengthening contractions in human muscle. *FASEB J* 29:2894-2904, 2015.

36. Janda, V. Muscles and motor control in low back pain: Assessment and management. In *Physical Therapy of the Low Back.* Twomey, LT, ed. New York: Churchill Livingstone, 253-278, 1987.

37. Jandačka, D and Beremlijski P. Determination of strength exercise intensities based on the load-power-velocity relationship. *J Hum Kin* 28:33-44, 2011.

38. Jidovtseff, B, Harris, NK, Crielaard, J-M, and Cronin, JB. Using the load-velocity relationship for 1RM prediction. *J Strength Cond Res* 25:267-270, 2011.

39. Jordan, MJ. *Loading Parameter Table*. Figshare, 2023.

40. Jovanović, M. *Strength Training Manual: The Agile Periodization Approach. Theory.* Volumes One and Two. Mladen Jovanović, 2020.

41. Jovanović, M, and Flanagan, EP. Researched applications of velocity based strength training. *J Aust Strength Cond* 22:58-69, 2014.

42. Kawamori, N, Crum, AJ, Blumert, PA, Kulik, JR, Childers, JT, Wood, JA, Stone, MH, and Haff, GG. Influence of different relative intensities on power output during the hang power clean: Identification of the optimal load. *J Strength Cond Res* 19:698-708, 2005.

42a. King, I. How to write strength training programs. In *Speed of Movement*, p. 123, 1998.

43. Komi, P. Training of muscle strength and power: Interaction of neuromotoric, hypertrophic, and mechanical factors. *Int J Sports Med* 7:S10-S15, 1986.

44. Kraska, JM, Ramsey, MW, Haff, GG, Fethke, N, Sands, WA, Stone, ME, and Stone, MH. Relationship between strength characteristics and unweighted and weighted vertical jump height. *Int J Sport Physiol* 4:461-473, 2009.

45. Kubo, K, Kanehisa, H, Ito, M, and Fukunaga, T. Effects of isometric training on the elasticity of human tendon structures in vivo. *J Appl Physiol* 91:26-32, 2001.

46. Lee, M, Gandevia, SC, and Carroll, TJ. Unilateral strength training increases voluntary activation of the opposite untrained limb. *Clin Neurophysiol* 120:802-808, 2009.

47. Leong, C, McDermott, W, Elmer, S, and Martin, J. Chronic eccentric cycling improves quadriceps muscle structure and maximum cycling power. *Int J Sports Med* 35:559-565, 2014.

48. McGuigan, M. *Developing Power*. Champaign, IL: Human Kinetics, 2017.

49. McLellan, CP, and Lovell, DI. Neuromuscular responses to impact and collision during elite rugby league match play. *J Strength Cond Res* 26:1431-1440, 2012.

50. Mirkov, DM, Nedeljkovic, A, Milanovic, S, and Jaric, S. Muscle strength testing: Evaluation of tests of explosive force production. *Eur J Appl Physiol* 91:147-154, 2004.

51. Mitchell, CJ, Churchward-Venne, TA, West, DW, Burd, NA, Breen, L, Baker, SK, and Phillips, SM. Resistance exercise load does not determine training-mediated hypertrophic gains in young men. *J Appl Physiol* 113:71-77, 2012.

52. Morrissey, MC, Harman, EA, and Johnson, MJ. Resistance training modes: Specificity and effectiveness. *Med Sci Sports Exerc* 27:648-660, 1995.

53. Oliveras, R, Bizzini, M, Brunner, R, and Maffiuletti, NA. Field-based evaluation of hip adductor and abductor strength in professional male ice hockey players: Reference values and influencing factors. *Phys Ther Sport* 43:204-209, 2020.

54. Peterson, MD, Alvar, BA, and Rhea, MR. The contribution of maximal force production to explosive movement among young collegiate athletes. *J Strength Cond Res* 20:867-873, 2006.

55. Rassier, D, and Macintosh, B. Coexistence of potentiation and fatigue in skeletal muscle. *Braz J Med Biol Res* 33:499-508, 2000.

56. Rowlands, AV, Marginson, VF, and Lee, J. Chronic flexibility gains: Effect of isometric contraction duration during proprioceptive neuromuscular facilitation stretching techniques. *Res Q Exerc Sport* 74:47-51, 2003.

57. Sale, DG. Neural adaptation to resistance training. *Med Sci Sports Exerc* 20:S135-145, 1988.

58. Schaefer, LV, and Bittmann, FN. Are there two forms of isometric muscle action? Results of the experimental study support a distinction between a holding and a pushing isometric muscle function. *BMC Sports Science, Medicine and Rehabilitation* 9:1-13, 2017.

59. Schoenfeld, BJ, Peterson, MD, Ogborn, D, Contreras, B, and Sonmez, GT. Effects of low-vs. high-load resistance training on muscle strength and hypertrophy in well-trained men. *J Strength Cond Res* 29:2954-2963, 2015.

60. Secomb, JL, Kelly, M, and Dascombe, BJ. Hip strength profiling of ice hockey athletes across various joint-specific angles: Monitoring and injury implications. *J Strength Cond Res* 37:e422-e429, 2023.

61. Stone, MH, Sanborn, K, O'Bryant, HS, Hartman, M, Stone, ME, Proulx, C, Ward, B, and Hruby, J. Maximum strength-power-performance relationships in collegiate throwers. *J Strength Cond Res* 17:739-745, 2003.

62. Tillin, NA, Jimenez-Reyes, P, Pain, MTG, and Folland, JP. Neuromuscular performance of explosive power athletes versus untrained individuals. *Med Sci Sports Exerc* 42:781-790, 2010.

63. Tyler, TF, Nicholas, SJ, Campbell, RJ, and McHugh, MP. The association of hip strength and flexibility with the incidence of adductor muscle strains in professional ice hockey players. *Am J Sport Med* 29:124-128, 2001.

64. Vanhelder, W, Radomski, M, and Goode, R. Growth hormone responses during intermittent weightlifting exercise in men. *Eur J Appl Physiol Occup Physiol* 53:31-34, 1984.

65. Verkhoshansky, Y. Organization of the training process. *New Studies in Athletics* 13:21-32, 1998.

66. Verkhoshansky, Y, and Siff, M. Strength training methods. In *Supertraining*. Rome: Verkhoshansky SSTM, 393-402, 2009.

67. Viru, A. *Adaptation in Sports Training*. Boca Raton, FL: CRC Press, 1995.

68. Weir, JP, Housh, DJ, Housh, TJ, and Weir, LL. The effect of unilateral eccentric weight training and detraining on joint angle specificity, cross-training, and the bilateral deficit. *J Orthop Sports Phys Ther* 22:207-215, 1995.

69. Wilson, JM, Marin, PJ, Rhea, MR, Wilson, SM, Loenneke, JP, and Anderson, JC. Concurrent training: A meta-analysis examining interference of aerobic and resistance exercises. *J Strength Cond Res* 26:2293-2307, 2012.

70. Winter, EM, and Brookes, FBC. Electromechanical response times and muscle elasticity in men and women. *Eur J Appl Physiol Occup Physiol* 63:124-128, 1991.

71. Zaryski, C, and Smith, DJ. Training principles and issues for ultra-endurance athletes. *Curr Sports Med Rep* 4: 165-170, 2005.

72. Zourdos, MC, Klemp, A, Dolan, C, Quiles, JM, Schau, KA, Jo, E, Helms, E, Esgro, B, Duncan, S, and Merino, SG. Novel resistance training–specific rating of perceived exertion scale measuring repetitions in reserve. *J Strength Cond Res* 30:267-275, 2016.

Chapter 6

1. Bompa, T. *Theory and Methodology of Training*, 3rd ed. Dubuque, IA: Kendall Hunt, 1994.

2. Carr, K, and Feit, MK. *Functional Training Anatomy*. Champaign, IL: Human Kinetics, 121-145, 2023.

3. Donskov, A. *Physical Preparation for Ice Hockey: Biological Principles and Practical Solutions*. Bloomington, IN: AuthorHouse, 99-121, 2016.

4. Krause, M, and Febles, R. Lower Body Exercise Technique. In *Strength Training for Baseball*. Coleman, AE, and Szymanski, D, eds. Champaign, IL: Human Kinetics, 99-127, 2022.

5. McBride, JM. Biomechanics of resistance exercise. In *Essentials of Strength Training and Conditioning*, 4th ed. Haff, GG, and Triplett, NT, eds. Champaign, IL: Human Kinetics, 19-42, 2016.

6. Neeld, K, and Pollen, T. *Speed Training for Hockey: 12 Weeks to Game-Changing Speed*. 1-6, 38-50, 2018.

Chapter 8

1. Kibler, WB, Press, J, and Sciascia, A. The role of core stability in athletic function. *Sports Med* 36:189-198, 2006.

Chapter 9

1. Adams, K, O'Shea, JP, O'Shea, KL, and Climstein, M. The effect of six weeks of squat, plyometric and squat-plyometric training on power production. *J Strength Cond Res* 6(1):36-41, 1992.

2. Comyns, TM, Harrison, AJ, Hennessy, LK, and Jensen, RL. The optimal complex training rest interval for athletes from anaerobic sports. *J Strength Cond Res* 20(3):471-476, 2006.

3. Ebben, W. Complex training: A review of combined weight training and plyometric training modes. *Strength Cond J* 20(5):18-27, 1998.

4. Giakoumis, M. To Nordic or not to Nordic? A different perspective with reason to appreciate semitendinosus more than ever. Sport Performance & Science Reports [website], 2020. https://sportperfsci.com/wp-content/uploads/2020/05/SPSR93_Giakoumis_final.pdf.

5. González-Badillo, JJ, and Sánchez-Medina, L. Movement velocity as a measure of loading intensity in resistance training. *Int J Sports Med* 31(5):347-352, 2010.

6. Kawamori, N, and Newton, R. Velocity specificity of resistance training: Actual movement velocity versus intention to move explosively. *Strength Cond J* 28(2):86-89, 2006.

7. Mihalik, JP, Libby, JJ, Battaglini, CL, and McMurray, RG. Comparing short-term complex and compound training programs on vertical jump height and power output. *J Strength Cond Res* 22:47-53, 2008.

8. Włodarczyk, M, Adamus, P, Zieliński, J, and Kantanista, A. Effects of velocity-based training on strength and power in elite athletes—A systematic review. *Int J Env Res Pub He* 18(10):5257, 2021.

Chapter 10

1. Mann, B. *Developing Explosive Athletes: Use of Velocity-Based Training in Athletes.* Ultimate Athlete Concepts, 2016.

Chapter 11

1. Brocherie, F, Babault, N, Cometti, G, Maffiuletti, N, and Chatard, JC. Electrostimulation training effects on the physical performance of ice hockey players. *Med Sci Sports Exerc* 37(3):455-460, 2005.

2. Nichol, M. Performance demands of ice hockey. In *Science and Application of High Intensity Interval Training*. Laursen, P, and Buchheit, M, eds. Champaign, IL: Human Kinetics, 477-494, 2019.

Chapter 12

1. Carroll, TJ, Herbert, RD, Munn, J, Lee, M, and Gandevia, SC. Contralateral effects of unilateral strength training: Evidence and possible mechanisms. *J Appl Physiol* 101(5):1514-1522, 2006.

INDEX

Note: The italicized *f* and *t* following page numbers refer to figures and tables, respectively.

ABOUT THE NSCA

The **National Strength and Conditioning Association (NSCA)** is the world's leading organization in the field of sport conditioning. Drawing on the resources and expertise of the most recognized professionals in strength training and conditioning, sport science, performance research, education, and sports medicine, the NSCA is the world's trusted source of knowledge and training guidelines for coaches and athletes. The NSCA provides the crucial link between the lab and the field.

ABOUT THE EDITORS

Kevin Neeld, PhD, CPSS, CSCS, RSCC*D, is the head performance coach for the Boston Bruins, where he oversees the organization's performance training program and sport science initiatives. He previously worked as a strength and conditioning coach with the San Jose Sharks and USA Hockey's women's team. Neeld earned his PhD in human and sport performance from Rocky Mountain University, where his research focused on the relationship between workload and performance in elite hockey. He has published several articles in peer-reviewed journals and is the author of *Ultimate Hockey Training* and *Speed Training for Hockey*. He has been an invited guest speaker at events hosted by the National Hockey League (NHL), National Strength and Conditioning Association (NSCA), and USA Hockey. Neeld is certified as a strength and conditioning coach and as a performance and sport scientist through the NSCA.

Brijesh Patel, MA, CSCS, RSCC*E, has been an innovator, leader, and highly regarded coach in the health and performance field for over 20 years. His passion for improvement, growth, and development has played a major role in the success and well-being of hundreds of individuals. Patel is a sought-after speaker and consultant as well as a mentor for coaches across all sports. He currently serves as the associate athletic director and director of athletic performance at Quinnipiac University. Patel has built the strength  and conditioning department from scratch, instilling his philosophy and approach to creating the best overall environment. He prides himself in leading a department in which each student-athlete is given his or her own individualized program that is designed to improve movement skills, core strength, power, speed, strength, balance, and flexibility. Although Patel oversees the strength and conditioning development for all 21 varsity sports at Quinnipiac, he works primarily with the men's and women's basketball and ice hockey teams.

Vicki Bendus, is the director of performance for PWHL Montreal. She was previously a sport performance coach at Brock University, where she led the men's and women's hockey and soccer teams. Bendus has worked with multiple national sport organizations since 2016, including Hockey Canada and Wrestling Canada. She is currently the lead strength and conditioning coach with the senior national women's hockey team, after previously working with the U18 and development programs. Bendus is currently pursuing her PhD, with a focus on identifying, measuring, and improving off-ice key performance indicators for linear skating speed.

Cam Davidson, CSCS, RSCC, USAW L2, is the director of strength and conditioning at Colorado College (CC) and works with men's hockey and women's soccer. He came to CC after serving as the assistant director of performance enhancement at Penn State University (PSU). While at PSU, Davidson trained the women's volleyball team, a program that went undefeated for 109 matches and won four4 national championships in six years. Davidson also worked with the track and field and

men's hockey programs, winning a combined 11 B1G championships. He worked with multiple national champions, Olympians such as Joe Kovacs and Darrell Hill, and two-time world champion Ryan Whiting.

Anthony Donskov, PhD, CSCS, is the founder of Donskov Strength and Conditioning. He has coached professional, collegiate, and youth hockey players for 25 years. Donskov earned a PhD at the University of Western Ontario. His research interests include biomechanics, on- ice performance, and return to play. He has authored two books: *Physical Preparation for Ice Hockey I* and *Physical Preparation for Ice Hockey II*. Donskov is a head instructor at Donskov Hockey Development, a family-run hockey school with a renowned reputation for developing players. Donskov played two years of minor professional hockey (2001-2003) for the Lubbock Cotton Kings (Central Hockey League), and he played collegiate hockey at Miami University in Ohio (1997-2001).

Adam Douglas, PhD, CSCS, RSCC*D, is the director of sport science and performance with the Montreal Canadiens. He has spent his career working with hockey players at the elite level and international level. Prior to joining the Canadiens, Douglas spent over 10 years working with Hockey Canada's national men and women's programs, including teams who won a gold medal at the 2014 Olympic Games; 2012 World Championship; and 2015, 2018, and 2020 World Junior Championships. His research focuses on the application of on-ice load monitoring and wearable technology to better understand the demands of the game.

Meghan Duggan is a champion with proven success at the highest levels of hockey. Over a 14-year career with Team USA, she won three Olympic medals (one gold and two silver) and seven World Championship gold medals. She competed collegiately for the University of Wisconsin, winning three NCAA Championships, and was honored with the Patty Kazmaier Memorial Award for the top player in college hockey. As the current director of player development for the New Jersey Devils, Duggan works on all levels of the development department's operations, with a specific focus on on- and off-ice information and strategy.

Mark Fitzgerald has spent over 20 years in the field of sport performance, working with teams and private athletes. During his tenure in the National Hockey League (NHL), he worked with the Toronto Maple Leafs as well as the Anaheim Ducks. Fitzgerald is the founder of Elite Training Systems (ETS), a company in Ontario, Canada, that supports all levels of athletes. He is also the cofounder of Kelowna High Performance (KHP), located in Kelowna, British Columbia, where he resides currently. From guiding young prospects to

molding seasoned professionals, Fitzgerald's holistic approach to training encompasses physical, mental, and tactical aspects. His track record of success speaks volumes, solidifying his reputation as a transformative force in the world of hockey performance coaching.

Tim Lebbossiere, MS, CSCS, has been the assistant performance coach for the Boston Bruins since 2021. He designs, implements, and oversees the off-ice performance and reconditioning programming for the organization and its prospects. Prior to his time in Boston, Lebbossiere spent time in the American Hockey League and in collegiate, high school, and private settings, all working with men's and women's ice hockey. He holds a master of science degree in human performance and a bachelor of science degree in applied exercise science.

Devan McConnell is the high-performance director for the Arizona Coyotes. In this role, he oversees all aspects of the performance department, including sport science, strength and conditioning, nutrition, and reconditioning. McConnell handles much of the day-to-day applied sport science integration while managing the vision and direction of the performance development of all players in the Coyotes organization. Before joining the Coyotes, he was the director of performance science

and reconditioning for the New Jersey Devils. In this role, he oversaw the integration and application of sport and performance science technologies, systems, and practices. In addition, McConnell assisted with the day-to-day performance training of all National Hockey League athletes within the organization, oversaw the return-to-play training of injured athletes, and assisted with the organizational vision of the performance department at both the NHL and AHL levels.

Maria Mountain, MSc, CSCS, is an exercise physiologist, speaker, and dedicated hockey goalie training consultant. As the founder of GoalieTrainingPro.com, she's committed to developing effective, scientifically backed off-ice training programs. Mountain has guided goalies at various levels, including minor league hockey and the NHL. As the founder of Revolution Sport Conditioning, she has trained four Olympic champions from figure skating, soccer, and track and field. Mountain's experience with elite athletes has reinforced her mission to provide the guidance they need to unlock their potential, win more competitions, and prevent injuries along the way.

Matt Nichol, MKin, BEd, is the director of player health and performance for the Ottawa Senators (NHL) and the Hamilton Tiger-Cats (CFL). He also runs his own private consulting business in Toronto, Canada. Nichol has coached hundreds of professional and Olympic athletes across a wide variety of sports over the past three decades and is recognized as one of the preeminent authorities in the world of sport performance.

Mike Potenza, MEd, CSCS, TSAC-F, RSCC*E, is the director of performance for the Golden State Warriors and is a managing partner and the director of performance for Tactical Fitness and Performance. At Golden State, Potenza oversees player training, provides support to the performance nutritionist, coordinates and administers annual performance testing, creates return-from-injury programs, and works with the coaching and development staff on daily scheduling. Before coming to the Warriors, Potenza spent 16 years in the NHL with the San Jose Sharks. During that time, he worked with two U.S. Air Force pararescue teams to implement a performance-enhancement program that has become a standardized model among all five National Guard Bureau pararescue teams.

Matt Shaw, MEd, RSCC, is the senior associate athletic director of sport performance at the University of Denver. In his role, he oversees the physical development and athlete monitoring for hockey and men's soccer, while supervising the sport performance department's work with all 19 sport programs. During his tenure, Shaw has been part of two national hockey championships (2017 and 2022). Additionally, he oversees off-season training for more than 25 NHL and AHL players each summer. Shaw was the NSCA's College Assistant Strength and Conditioning Coach of the Year in 2016.